QuickBooks® Online 7e
for Accounting

Glenn Owen

✲ Cengage

Australia • Brazil • Canada • Mexico • Singapore • United Kingdom • United States

QuickBooks® Online For Accounting,
Seventh Edition
Glenn Owen

SVP, Product: Cheryl Costantini

VP, Product: Thais Alencar

Portfolio Product Director: Joe Sabatino

Portfolio Product Manager: Jonathan Gross

Content Manager: Valarmathy Munuswamy, Lumina Datamatics, Inc.

Product Assistant: Flannery Cowan

Marketing Manager: Colin Kramer

Content Acquisition Analyst: Nichole Nalenz

Content Acquisition Project Manager: Anjali Kambli, Lumina Datamatics, Inc.

Production Service: Lumina Datamatics, Inc.

Art Director and Cover Designer: Christopher Doughman

Cover Image: erhui1979/DigitalVision Vectors/ Getty Images, Berkah/Moment/Getty Images

For product information and technology assistance, contact us at
Cengage Customer & Sales Support, 1-800-354-9706 or
support.cengage.com.

For permission to use material from this text or product, submit all requests online at **www.cengage.com/permissions**.

Intuit and QuickBooks are trademarks and service marks of Intuit Inc., registered in the United States and other countries.

Library of Congress Control Number: 2023904643

ISBN: 978-0-357-90118-2

Cengage
200 Pier 4 Boulevard
Boston, MA 02210
USA

Cengage is a leading provider of customized learning solutions. Our employees reside in nearly 40 different countries and serve digital learners in 165 countries around the world. Find your local representative at **www.cengage.com**.

To learn more about Cengage platforms and services, register or access your online learning solution, or purchase materials for your course, visit **www.cengage.com**.

Printed at CLDPC, USA, 04-23

Brief Contents

Contents

Overview

Accounting has arrived in the Cloud and its time has come. *Cloud computing* is a general term for anything that involves delivering hosted services over the Internet. According to a recent study by KPMG (a global network of professional firms), businesses—large, medium, and small—are using the Cloud to drive cost efficiencies, better enable a mobile workforce, and improve alignment with their customers and vendors.

Imagine being able to update your business's accounting information system from anywhere on any device using any operating system. That is where the global economy is going. Are you on the path?

Is This Text for You?

This text is for you if you are an instructor who desires a self-paced, self-directed environment for your students to learn the essentials of QuickBooks Online (QBO) and to review their understanding of financial accounting and reporting.

This text is for you if you are a business owner looking for a self-paced, self-directed environment for yourself to learn the essentials of QBO as well as a means to refresh your understanding of financial accounting and reporting.

This book focuses on QBO. It is not designed for users of QuickBooks Pro, Accountant, or any other desktop version of QuickBooks. In that case, Glenn Owen's QuickBooks Accountant books are a better fit. The desktop version and online versions are different, and though you can import files created in the desktop version into the online version, significant differences exist as discussed in Chapter 1.

New to This Edition (VIP)

In the prior editions of this text, Intuit limited students to creating only one company. Thus, the author had to use Inuit's Sample Company to demonstrate QBO features. In this edition, with the new ability to use multiple companies (up to 4), the author has chosen to use one of those 4 to demonstrate QBO features in Chapters 3 to 10. Thus, the Sample Company is only used in Chapter 1. Later in this Preface the instructor will be shown how to assign the Wild Water Sports company to each student. This assignment will only give the student the ability to modify a QBO file as instructed in Chapters 3–10. Later the instructor can assign a second QBO company to a student so that they can complete one of 6 cases found at the end of Chapters 3–10. Ultimately, the instructor can only assign 4 QBO files to each student.

Multiple Companies

Intuit has finally seen the light and has agreed to give students and instructors the ability to create more than one company. They have also developed a more streamlined means to access QBO.

See overview at: https://www.intuit.com/partners/education-program/products/quickbooks/

Instructors

To give your students access to creating multiple companies:

1 First step, register yourself as a QBO Educator: Access the Educator Portal by navigating your web browser to https://www.intuit.com/partners/education-program/products/quickbooks/educator-qbo-signup/

2 Intuit will then attempt to validate you as an instructor at your educational institution.

3 After validation, navigate your web browser to https://accounts.intuit.com/index.html?redirect_url=https%3A%2F%2Feducation-portal.app.intuit.com%2Fapp%2Fdashboard&appfabric=true

Figure Preface 1

Sign in to the Education Portal

4 Provide your email in the space shown in Figure Preface 1 above and then click **Sign In**.

5 Provide your password in the window presented next and then click **Continue**. A Welcome to the Intuit Educator Portal window should appear as shown in Figure Preface 2.

6 Click the video box titled **How the Educator Portal Works** to see an overview of the Educator Portal.

7 To access the Sample Company this text uses to demonstrate QBO features, you will click **QuickBooks Online test drive**. Don't do this now.

8 To access QBO tutorials, you will click **Tutorials**. Don't do this now, instead proceed to the next step below.

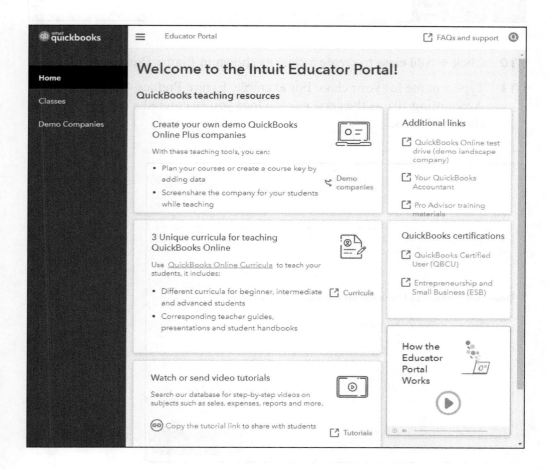

Figure Preface 2

Welcome to the Intuit Educator Portal

9 Click **Classes** from the navigation bar on the left to view the screen shown in Figure Preface 3. Ignore the reference to an existing Accounting 100 class. Your screen will not show the Accounting 100 class.

Figure Preface 3

Classes

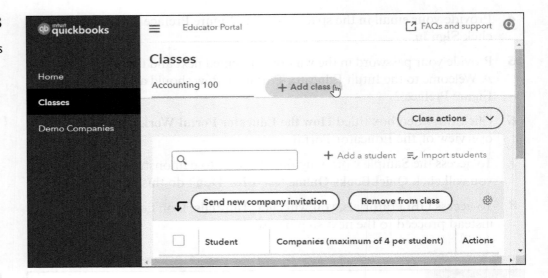

10 Click **+ Add class** to create a class as shown in Figure Preface 3.

11 Type a name for your class. For example, Figure Preface 4 shows Accounting 101 as the class name. Once you've entered a class name, click **Add class**.

Figure Preface 4

Add class

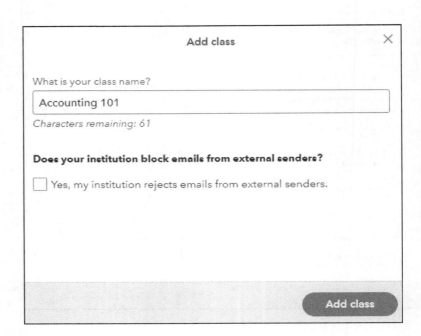

12 Click **Add class**. Your window should look like Figure Preface 5. Add your students to a class either by uploading a roster or clicking Add students manually.

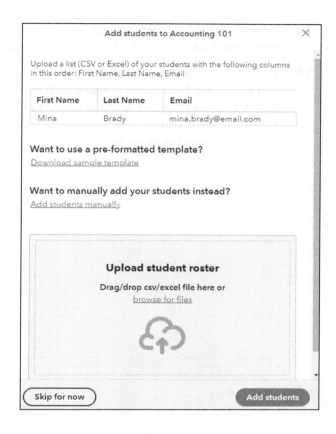

Figure Preface 5

Add students

13   In this example, click **Add students manually** to view Figure Preface 6.
     The student information will be empty until you perform step 14.

Figure Preface 6

Adding students manually

14 Type your student's first name, last name, and email address, then click **Save and close**. A sample student was added in this example.

15 To assign a company to a student, place a **check** next to a student's name and then click **Send new company invitation** as shown in Figure Preface 7. Below is an example of sending an invitation to one student. If you wanted to send this invitation to more students you would simply place a check next to all student names.

Figure Preface 7

Sending an invitation to a student to complete a case

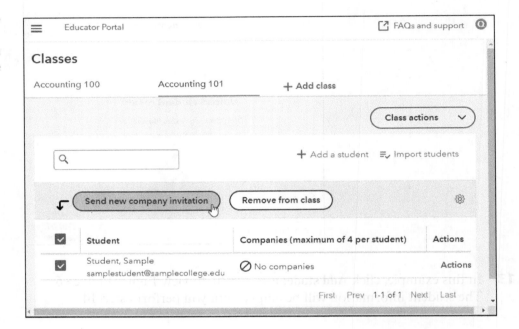

16 Type **Wild Water Sports** in the Choose a name text box as shown in Figure Preface 8. All students should be assigned the Wild Water Sports company so they can complete the chapter instructions provided by the author in Chapters 3–10. Later you can assign additional cases (Case 1–6) as desired up to a maximum of 4 remembering that 1 of those 4 is used up by the Wild Water Sports company. As an instructor you get to choose the name, however, it is recommended that you match the name with the case you've chosen to assign from the text (either Case 1, 2, 3, 4, 5, or 6).

Figure Preface 8

Entering a name for the company you're assigning to a student

17 Click **Next: Preview invitation** to view Figure Preface 9.

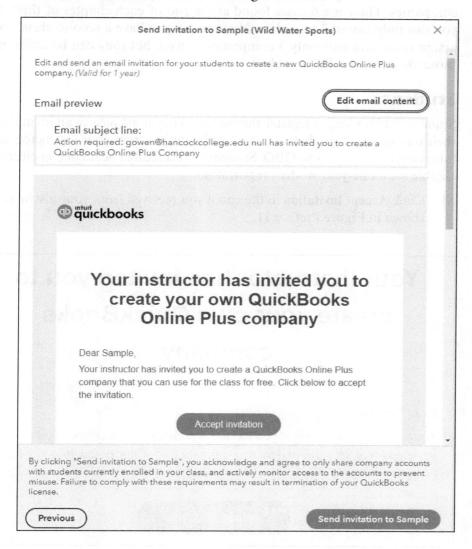

Figure Preface 9

Partial view of invitation preview

18 Click **Send invitation to Sample** (your student's first name will appear in place of Sample).

19 You should receive confirmation that your invitation was sent. Your student listing should then be updated to indicate an invitation was sent and give you the opportunity to resend the invitation if necessary. This update should look like Figure Preface 10.

Figure Preface 10

Updated student information

20 Click your account information icon located in the upper right-hand corner of the QBO window, then click **Sign out**.

Keep in mind that you, as an instructor, may assign your class up to 3 additional companies. There are 6 cases found at the end of each chapter of this text, but you can only assign 3 to a class. However, if you have a second class, you may assign those students only 3 companies as well, but they can be different than those assigned in a different class.

Students

Students can no longer register themselves. They must receive an invitation from their instructor. If you have received an invitation from your instructor, read the following to get access to QBO. Students at accredited academic institutions are eligible for a one-year student registration.

1   Click **Accept Invitation** in the email you received from your instructor as shown in Figure Preface 11.

Figure Preface 11

Accepting an instructor's invitation to create a QBO company

Your instructor has invited you to create your own QuickBooks company

Dear Sample,

Your instructor has invited you to create a QuickBooks Online Plus company that you can use for the class for free. Click below to accept the invitation.

Accept invitation

2   If you have already registered and been validated (see above), click **Sign In** and provide Intuit with your username and password as shown in Figure Preface 12. If you have not registered, provide your information as shown below and click **Create Account**.

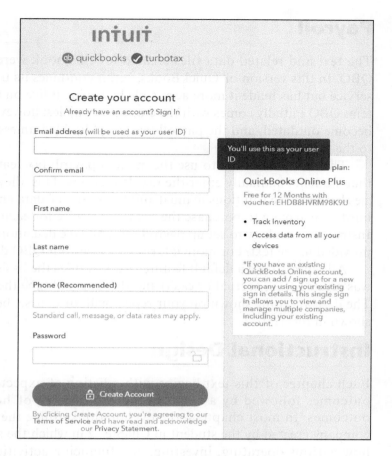

3   Type your **email address** twice, **first name**, **last name**, **phone** (if you wish), a **password** twice, and then click **Create Account**. You should now see a QBO window like Figure Preface 13.

Figure Preface 13

QBO Welcome

4   For now, do not click Next, instead just close the browser window. You will return to your company in Chapter 2.

Payroll

The text and related data files created for this book were constructed using QBO. In this version of QuickBooks, Intuit continues its use of a basic payroll service but has made it more accessible by having it live on its Cloud-based system. QBO initially comes with the current tax tables; however, these tables soon become outdated, and the payroll feature is disabled unless the user subscribes to the payroll service.

The author decided to use the manual payroll tax feature, which requires that students manually enter the tax deductions. This alleviates the discrepancies between the solutions manual and the students' data entry and removes the burden of having to purchase the tax table service for each copy of QBO used. Instructions on how to set up payroll for manual calculation of payroll taxes are provided in the text. For more information, see your QBO documentation.

All reports have a default feature that identifies the basis in which the report was created (e.g., accrual or cash) and the date and time the report was printed. The date and time shown on your report will, of course, be different from that shown in this text.

Instructional Design

Each chapter of this text begins with a listing of expected student learning outcomes followed by a step-by-step explanation of how to obtain those outcomes. In most chapters, the explanations utilize the Wild Water Sports company created by the student in Chapter 2 in which the author demonstrates how various operating, investing, and financing activities of a business are captured and then reported in QBO.

End-of-chapter questions, matching, and student cases follow these explanations. The questions help you to review the text-explained concepts and processes, whereas the matching section helps with terms and definitions. The student cases provide the information necessary to add data to the student's company file. Each chapter requires the student to add information to the previous chapter's rendition. Thus, for success in learning, each student must complete the previous chapter's student case before attempting the next chapter's student case.

Solutions to each chapter's student cases are provided in the instructor manual. The following is a matrix of all end-of-chapter cases that identifies key differences between cases key processes assessed. For example, Cases 1, 2, 4, and 6 are corporations, whereas Cases 3 and 5 are sole proprietors. Cases 1 and 2 do not require sales tax collections, whereas Cases 3, 4, and 5 do. All cases involve business entities that sell products, provide services, and have checking accounts, customers, vendors, employees, and so on.

	Case 1	Case 2	Case 3	Case 4	Case 5	Case 6
Company Setup:						
Date company started using QBO	1/1/24	1/1/25	1/1/26	1/1/27	1/1/22	1/1/23
Location	La Jolla, CA	La Jolla, CA	La Jolla, CA	Hollywood, CA	Huntsville, AL	Sumner, WA
Company organization	Corporation	Corporation	Sole Proprietor	Corporation	Sole Proprietor	Corporation
Business	Distributor	Distributor	Retail	Sports Gym	Engineering	Automotive Dealer
Inventory products sold	Surf boards	Toys	Cell Phones	T-Shirts	Computers	Recreational Vehicle
Services provided	Consulting	Repairs	Repairs	Monthly Fees	Program Support	Repairs
Track expenses	Yes	Yes	Yes	Yes	Yes	Yes
Bill payment terms (default)	Net 30	Net 30	Net 30	Net 30	Net 30	Net 30
Hourly employees	Yes	Yes	Yes	Yes	Yes	Yes
Salary employees	Yes	Yes	Yes	Yes	Yes	Yes
Sales tax applicable	No	No	Yes	Yes	Yes	Yes
Add customers	Yes	Yes	Yes	Yes	Yes	Yes
Add employees	Yes	Yes	Yes	Yes	Yes	Yes
Add inventory items	Yes	Yes	Yes	Yes	Yes	Yes
Add service items	Yes	Yes	Yes	Yes	Yes	Yes
Add vendors	Yes	Yes	Yes	Yes	Yes	Yes
Add/delete accounts	Yes	Yes	Yes	Yes	Yes	Yes
Enter beginning balances	Yes	Yes	Yes	Yes	Yes	Yes
Accounts Used:						
Checking account	Yes	Yes	Yes	Yes	Yes	Yes
Accounts receivable	Yes	Yes	Yes	Yes	Yes	Yes
Prepaid expenses/supplies	Yes	Yes	Yes	Yes	Yes	Yes
Investments	Yes	Yes	Yes	Yes	Yes	Yes
Fixed assets	Yes	Yes	Yes	Yes	Yes	Yes
Accounts payable	Yes	Yes	Yes	Yes	Yes	Yes
Notes payable	Yes	Yes	Yes	Yes	Yes	Yes
Common stock	Yes	Yes	No	Yes	No	Yes
Owner's equity	No	No	Yes	No	Yes	No
Business Transactions:						
Record additional investment by owners	No	No	Yes	No	Yes	No
Record adjusting (accrual) entries	Yes	Yes	Yes	Yes	Yes	Yes
Record bills	Yes	Yes	Yes	Yes	Yes	Yes
Record bills received with purchase orders	Yes	Yes	Yes	Yes	Yes	Yes
Record bills received without purchase orders	Yes	Yes	Yes	Yes	Yes	Yes
Record checks	Yes	Yes	Yes	Yes	Yes	Yes
Record journal entries	Yes	Yes	Yes	Yes	Yes	Yes
Record payments made on account	Yes	Yes	Yes	Yes	Yes	Yes
Record payments received on accounts	Yes	Yes	Yes	Yes	Yes	Yes
Record payroll	Yes	Yes	Yes	Yes	Yes	Yes

Record purchase orders	Yes	Yes	Yes	Yes	Yes	Yes
Record sales invoices	Yes	Yes	Yes	Yes	Yes	Yes
Record sales receipts	Yes	Yes	Yes	Yes	Yes	Yes
Record the sale of common stock	Yes	Yes	No	Yes	No	Yes
Reports Created:						
Reports—A/P Aging Summary	Yes	Yes	Yes	Yes	Yes	Yes
Reports—A/R Aging Summary	Yes	Yes	Yes	Yes	Yes	Yes
Reports—Balance Sheet	Yes	Yes	Yes	Yes	Yes	Yes
Reports—Export Reports to Excel	Yes	Yes	Yes	No	No	Yes
Reports—Income Statement	Yes	Yes	Yes	Yes	Yes	Yes
Reports—Inventory Valuation Summary	Yes	Yes	Yes	Yes	Yes	Yes
Reports—Statement of Cash Flows	Yes	Yes	Yes	Yes	Yes	Yes
Reports—Transaction Detail by Account	Yes	Yes	Yes	Yes	Yes	Yes
Reports—Trial Balance	Yes	Yes	Yes	Yes	Yes	Yes

Comprehensive Problems

Additional transactions for Cases 1, 2, 3, 4, and 6 can be found in Appendix 2. Students who have successfully completed a case in the text through Chapter 10 can be assigned these comprehensive problems. Each pick up in the month following the chapter work. For example in Case 1, chapter work occurred in January 2024, thus the comprehensive problem will describe transactions occurring in February 2024. The transactions included in February are similar in nature to those described in Chapters 3 to 10. Students assigned Case 1 would be able to complete comprehensive Case 1. Those assigned Case 2 would only be able to complete comprehensive Case 2 and the like. Ultimately your instructor can assign you up to 4 companies. All students will be assigned the Wild Water Sports company. After that your instructor can assign an additional 3 companies from the following list: Case 1, 2, 3, 4, 5, or 6.

Textbook Goals

This textbook takes a user and a preparer perspective by illustrating how accounting information is created and then used for making decisions. QBO is user-friendly and provides point-and-click simplicity and sophisticated accounting reporting and analysis tools. The textbook uses proven and successful instructional design (described earlier) to demonstrate the application's features and elicit student interaction.

The first and foremost goal of this text is to help students review fundamental accounting concepts and principles through the use of the QBO application and the analysis of business events. The content of this text complements the first course in accounting principles or financial accounting. Thus, this text should either be used concurrently with an accounting principles or financial accounting course or be used subsequent to completion of such a course.

A second goal of this text is to teach students how to set up QBO for a business, use it to record business events, and use it to generate financial statements and reports. Acquiring these skills will help students improve their job prospects whether the company they work for uses QuickBooks or not.

A third goal of this text is to teach students the value of a computerized accounting information system and how it can be used to communicate important information to business owners, investors, and creditors.

Date Warning

The Sample Company (created and maintained by Intuit) is used in Chapter 1 only and is used to demonstrate many aspects of QBO. The author has no control over the dates used by Intuit and those dates may change depending on when you are accessing the file online. The dates that appear in the figures supplied by the author in this text may not be the dates that appear on your screen. Instructions to generate reports in this text often suggest the user set the report period to the month before or in the month of the current system date. If you are entering data at the beginning of the month (your system date is between the 1st and the 15th of a month), you should set your report period to the month prior to your current system date. If you are entering data at the end of the month (your system date is between the 15th and the 31st of a month), you should set your report period to the current month of your current system date. For example, if you are entering data on 10/09/2023, use 10/01/2023 to 10/31/2023 as your reporting period. For example, if you are entering data on 10/21/2024, use 10/01/2024 to 10/31/2024 as your reporting period.

The student cases (Cases 1–6) are set in 2024, 2025, 2026, 2027, 2022, and 2023, respectively. If transactions are entered into the student case in other than the proper period, answers will be wrong. Be careful about entering dates into QBO when you are working on this case. The default date when entering new transactions into QBO is the computer's system date that may or may not be in those years.

Update Warning

QBO is frequently upgraded by Intuit to provide new features, correct errors, or improve functionality. This book was written in late 2022 and early 2023, and all figures are based on how QBO looked at that time. If you are using this text in 2023 or later, Intuit may have made modifications in how QBO looks and feels or functions. Differences will occur, which are out of the author's control.

Keep in mind that sales tax rates change year to year, state to state. The solutions provided by the author for each case were based on tax rates in effect for that particular year. If a rate changes your answers for sales tax payable and related accounts may be different.

Instructor as Your Accountant

Your instructor may choose to have you assign them as your accountant so that they can see your work and progress at their convenience without having you to "send" the file. In fact, you cannot "send" your file, since all the files are on the Cloud. Instructions on how to set your instructor as your accountant are provided in Chapter 2.

Video Tutorials Developed by Intuit

Intuit, developer of QBO, and others have made video tutorials to help you get started with QBO. These tutorials can be viewed and/or sent to students from the Welcome to the Intuit Educator Portal described earlier in this text.

Instructors

To access these tutorials:

1   Login to the Educator Portal as shown in Figure Preface 1.

2   Click **Tutorials** shown at the bottom of the window to view Figure Preface 2.

3   View as many tutorials as you like and send them to students if you desire.

Students

To access these tutorials:

1   Navigate your browser to https://quickbooks.intuit.com/global/learn-and-support/video-tutorials/

2   Type a topic for a video into the text box labeled **Search for anything**.

3   View the video.

About the Author

Glenn Owen is a retired member of Allan Hancock College's Accounting and Business faculty, where he lectured on accounting and information systems from 1995 to 2016. In addition, he is a retired lecturer at the University of California at Santa Barbara, where he taught accounting and information systems courses from 1980 to 2011. His professional experience includes five years at Deloitte & Touche as well as vice president of finance positions at Westpac Resources, Inc., and ExperTelligence, Inc. Mr. Owen completed his fourth edition of Using Microsoft Excel and Access in Accounting text in 2016, which gives accounting students specific, self-paced instruction on the use of spreadsheets (Excel 2016) and database applications (Access 2016) in accounting. He has also written the 15th edition of his *Using QuickBooks Accountant for Accounting 2018* text, which is also a self-paced, case-based instruction on the use of a commercial accounting application (QuickBooks 2018). His innovative teaching style emphasizes the decision maker's perspective and encourages students to think creatively. His graduate studies in educational psychology and 41 years of business experience yield a balanced blend of theory and practice. Mr. Owen was presented the Lifetime Achievement Award in August 2016 by the Two-Year Section of the American Accounting Association.

Dedication

I would like to thank my wife Kelly, my boys Michael, Nathan, Kyle, and Casey, my grandchildren Graham, Julia, Beckett, Emelia, Oliver, Anastasia, and Kayden for their support and assistance during the creation of this and previous editions of this text. Though our boys are out of the house and pursuing their own interests, Kelly continues to listen to my often crazy ideas for new cases and experiences with college students, providing an excellent sounding board and reality check. You, the boys, their wives, and our grandchildren continue to define what life is all about.

An Introduction to QuickBooks Online Using the Sample Company

Student Learning Outcomes

Upon completion of this chapter, the student will be able to do the following:

- Open the Sample Company provided by Intuit to explore QBO
- Access customer, vendor, and employee information
- Explore banking transactions
- Explore sales and expense transactions
- Explore the chart of accounts
- Explore lists
- Access reports
- Use the Gear icon to view company settings

Overview

Intuit has provided a Sample Company online to provide new users a test-drive of its QBO product. You will open this Sample Company and explore various features of QBO. In this chapter, you will be viewing the Sample Company looking at customer, vendor, and employee information. You will also be viewing banking, sales, and expense transactions and will be looking at the chart of accounts, lists, reports, and company settings. You will not be making any changes, such as adding a customer, invoice, check, and so on. That will occur in the next chapter.

The author has no control over the dates used by Intuit, and those dates may change, depending on when you are accessing the file online. The dates in the figures supplied by the author in this text may not be the dates on your screen.

Begin Your Sample Company Walkthrough

You can use this Sample Company to explore QBO as often as you like. No matter what you do to modify this Sample Company, you will be unable to save it. When you leave and later return, it will look the same as it did initially. Each time you open this Sample Company, it will retrieve your current system date (the actual date you are working on your computer) and place that date under the company name on the home page.

To open the Sample Company, do the following:

1 Open your Internet browser.

2 Type **https://qbo.intuit.com/redir/testdrive** into your browser's address text box, press [**Enter**] to view the Sample Company Dashboard shown in Figure 1.1. Transaction dates may differ on your screen from the figures shown throughout this text.

Figure 1.1

Sample Company Dashboard

3 Click the `+ New` icon to view the Create menu shown in Figure 1.2.

Figure 1.2

Create menu

CUSTOMERS	VENDORS	EMPLOYEES	OTHER
Invoice	Expense	Single time activity	Bank deposit
Receive payment	Check	Weekly timesheet	Transfer
Estimate	Bill		Journal entry
Credit memo	Pay bills		Statement
Sales receipt	Purchase order		Inventory qty adjustment
Refund receipt	Vendor credit		Pay down credit card
Delayed credit	Credit card credit		
Delayed charge	Print checks		

Customers, Vendors, and Employees

QBO provides easy access to customer information using the navigation bar. In this section, you will open the Customers section in a new tab and drill down to a specific customer and specific transactions related to that customer.

To access customer information, do the following:

1 Click **Sales** and then click **Customers** as shown in Figure 1.3.

Trouble? If the navigation menu does not appear, click the **Show Navigation** icon located next to the words Sample Company. Clicking this icon should reveal and hide the navigation menu each time it's clicked.

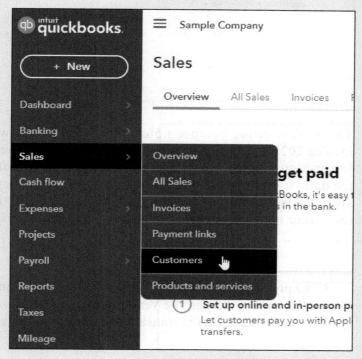

Figure 1.3

Accessing the Customers window

2 The resulting Customers window is then revealed as shown in Figure 1.4.

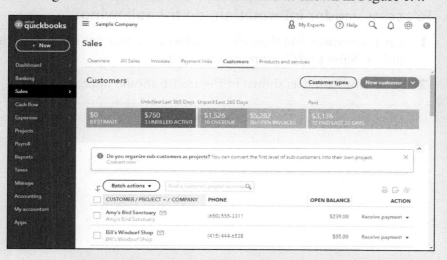

Figure 1.4

Customers window

3   Click on the **Amy's Bird Sanctuary** text to view detailed transactions related to that particular customer shown in Figure 1.5.

Figure 1.5

Amy's Bird Sanctuary

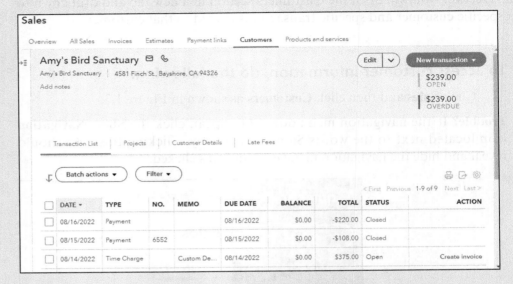

The $239 overdue balance noted at the top of the window correlates to invoice 1021 shown near the bottom of the list. To view it, scroll down the transactions list for Amy's Bird Sanctuary. (The author has no control over the dates used by Intuit, and those dates may change depending on when you are accessing the file online. The dates, which appear in the figures supplied by the author in this text, may not match the dates that appear on your screen.)

QBO provides easy access to vendor information using the navigation bar. In this section, you will open the Vendors section in a new tab and drill down to a specific vendor and specific transactions related to that vendor.

To access vendor information, do the following:

1   Click **Expenses** and then click **Vendors** (in a manner similar to what you did for Sales and Customers previously).

2   A vendor listing as shown in Figure 1.6 should appear.

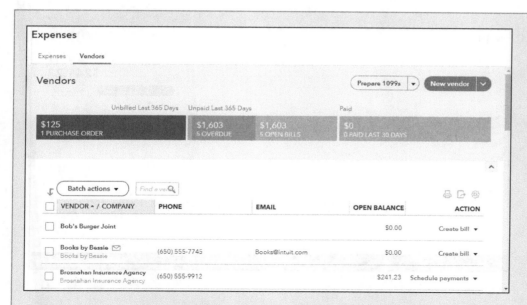

Figure 1.6

Vendors information

3 Click on the **Brosnahan Insurance Agency** text to view detailed transactions related to that particular vendor shown in Figure 1.7.

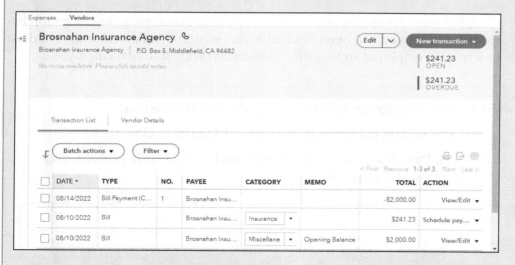

Figure 1.7

Brosnahan Insurance Agency

4 Click on the **$241.23** balance to view the bill received as shown in Figure 1.8.

Figure 1.8

Bill from Brosnahan
Insurance Agency

The $241.23 overdue balance noted at the top of the window correlates to a
bill received from an earlier month.

QBO provides easy access to employee information using the navigation bar.
In this section, you will open the Employees section in a new tab and drill down
to a specific employee and specific transactions related to that employee.

To access employee information, do the following:

1   Click the **X** in the upper-right corner of the Bill to close it.

2   Click **Payroll** and then select **Employees** to reveal an employee listing
as shown in Figure 1.9.

Figure 1.9

Employees information

3 Click **Edit** for John Johnson to view employee information for John Johnson as shown in Figure 1.10.

Figure 1.10

Employee Information for John Johnson

4 Click **X** to close this window.

5 Click the **R** icon located in the upper right-hand corner of your window, and then click **Sign out** to close the Sample Company.

Banking Transactions

QBO has an online banking feature that lets you automatically connect to your bank and download banking-related transactions. The application automatically matches the banking transaction with a previously recorded QBO transaction. QBO calls this "Recognizing." This feature is briefly reviewed as this text is academically based and no "real" bank account is linked to this sample, and no "real" bank account will be linked to your student company.

To view banking transactions, do the following:

1 Open your Internet browser.

2 Type **https://qbo.intuit.com/redir/testdrive** into your browser's address text box and then press [**Enter**] to view the Sample Company home page shown in Figure 1.1. You may be asked to provide security information before proceeding. Click **Continue**.

3 Click **Banking** from the navigation bar and then click the **X** in the Your bank connection is all set window to view the Checking page as shown in Figure 1.11.

Figure 1.11

Checking (partial view)

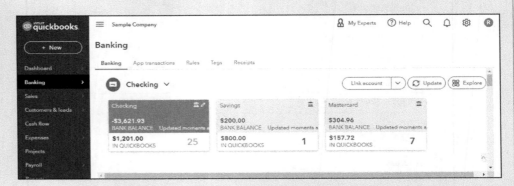

4 Scroll down the Checking page to view banking transactions as shown in Figure 1.12.

Figure 1.12

Checking transactions (partial view)

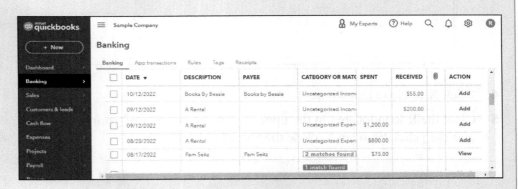

5 Scroll back up the Checking page and then click **Go to bank register** on the right to view the traditional checking account register listing each QBO-recorded check, deposit, or cash transaction affecting the checking account shown in Figure 1.13. Close any messages that may appear. You may have to enlarge your window to view the Deposit and Balance columns.

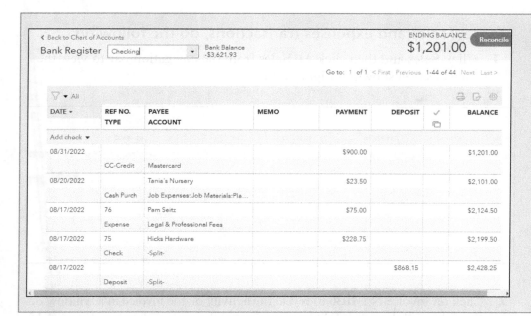

Figure 1.13

Bank Register (partial view)

Bank deposits, which have not been recorded in QBO, are not recognized and are temporarily classified as Uncategorized Income. Bank charges that have not been recorded in QBO are not recognized and are temporarily classified as Uncategorized Expense.

The Bank Register seen in Figure 1.13 is similar to the general ledger account concept seen in traditional accounting without the debits and credits. The balance is shown after every increase or decrease in the account. In a bank account, increases are deposits and decreases are payments. Registers exist for all assets, liabilities, and equity accounts, and they are a great way to identify and/or correct errors if they occur.

Sales and Expense Transactions

The next two choices in the navigation bar are sales and expense transactions. The Sales Transactions section provides a listing of recent sales invoices and payments: Some are closed and others are open, meaning payment has not been received. Thus, the action item of receiving payment is listed for all open invoices. This screen also highlights unbilled activity, open balances, overdue balances, and those invoices paid in the last 30 days across the top. You can decide to drill down to view a particular invoice.

To view sales and expenses transactions, do the following:

1 Click **Sales** and then click **All Sales** from the navigation bar to view the Sales section shown in Figure 1.14.

Figure 1.14

Sales Transactions (partial view)

2 Click on Invoice No. **1036** to reveal the activity of the invoice in a window on the right, and then click **Edit invoice** to reveal the invoice shown in Figure 1.15.

Figure 1.15

Invoice #1036

3 Click **Cancel** to close Invoice No. 1036.

The Expense Transactions section will provide a listing of recent credit card charges, bills, expenses, purchase orders, checks, bill payments, and cash payments. You can decide to drill down to view a particular credit card transaction.

4 Click **Expenses** and then click **Expenses** again from the navigation bar to view the Expense Transactions section shown in Figure 1.16.

Figure 1.16

Expense Transactions (partial view)

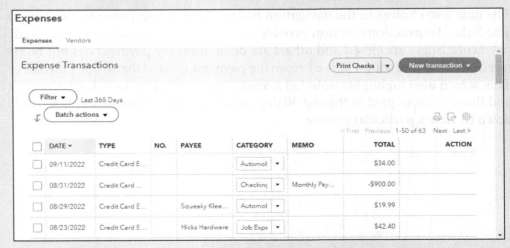

5   Click **Squeaky Kleen Car Wash** to reveal the charge as shown in
Figure 1.17.

Figure 1.17

Expense window (credit card charge for $19.99)

6   Click **Cancel** to close the credit card charge window.

Settings

The Settings window (also known as the Gear window) is accessed by clicking the Gear icon located in the upper-right portion of the QBO window. Here you can modify your company settings, products and services, and budgets as well as reconcile bank accounts.

To view the Settings window and examine the Sample Company's settings:

1   Click the **Gear** icon as shown in Figure 1.18.

Figure 1.18

Company Settings window

2 Click **Account and settings** to view company name, type, address and so on as shown in Figure 1.19.

Figure 1.19

Account and Settings window

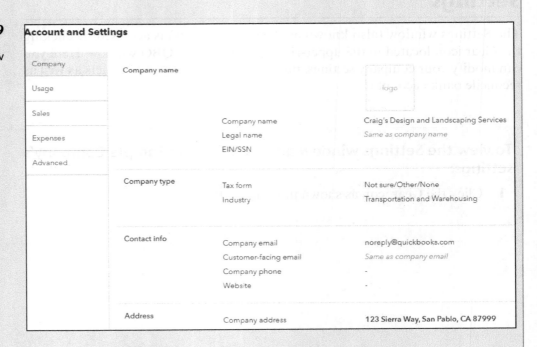

3 Click **X** to close the Account and Settings window.

Chart of Accounts

A chart of accounts is a listing of all accounts available. Each account is assigned a type and a detailed type. The Sample Company's chart of accounts has been modified from the default chart of accounts and tailored to this company's needs. Not all companies need these particular accounts, and some will need additional accounts.

To view the Sample Company's chart of accounts, do the following:

1 Click the **Gear** icon and then click **Chart of Accounts** to view the Chart of Accounts section. Then click **See your Chart of Accounts** to view the Sample Company's chart of accounts as shown in Figure 1.20.

Figure 1.20

Chart of Accounts (partial view)

2 Scroll down the chart of accounts. Each asset, liability, and equity account has a View register action item listed.

3 As you scroll down, you will see that the balance in the chart of accounts for accounts payable (A/P) is $1,602.67.

4 Click **View register** on the Accounts Payable line of the chart of accounts to view the register for accounts payable shown in Figure 1.21. The ending balance in the A/P Register matches the $1,602.67 balance specified in the chart of accounts listing. (Remember to ignore dates in this Sample Company problem. Also click **X** to close any pop up windows that may display.)

Figure 1.21

A/P Register

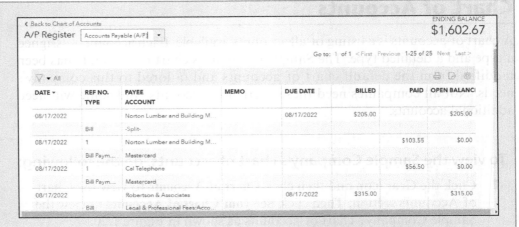

5 Click **Back to Chart of Accounts** located at the top of the A/P Register.

6 Scroll down the chart of accounts to see that each revenue and expense account has a Run Report action item listed. Click **Run Report** on the Landscaping Services account line to view an Account QuickReport for this account.

7 Scroll to the top of this Account QuickReport. Select **Since 90 Days Ago** from the Report period drop-down list, and then click **Run report** to view the report shown in Figure 1.22.

Figure 1.22

Account QuickReport

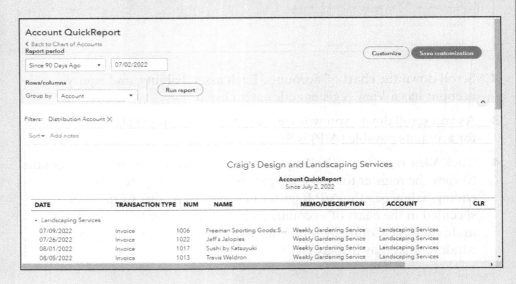

Lists

Lists in QBO provide you with an easy and quick way to view a collection of common items. Some of the more common lists include the chart of accounts, products and services, and terms. You can decide to view a summary of all the lists available in QBO and explore the list of terms.

To view a list of lists and the list of terms, do the following:

1 Click the **Gear** icon and then click **All Lists** to view all lists shown in Figure 1.23.

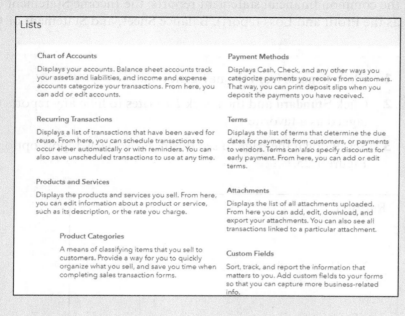

Figure 1.23

Lists

Lists

Chart of Accounts

Displays your accounts. Balance sheet accounts track your assets and liabilities, and income and expense accounts categorize your transactions. From here, you can add or edit accounts.

Recurring Transactions

Displays a list of transactions that have been saved for reuse. From here, you can schedule transactions to occur either automatically or with reminders. You can also save unscheduled transactions to use at any time.

Products and Services

Displays the products and services you sell. From here, you can edit information about a product or service, such as its description, or the rate you charge.

Product Categories

A means of classifying items that you sell to customers. Provide a way for you to quickly organize what you sell, and save you time when completing sales transaction forms.

Payment Methods

Displays Cash, Check, and any other ways you categorize payments you receive from customers. That way, you can print deposit slips when you deposit the payments you have received.

Terms

Displays the list of terms that determine the due dates for payments from customers, or payments to vendors. Terms can also specify discounts for early payment. From here, you can add or edit terms.

Attachments

Displays the list of all attachments uploaded. From here you can add, edit, download, and export your attachments. You can also see all transactions linked to a particular attachment.

Custom Fields

Sort, track, and report the information that matters to you. Add custom fields to your forms so that you can capture more business-related info.

2 Click **Terms** to view the list shown in Figure 1.24.

Figure 1.24

Terms

Terms
‹ All Lists

Run Report   New

Filter by name

Previous 1-5 Next

NAME ▲	ACTION
Due on receipt	Run report ▼
Net 10	Run report ▼
Net 15	Run report ▼
Net 30	Run report ▼
Net 60	Run report ▼

Previous 1-5 Next

Reports

QBO comes with many predesigned reports for use in business, all of which you can customize for your particular needs. For instance, you can decide to focus on the common financial statement reports: the Income Statement (known in QBO as the Profit and Loss report), Balance Sheet, and Statement of Cash Flows.

1 Click **Reports** from the navigation bar.

2 Click **Standard** and then click **Favorites** to hide any reports QBO had tagged as a favorite.

3 Scroll down the page to see Business overview report options shown in Figure 1.25.

Figure 1.25

Business overview reports

4 Scroll down the page and then click **Profit and Loss**. Click **Collapse** and then scroll to the top of the report to view the top part of the Profit and Loss Report shown in Figure 1.26. (If you view the entire report, you would note that clicking the **Collapse** text summarizes details under a heading. For example, Landscaping Services is shown as one number when Collapse is selected. Clicking **Expand** would show more detail. You will learn more about customizing and creating other reports in Chapter 10. Remember, the dates on your screen may differ from those shown in the figure.)

Figure 1.26

Profit and Loss Report (partial view)

5   Click **Reports**, then scroll to find and click **Balance Sheet**, and then scroll to the top of the report to view the top part of the Balance Sheet Report shown in Figure 1.27.

Figure 1.27

Balance Sheet Report (partial view)

6   Click **Reports**, then scroll to find and click **Statement of Cash Flows**, and then scroll to the top of the report to view the top part of the Statement of Cash Flows Report shown in Figure 1.28.

Figure 1.28

Statement of Cash Flows Report

Statement of Cash Flows Report

‹ Back to report list
Report period

| This Year-to-date ▾ | 01/01/2022 | to | 09/30/2022 |

Customize   Save customization

Display columns by   Show non-zero or active only

| Total Only ▾ | | Active rows/active colui ▾ | Run report

Sort ▾ Add notes

Craig's Design and Landscaping Services

Statement of Cash Flows
January - September, 2022

	TOTAL
▾ OPERATING ACTIVITIES	
Net Income	1,642.46
▾ Adjustments to reconcile Net Income to Net Cas...	
Accounts Receivable (A/R)	-5,281.52
Inventory Asset	-596.25
Accounts Payable (A/P)	1,602.67

Alternatively, you can easily find a report if you know its name or part of its name. For example, if you wanted to access a report dealing with accounts receivable (A/R), you would type Accounts receivable into the report search box located in the Reports section.

To find a report related to accounts receivable, do the following:

1 Click **Reports** and type **Accounts receivable** in the Find report by name search box. Note the two reports that match your search as shown in Figure 1.29.

Figure 1.29

Reports

Reports

🔍 Accounts receivable

Standard	Custom reports	Management reports

Accounts receivable aging detail

Accounts receivable aging summary

Company Settings

Five tabs are in the Settings section of QBO: Company, Usage, Sales, Expenses, and Advanced. You can edit these by clicking on the Pencil icon to the right of each section. The settings for the Sample Company have been modified from the default settings provided when QBO first creates a company. These options in the Settings section change the way QBO appears to the user. For example, in the Advanced section, if time tracking is turned off, no time tracking features will be available in QBO. Also, if purchase orders are turned off in the Expenses section, no purchase orders will be available in QBO. You can decide to view each of these sections to learn more about what options you are given in QBO.

1 Click the **Gear** icon and then click **Account and settings**, and click the **Company** tab to view the Company Settings section shown in Figure 1.30.

Figure 1.30

Company settings

2 Click the **Sales** tab in the Account and Settings window to view options provided as shown in Figure 1.31.

Figure 1.31

Sales settings

3 Click the **Expenses** tab in the Account and Settings window to view options provided as shown in Figure 1.32. Note that this is where you can turn purchase orders on or off.

Figure 1.32

Expenses settings

4 Click the **Advanced** tab in the Account and Settings window to view options provided as shown in Figure 1.33. Note that this is where you change your company type to corporation, sole proprietor, and so on.

Figure 1.33

Advanced settings

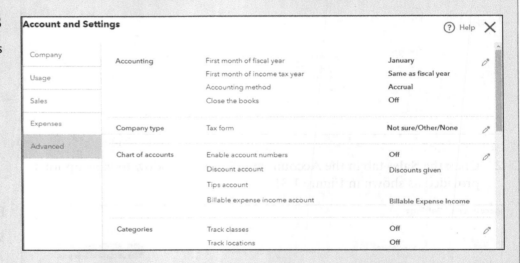

5 Click **Done** to close the Settings window.

End Note

In this chapter, you have used Intuit's Sample Company to practice navigating QBO. You have accessed customer, vendor, and employee information; viewed various transactions; and viewed the chart of accounts, lists, reports, and company settings. In Chapter 2, you will accept an invitation to work a case your instructor assigns you. In Chapter 3, you will use the Wild Water Sports company to learn how to modify settings, the chart of accounts, beginning balances, and products and services. In Chapters 4 through 10, you will use the Wild Water Sports company to learn how to add operating, investing, and financing activities; reconcile a bank account; create a budget; add adjusting entries; and prepare financial statements and reports.

Chapter 1 Questions

1   What steps do you take to view customer information?

2   What steps do you take to view detailed transactions related to a particular customer?

3   What steps do you take to view a specific bill from a specific vendor?

4   What steps do you take to view a specific employee's information?

5   How are bank deposits, which have not been recorded in QBO, classified?

6   How are bank charges, which have not been recorded in QBO, classified?

7   Opening the Sales Transaction section of QBO will provide a listing of _____.

8   Opening the Expense Transaction section of QBO will provide a listing of _____.

9   What lists are available in QBO?

10   What steps do you take to view all reports related to accounts payable (A/P)?

Chapter 1 Matching

a. Navigation bar   _____   An employee in the Sample Company

b. Amy's Bird Sanctuary   _____   Bank deposits not yet recognized

c. Brosnahan Insurance Agency _____   Exist for all asset, liability, and equity accounts

d. Recognizing   _____   Specify due dates for payment to/from vendors/customers

e. Uncategorized Income   _____   Used to access a list of sales and expense transactions

f. Uncategorized Expense   _____   A vendor in the Sample Company

g. Registers   _____   A listing of all accounts available

h. John Johnson   _____   Bank charges not yet recognized

i. Terms   _____   A customer in the Sample Company

j. Chart of accounts   _____   Matching a banking transaction with a QBO transaction

2

An Overview of QuickBooks Online

Upon completion of this chapter, the student will be able to do the following:

- Identify the basic features of QuickBooks Online (QBO)
- Explain how QBO is similar to and differs from the desktop version of QuickBooks
- Open the QBO company you created in the Preface to this text
- Provide information to QBO about your company
- Successfully navigate the QBO Dashboard
- Assign their instructor as their "Accountant"
- Use QBO's help feature

Overview

The focus of this chapter is to introduce you to QuickBooks Online (QBO) and get your account and company established. A description of QBO will be provided along with a brief comparison of how QBO differs from its desktop version. This text includes instructions provided by Intuit to create your own personal account with Intuit and create up to four companies. You will assign your company a name that includes your name for identification purposes. Welcome to the journey.

What Is QBO?

Navigate your browser to the Video Tutorials provided by Intuit (see website address specified in the Preface to this text) and then search on how to get started in QuickBooks Online.

QBO is an online version of the popular QuickBooks accounting software developed by Intuit. The software is designed to capture common business events like purchases from and payments to vendors; sales to and collections from customers; payments and receipts to/from other operating, investing, and financing activities; period end accrual adjustments; and reports. Reports include the standard financial statements, including the income statement, statement of stockholders' equity, balance sheet, statement of cash flows, and other useful reports like accounts receivable aging. All interaction with QBO is done via an Internet connection. In other words, if you have not connected to the Internet, you will have no QBO. In other words, QBO cannot work offline.

All interaction with QBO is done online; there are no files to maintain on a computer, and everything is saved online. Thus, there is no need for backup files. The monthly fee for using QBO in its commercial (non-educational) version covers up to four companies. This text includes access to QBO for the user to create up to four companies online for a limited amount of time.

How Is QBO Similar to/Different Than the Desktop Version of QuickBooks Accountant?

Even though these two products share the name "QuickBooks," they are unrelated. QBO isn't a copy of QuickBooks that has been web enabled. They are different products with different database structures and approaches to solving problems even though both were developed in-house by Intuit to capture and report on accounting events.

Not all features available in QBO are available in the Windows desktop version of QuickBooks Accountant (QBDT). Likewise, not all features of QBDT are available in QBO. QBO requires an Internet connection. QBDT requires installation of software on to a computer. QBO requires a monthly fee. QBDT requires a one-time purchase and no monthly fees.

A key difference is that because QBO is online, it works on multiple operating systems (Windows, Apple, etc.) and multiple devices (desktops, laptops, smart phones, or tablets). The same cannot be said for QBDT. Intuit requires different software for QBDT to run on a Windows-based or an Apple-based computer. In this text, QBDT will always mean the Windows version of QuickBooks Accountant.

Some additional notable differences are the following:

- QBDT can be used for an unlimited number of companies; QBO limits you to four companies as assigned by your instructor. Need to manage more than four companies outside of your class using QBO? Each will cost you another monthly fee.

- QBO can automatically download bank transactions for no additional cost.

- QBDT can track inventory purchases and sales based on an average cost assumption or a first-in-first-out assumption.

- QBO can track inventory purchases and sales based only on a first-in-first-out assumption.

- QBDT can account for the receipt of inventory items (receive items function) based on a purchase order; QBO cannot and calls inventory products and services.

- QBO can automatically schedule and send invoices, whereas QBDT cannot.

- QBDT can perform manual payroll without paying Intuit a monthly payroll processing fee. QBO encourages you to sign up for its payroll service and makes manually processing payroll difficult.

- QBO can be accessed from anywhere in the world where you have access to the Internet. QBDT requires a computer with the QuickBooks application and data files installed.

- QBDT provides for profit and loss as well as balance sheet budgeting. QBO only provides for profit and loss budgeting.

- QBO operates irrespective of platform (desktop, laptop, mobile device, or tablet) or operating system (Microsoft Windows or Apple iOS). QBDT does have a version of QuickBooks for both of those operating systems, but they are different and require two separate application purchases.

- QBDT includes a fixed asset management system, which will calculate depreciation and maintain detailed fixed asset records by individual asset, whereas QBO does not calculate depreciation and does not maintain detailed records of fixed assets.

- QBO provides automatic upgrades; this is a good and a bad feature. With QBO, you are almost always running the most current version (whether you want to or not).

How to Open the QBO Company You Created in the Preface

Instructions for both instructors and students are found in the Preface to this text. You must complete the registration process before you can proceed in this chapter.

Once you completed your QBO registration, you were presented with a QBO company shell (meaning a QBO company without any details). You were then instructed to sign out of QBO. In this section of the text, you are to return to that QBO company and add some additional information. When you return you will be presented a series of questions to set up your company in QBO. Since you exited QBO before answering questions in the Preface, QBO automatically returns you to the setup questions. Once you have completed this setup process, QBO will open your company dashboard.

To login to the company you created in the Preface to this text:

1. Type **https://qbo.intuit.com/** into your web browser.

2. Enter your User ID and password and then click **Sign In**.

3. Click **Skip for now** if asked to verify your number. Your company welcome window should now appear and look like Figure 2.1.

Figure 2.1

Welcome window

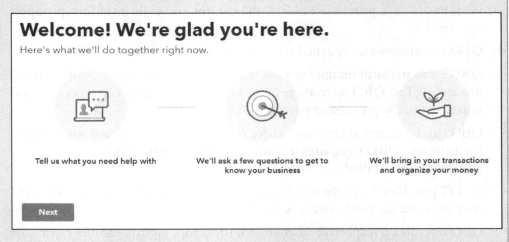

4. Click **Next** to answer the business name question. Type **Wild Water Sports - Student Name (ID Number)** or whatever name your instructor specifies as shown in Figure 2.2.

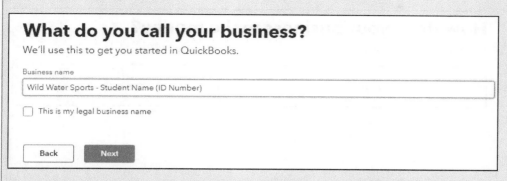

Figure 2.2

Business name

5   When asked how you have been managing your finances, click **Nothing, I'm just getting started**, then click **Next**.

6   When asked What's your industry, click **Skip for now**.

7   Click **C Corp** to answer the type of business question as shown in Figure 2.3.

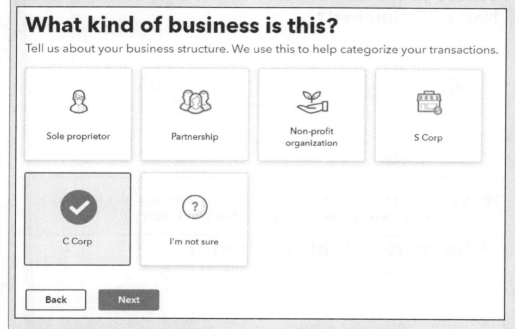

Figure 2.3

Type of business

8   Click **Next** to answer the question about how your business makes money. Click **Provides services** and **Sells products** as shown in Figure 2.4.

Figure 2.4

How your business makes money

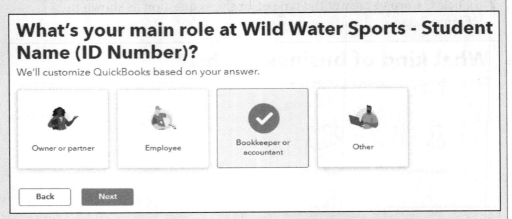

9   Click **Next** to answer the question about your main role. Click **Bookkeeper or accountant** as shown in Figure 2.5.

Figure 2.5

Your main role

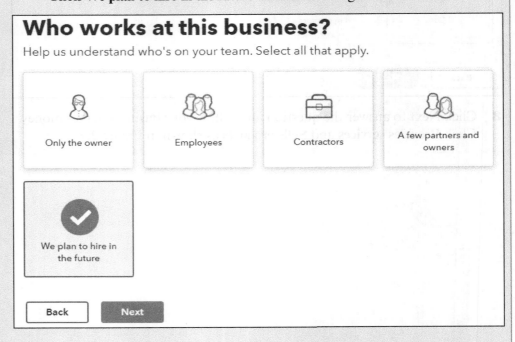

10   Click **Next** to answer the question about who works at this business. Click **We plan to hire in the future** as shown in Figure 2.6.

Figure 2.6

Who works at this business

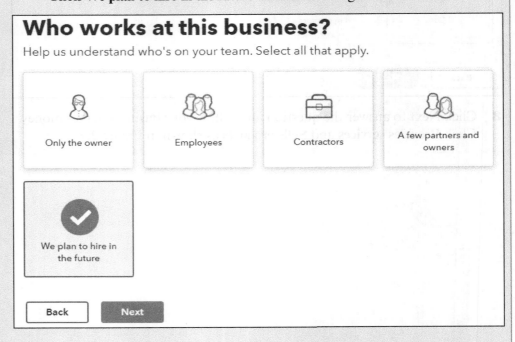

11 Click **Next** to answer the question about what apps you use. Click **Skip for now**.

12 Click **Skip for now** in the Link your accounts window.

13 Click the choices specified in Figure 2.7. Click **Next** to move to the next window.

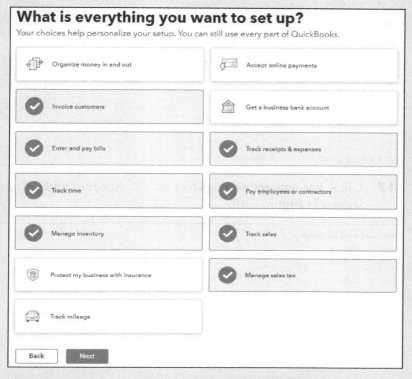

Figure 2.7

Choices to build your setup guide

14 Click **No, I don't want** to add payroll when asked if you are ready for a free trial of QuickBooks Payroll, then click **Next**.

15 Click **Let's go** to complete the setup process. At this point, click **Take a quick tour** or close the Welcome to QuickBooks window to view your company dashboard as shown in Figure 2.8.

Figure 2.8

Company dashboard

16 Click the **Gear** icon to view the settings menu shown in Figure 2.9.

Figure 2.9

Settings menu

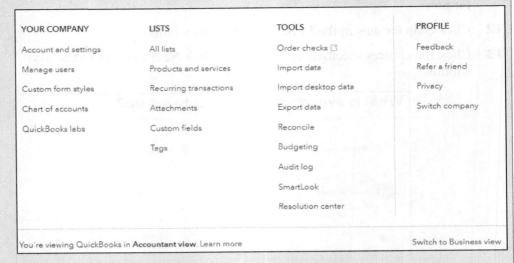

17 Click **Account and settings** to view the Account and Settings section shown in Figure 2.10.

Figure 2.10

Account and Settings section

18 Click the **Company** tab and then click the **Pencil** icon in the Company name section of Account and Settings.

19 Type **Wild Water Sports - Student Name (ID Number)** replacing Student Name with your name and ID Number in the Company Name text box and then place a check in the **Same as company name** check box as shown in Figure 2.11.

Figure 2.11

Changing your company name

20 Click **Save** to save your company name change.

21 Click the **Pencil** icon in the Company type section of Account and Settings.

22 Confirm that Corporation is selected as the tax form as shown in Figure 2.12. The other options for Company type are shown. Depending on the case you're assigned, these may be more appropriate selections.

Figure 2.12

Choosing company type

23 Click **Save**.

24 Click the **Pencil** icon in the Address section of Account and Settings.

25 Type the address shown in Figure 2.13 into the Address section of Account and Settings. Remember that, depending on the case you're assigned, your case address may be different.

Figure 2.13

Company address

Address	Company address	Street address
	Address where your company is based. This address is used to calculate applicable taxes for your QBO subscriptions and is your default company address.	5500 E Colonial Dr
		City
		Orlando
		State
		Florida
		ZIP code
		32807

Cancel   Save

26   Click **Save**.

27   Click the **Sales** tab.

28   Make sure that the Preferred invoice terms are set to Net 30 in the Sales form content section and that Track inventory quantity on hand is On in the Products and services section.

29   Close the Settings window.

30   Go to Appendix 1 and complete before moving on.

31   Click **Taxes** then **Sales tax** from the Navigation bar.

32   Click **Sales Tax Settings**.

33   Click **Edit** from the Agency Action column.

34   Type **01/01/2027** in the Start date text box.

35   Click **Save** then click Dashboard from the Navigation bar.

36   Sign out of your QBO file by clicking on your account. In Figure 2.14, this is illustrated by clicking on the **S** in the upper right-hand corner of your QBO window and then clicking **Sign out**. Your window will look different.

Figure 2.14

Signing out of QBO

S

Sample Student

basslakestudent@gmail.com

Manage your Intuit Account

Sign out

Navigating QBO

The Dashboard provides links to various tasks and resources. Clicking **Banking** in the navigation bar will let you set up a new checking account and view checking transactions. Clicking **Sales** in the navigation bar provides access to adding invoices and new customers, viewing existing balances, and highlighting overdue accounts. Clicking **Expenses** provides access to adding new expenses, new vendors, viewing existing balances, and highlighting overdue accounts. Clicking **Payroll** provides access to adding new employees and viewing payroll information. The Transactions and Reports links will be addressed later in this text.

Navigate your browser to the Video Tutorials provided by Intuit (see website address specified in the Preface to this text) and then search on how to Navigate QuickBooks Online: Menus, Transactions, and Set Up.

First you'll need to login to your account and retrieve your QBO company.

Keep in mind that in this section, you'll be navigating QBO but not making any substantial changes to your Company. Modifications to your Company will occur in Chapter 3.

To login to the case you modified earlier in this chapter:

1 Type **https://qbo.intuit.com/** into your web browser.

2 Enter your User ID and password and then click **Sign In**.

3 Click **Skip for now** if asked to verify your number.

4 Your window should show the QBO dashboard as shown in Figure 2.15.

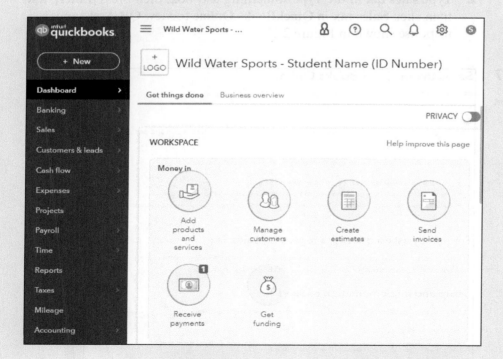

Figure 2.15

Dashboard for Wild Water Sports

Now that you're back into your QBO Company it's time to explore QBO's help features.

To use QBO help:

1   Click the ⑦ **Help** button located in the upper-right portion of your window. Type **Add an account** in the Type something text box, then press **[Enter]** to view QB Assistance's response, and then click **Add to my Chart of accounts** to view QB Assistance's response shown in Figure 2.16.

Figure 2.16

Using QuickBooks Online help to learn how to add an account

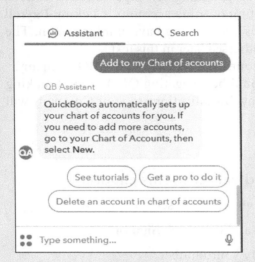

2   Type **sales tax** in the Type something text box, then press **[Enter]**, and then click **Sales tax in QuickBooks Online** to view QB Assistance's response shown in Figure 2.17.

Figure 2.17

Help with sales tax

QuickBooks help is, to be frank, not very helpful. Most of what you need to be effective using QBO is outlined in this text. Now let's learn how to navigate QBO.

To navigate QBO:

1 Close the Help window, then click the [+ New] button at the top of the Dashboard to view the menu items available as shown in Figure 2.18.

CUSTOMERS	VENDORS	EMPLOYEES	OTHER
Invoice	Expense	Payroll 🔋	Bank deposit
Receive payment	Check	Time entry	Transfer
Estimate	Bill		Journal entry
Credit memo	Pay bills		Statement
Sales receipt	Purchase order		Inventory qty adjustment
Refund receipt	Vendor credit		Pay down credit card
Delayed credit	Credit card credit		
Delayed charge	Print checks		

Show less

Figure 2.18

The + New menu

2 Click outside the + New menu to close the + New menu, then click **Sales** from the navigation bar, and then click **Customers** as shown in Figure 2.19.

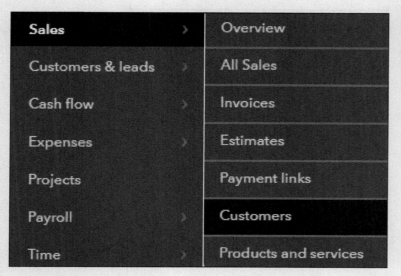

Figure 2.19

Adding customers

3   Then click **Add customer manually** to view Figure 2.20. As you have not
yet entered any customers, QBO will ask you to add your first customer.
You will do this later in Chapter 3. Remember QBO is an online
application, and Intuit will change it often.

Figure 2.20

Customer information window

4   Click **X** from the Customer information window to close the Customer
window, then click **Expenses** from the navigation bar, then click **Vendors**,
and then click **Add vendor manually** to view Figure 2.21.

Figure 2.21

Vendor Information window

5 Click **X** to close the Vendor Information window, then click **Payroll** from the navigation bar, and then click **Employees** to view Figure 2.22. In Chapter 3, you'll add employees by clicking **Add an employee** located at the bottom of the window shown. Do not click Add an employee now. Once again in this chapter, we're just showing you how to navigate QBO.

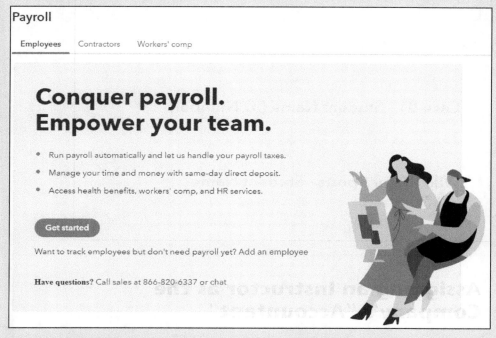

Figure 2.22

Getting started with payroll

6 Click the **Gear** icon located in the upper-right corner to view Figure 2.23. This menu gives you access to details about your company, lists (such as the chart of accounts, products and services, terms, etc.), tools (such as reconciling accounts and budgeting), and your profile, which will give you the ability to switch QBO companies.

YOUR COMPANY	LISTS	TOOLS	PROFILE
Account and settings	All lists	Order checks ☐	Feedback
Manage users	Products and services	Import data	Refer a friend
Custom form styles	Recurring transactions	Import desktop data	Privacy
Chart of accounts	Attachments	Export data	Switch company
QuickBooks labs	Custom fields	Reconcile	
	Tags	Budgeting	
		Audit log	
		SmartLook	
		Resolution center	

Figure 2.23

Gear window

7 If you had created more than one company you could click **Switch company** under the Profile heading to view Figure 2.24. Since you have only created one company, the Switch company text will not appear. However, if your instructor assigns you an additional case (they can assign you up to 3 more), more files will be shown such as you see in this figure. Click **Wild Water Sports** to return to your QBO company Dashboard.

Figure 2.24

Switching companies

"How to Give Your Accountant Access
to Your QuickBooks"

Assigning an Instructor as the Company's "Accountant"

Your instructor may require you to assign them as your company's accountant. You do this so they, as your accountant, will always have access to your company files for grading and evaluation purposes. This will also assist the instructor in answering questions you may have about your company. The process of assigning an accountant to your company involves a brief interview in which you will provide your instructor's email address and name. Make sure you have that information before beginning this process. Your instructor will receive an email inviting them to be your accountant. Once the instructor accepts your invitation, they will have access to your company and the instructor's name will appear in the Accounting Firms section of the Manage Users page.

However, if your instructor is using the Intuit Educator Portal, you will not have to assign them as your accountant. Once they have assigned you a case, they will always be able to view your QBO file.

To assign an accountant to your company, do the following:

1 Click **My Accountant** from the navigation bar.

2 Type your instructor's email address in the space provided as shown in Figure 2.25.

An accountant can be your best business partner

Make it easy to work together. Invite yours to your QuickBooks.

instructor@gmail.com | Invite

Your accountant and members of their firm will have admin access to your company data.

Figure 2.25

Inviting your instructor to be your accountant

3 Click the **Invite** button.

4 Once your instructor accepts your QuickBooks invitation, you'll be good to go.

Video Tutorials for QuickBooks Online (Developed and Maintained by Intuit)

Intuit, the developer of QBO, has made available video tutorials. The tutorials are step-by-step videos to learn your way around QuickBooks.

Throughout this text, the author will reference videos in the appropriate chapters. To view all tutorials, navigate your browser to https://quickbooks .intuit.com/global/learn-and-support/video-tutorials/.

To view two videos on QuickBooks Online, do the following:

1 Navigate your browser to the web address: https://quickbooks.intuit.com /global/learn-and-support/video-tutorials/. A partial view of that site is shown in Figure 2.26.

Figure 2.26

Video tutorials for QBO

2 Click Introduction to QuickBooks Online. Your window should look like Figure 2.27.

Figure 2.27

Accessing a video tutorial introducing QuickBooks Online

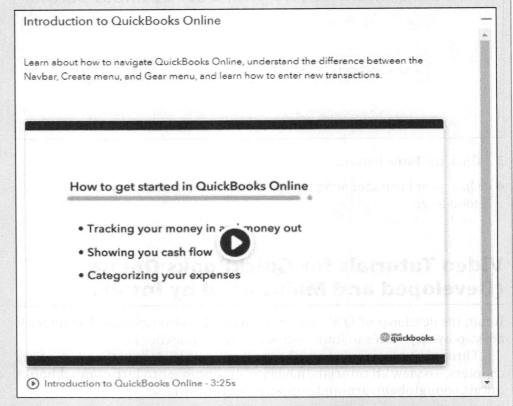

3 Click the **Play** arrow shown in Figure 2.27 and then click the **Play** arrow shown in Figure 2.28.

Figure 2.28

Playing the QuickBooks Online video

4 When you're done viewing the video close your browser windows and exit QBO.

End Note

You have now been introduced to QBO, its basic features, and how it is similar to but not the same as QBDT. You logged into your Intuit account and provided basic information about your company and learned how to navigate around the QBO application. After assigning your instructor as your accountant, learning more about the help features in QBO, exploring Intuit's video tutorials in this chapter, and exploring the Sample Company in Chapter 1, you're ready to start entering your company's information into your QBO file in Chapter 3. Chapter 3 will demonstrate how to set up your company using the Wild Water Sports company you created. After completing the instructions for Wild Water Sports found in the body of Chapter 3 you will be assigned a case by your instructor. This could be Case 1, 2, 3, 4, 5, or 6 found in the end of Chapter 3 materials.

2

Chapter 2 Questions

1 How are QBO and QBDT different in the number of companies they can manage per license?
2 Does QBO work offline, without an Internet connection?
3 Do you need to back up QBO files?
4 How are QBO and QBDT similar?
5 What information do you need to supply to assign your instructor as the company's accountant?

Chapter 2 Matching

a. QBO   _____   Click to access help
b. QBDT   _____   Click to find past transactions
c. Gear icon   _____   Click to access QBO employee information
d. Payroll   _____   Online version of QuickBooks
e. Navigation bar   _____   Click to add your instructor as your accountant
f. [+ New] icon   _____   Provides links to QBO tasks and resources
g. Magnifying glass   _____   Windows desktop version of QuickBooks
h. Help (?) icon   _____   Click to add any transaction
i. Manage Users   _____   Click to manage your subscription, users, and settings
j. Dashboard   _____   On the left of the Dashboard, it shows a menu of items

Setting Up a New Company: Establishing a Chart of Accounts, Beginning Balances, Customers, Vendors, and Products/Services

chapter **3**

Student Learning Outcomes

Upon completion of this chapter, the student will be able to do the following:

- Log into their account
- Change company settings
- Modify the chart of accounts; establish beginning balances; and create new customers, vendors, products, and services
- Close Opening Balance Equity and create and print a Balance Sheet
- Create, print, and export a Transaction Detail by Account report

Overview

You began this process in Chapter 2 when you created your account and provided basic information about the Wild Water Sports company, including the company name, address, industry, type, and so on.

Now you're going to revisit the Wild Water Sports company you worked on in Chapter 2. Each of the following chapters will work the same way. To begin, you will navigate your browser to Wild Water Sports company. The text will demonstrate how to do certain tasks, such as modify defaults, add a new account, add a new transaction, and so on. These demonstrations will occur in the Wild Water Sports company.

Each section of every chapter will begin with a demonstration using the Wild Water Sports company. That is followed by you completing an end-of-chapter case. In the case, you will be asked to perform tasks similar to those demonstrated in the Wild Water Sports company, but now in your new case. The tasks you accomplish on your Wild Water Sports company and your case are permanent and will be there even after you close your QBO browser window. There is no Save File or Save File As command in QBO. Everything is saved for you.

After you make changes to the Wild Water Sports company in each chapter, it is critical that you verify your work. Do that by comparing the trial balance you create at the end of each chapter with the trial balance figure shown at the end of each chapter in this text.

Company Settings

Your first task will be to update the Wild Water Sports company settings.

To modify Wild Water Sports company settings, do the following:

1   Open your Internet browser.

2   Type **https://app.qbo.intuit.com/app/login** into your browser's address text box. If you are using your own personal computer you may be presented with your email or user id. If so, click **Sign In** and then your password. If you are using any other computer you will be required to provide your email or user id as well as your password. You may have to click **Use a different user ID**.

3   From the Wild Water Sports company home page, click the **Gear** icon to manage your settings shown in Figure 3.1.

Figure 3.1

Settings

YOUR COMPANY	LISTS	TOOLS	PROFILE
Account and settings	All lists	Order checks ⧉	Feedback
Manage users	Products and services	Import data	Refer a friend
Custom form styles	Recurring transactions	Import desktop data	Privacy
Chart of accounts	Attachments	Export data	Switch company
QuickBooks labs	Custom fields	Reconcile	
	Tags	Budgeting	
		Audit log	
		SmartLook	
		Resolution center	

You're viewing QuickBooks in **Accountant view**. Learn more   Switch to Business view

4   Click **Account and settings**. The first screen is the Wild Water Sports company information shown in Figure 3.2. This is where you will change your company's name, tax form, industry, address, and so on.

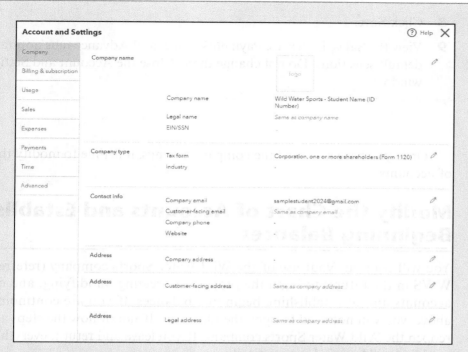

Figure 3.2

Company settings

5 Click the **pencil icon** in the Company type section then type **Misc** into the Industry text box. A drop-down list will appear. Select **Miscellaneous Store Retailers** as shown in Figure 3.3. Be sure that Form 1120 is selected as the tax form.

Figure 3.3

Selecting an Industry

6 Click **Save**.

7 Click the **pencil icon** in the Company name section and type **99-6854102** in the EIN text box and select the EIN button as shown in Figure 3.4.

Legal name
Used on forms like 1099s.

☑ Same as company name

EIN

◉ EIN   ○ SSN

99-6854102

Cancel   Save

Figure 3.4

Add an EIN

> **8** Click **Save**.
>
> **9** View the Sales, Expenses, Payments, Time, and Advance tabs noting
> default selections. Do not change these. Close the Account and Settings
> window.

Once you have modified the company settings, it is time to modify the chart
of accounts.

Navigate your browser to the Video
Tutorials provided by Intuit (see
website address specified in the
Preface to this text) and then search
on how to set up your chart of
accounts.

Modify the Chart of Accounts and Establish Beginning Balances

You will continue your use of the Wild Water Sports company (referred to as
WWS in the future) to learn the process of creating, modifying, and deleting
accounts and of establishing beginning balances. If you are continuing from
above, you will not need to open the file again. If not, follow the steps above to
reopen the Wild Water Sports company. If you leave and return, everything you
modified will be saved automatically.

Creating accounts and related beginning balances only occurs when you
are utilizing QBO for the first time and your business has been in operation for
some time. The transition to QBO from a previous accounting system will indicate
business events and balances that occurred prior to the first date of QBO use.

In this section, you will be adding new checking, inventory, prepaid rent, long-
term debt, and common stock accounts to the WWS company. You will also be
establishing beginning balances for checking, accounts receivable, prepaid rent,
inventory, and accounts payable. Every time you add a beginning balance, an
equal and opposite amount is recorded to the Opening Balance Equity account
(to keep debits and credits in balance).

QBO lets you establish a beginning amount for all of these accounts using
basic journal entries. We will do that for some accounts, such as accounts receivable and accounts payable. For the other accounts, such as checking, inventory,
prepaid rent, long-term debt, and common stock, you will set some beginning
balances when you set up a new account.

When a new account is added, its account type needs to be specified. Asset
account types include the following: bank, accounts receivable, other current assets,
fixed assets, and other assets. Liability account types include the following: accounts
payable, credit cards, other current liabilities, and long-term liabilities. Equity is
its own account type. Income account types include sales of product income and
services. Expense account types include cost of goods sold, expenses, and other
expense. Every account needs to be assigned to one of these account types. This will
dictate where the account appears in all reports, especially the income statement,
balance sheet, and statement of cash flows. The detail type will further define where
the account appears under its account type. Examples of bank account detail types
include cash on hand, checking, money market, and savings.

To begin, let's add a new checking account with a beginning balance of
$20,000.00.

To add a new checking account to the chart of accounts and establish a beginning balance, do the following:

1 Click the **Gear** icon and then click **Chart of Accounts**.

2 Click the **See your Chart of Accounts** button.

3 Click the **New** button in the upper-right corner of the chart of accounts.

4 Fill in the text boxes as shown in Figure 3.5.

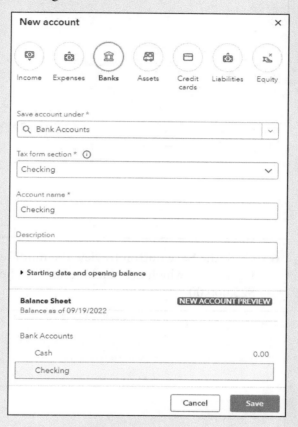

Figure 3.5

Account (adding a new bank account)

5 Click the text **Starting date and opening balance** and then fill in the text boxes as shown in Figure 3.6.

Figure 3.6

Account (completing the addition of a new checking account)

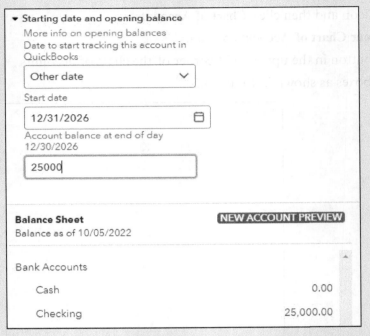

6 Click the **Save** button to view the modified chart of accounts shown in Figure 3.7, which now includes a new checking account with a balance of $25,000.00.

Figure 3.7

Chart of Accounts (modified with the new checking account)

So far, we have added $25,000 to the assets to the WWS company as of 12/31/2026. The Opening Balance Equity account has also increased as the result of this adjustment. To continue, let's add a new product. In QBO, products are merchandise a company purchases from a vendor, maintains in inventory, and then sells to customers. Services are efforts made by a company to add value to a customer. In the WWS company, an inventory account exists. If you create a new company, an inventory account may not exist. However, when you add a new product, a new inventory account, called inventory asset, will automatically be created.

Navigate your browser to the Video Tutorials provided by Intuit (see website address specified in the Preface to this text) and then search on how top create an inventory product.

To add a new product and service, do the following:

1 View the chart of accounts and note the Inventory account with a QuickBooks balance of $0.00.

2 Click the **Gear** icon and click **Products and Services** from the Lists column.

3 Click **New**.

4 Select **Inventory** from the Product/Service information list.

5 Type Malibu Sunset LX as the new product in the Name text box.

6 Click the **drop-down arrow** in the Category text box then click **Add New**. Type **Boats** as the Category name, then click **Save**.

7 Type **1** in the Initial quantity on hand text box and 12/31/2026 in the As of date text box.

8 Select **Inventory** as the Inventory asset account.

9 Type **Malibu Sunset LX** in the Description and Purchasing information text boxes.

10 Type **60000** in the Sales price/rate text box and **48000** in the Cost text box.

11 Select **Sales** as the Income account and **Cost of Goods Sold** as the Expense account.

12 Accept **Taxable - standard rate** from the Sales tax section. Type **Malibu Boats** in the Preferred Vendor text box then click **Add new Malibu Boats**, then click **Save**. Your window should look like Figure 3.8.

Figure 3.8

Product/Service information window

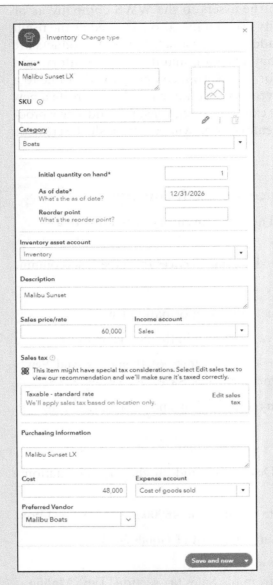

13 Click the down arrow in the Save and close button and then select **Save and new**.

14 Click on **Change type** next to the word Inventory at the top of the window. Click **Service**.

15 Type **Engine Service** as the name of a new service.

16 Check the **I sell this product/service to my customers** check box and then uncheck the **I purchase this product/service from a vendor** check box.

17 Type **Engine Service** as the Description in the sales forms text box and then select Services from the Category drop-down list. If Services is not listed as an option, type **Services** in the Category text box, then click **Add Services** and then click **Save**.

18 Type **250** in the Sales price/rate text box then click **Save and Close**.

19 Click the **Gear** icon then click **Chart of accounts**.

20 Click **New** then click **Income**.

21   Select **Income** from the Save account under drop-down list text box.

22   Select **Service/Fee Income** from the Tax form section drop-down list text box.

23   Type **Service Revenue** in the Account name text box then click **Save**.

24   Return to your recently created Service item by clicking the **Gear** icon, then clicking **Products and services**, then click **Edit** on the Engine Service service.

25   Click **Service Revenue** from the Income account drop-down list. See Figure 3.9.

Figure 3.9

Creating a new service

26   Click **Edit sales tax**, then select **Nontaxable**.

27   Click **Done** and then click the **Save and close** button.

28   Scroll down the list of products and services. Note the addition of the new Malibu Sunset LX product, with a quantity of 1, and the new Engine Service added.

29   Click the **Gear** icon and then **Chart of Accounts** and note the new balance in the Inventory account of $48,000.

Following the instructions for adding a new product above, create a new product (Name, Description, and Purchasing information: Malibu Sportster LX with a sales price of $52,000 and a cost of $41,600 on 12/31/26 with an initial quantify on hand of 3, Inventory asset account: Inventory, Category: Boats, Income account: Sales, Sales tax: Taxable – standard rate, Expense account: Cost of goods sold, and Preferred Vendor: Malibu Boats).

Following the instructions for adding a new service above, create a new service (Name and Description: Diagnostic Service with a rate of $500, Category: Services, Income account: Service Revenue, Sales tax: Nontaxable).

View the updated Chart of Accounts to see a $25,000 balance in the Checking account, a new Inventory account balance of $172,800, and a new Opening balance equity account of $197,800.

To continue, let's add opening balances to the Prepaid expenses, Long-term business loans, and Common stock accounts.

To add opening balances to Long-term business loans, Prepaid expenses, and Common stock accounts:

1 Continuing in the Chart of Accounts, click **View Register** in the Action column on the Long-term business loans account.

2 Click **Add journal entry**.

3 Type **12/31/2026** in the DATE column.

4 Type **1** in the REF NO. column.

5 Type **Chase Bank** in the PAYEE column then click **Add Chase Bank**.

6 Change Type to **Vendor** and then click **Save**.

7 Select **Opening balance equity** from the ACCOUNT drop-down list.

8 Type **50000** in the INCREASE column and then press the [**Tab**] key to view Figure 3.10.

Figure 3.10

Creating a beginning balance in the Long-term business loans account

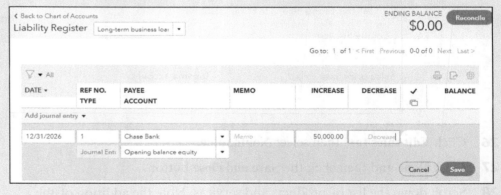

9 Click **Save**.

10 Click **Back to Chart of Accounts**, then click **View Register** in the Action column on the Prepaid expenses account.

11 Click **Add deposit**.

12 Type **12/31/2026** in the DATE column.

13 Type **Allstate Insurance** in the PAYEE column, then click **Add Allstate Insurance**.

14 Change Type to **Vendor** and then click **Save**.

15 Select **Opening balance equity** from the ACCOUNT drop-down list.

16 Type **15000** in the INCREASE column and then press the [**Tab**] key.

17 Click **Save**.

18 Click **Back to Chart of Accounts**, then click **View Register** in the Action column on the Common stock account.

19 Click **Add journal entry**.

20 Type **12/31/2026** in the DATE column.

21 Type **2** in the REF NO. column.

22 Type **Shareholders** in the PAYEE column then click **Shareholders**.

23 Change Type to **Vendor** and then click **Save**.

24 Select **Opening balance equity** from the ACCOUNT drop-down list.

25 Type **1000** in the INCREASE column and then press the [**Tab**] key.

26 Click **Save**.

27 Click **Reports** from the Navigation bar.

28 Type **Trial Balance** in the Find a report by name text box and then click **Trial Balance**.

29 Select **Custom** from the Report period drop-down list.

30 Type **1/1/2027** in both the first and second text boxes then click Run report to view the Trial Balance shown in Figure 3.11.

Figure 3.11

Trial Balance as of 1/1/2027

31 Click **Save customization** then click **Save**.

Now we will set up beginning balances in accounts receivable and accounts payable by using journal entries and add a new customer and vendor at the same time. Journal entries are commonly used to adjust accounts. A customer is an entity to whom you sell products or provide a service. A vendor is an entity from whom you purchase products or services.

Navigate your browser to the Video Tutorials provided by Intuit (see website address specified in the Preface to this text) and then search on how to use journal entries.

To create accounts receivable and accounts payable beginning balances:

1 Click the [+ New] icon, then click on **Journal Entry** from the Other column.

2 Type **12/31/2026** in the date text box.

3 Select **Accounts Receivable (A/R)** as the first account and type **70000** in the Debits column and type Refugio as a new customer in the Name text box and then click **Save** in the new Customer window.

4 Select **Accounts Payable (A/P)** as the second account, type **56000** in the Credits column, and type **Malibu Boats** in the Name text box.

5 Select **Opening Balance Equity** as the third account, type **14000** in the Credits column, then press the **[Tab]** key. Your screen should look like Figure 3.12.

Figure 3.12

Journal entry to create beginning account balances

6 Click **Save and close**.

7 Click **Reports**, click the Custom reports tab, and then click Trial Balance to view Figure 3.13.

Figure 3.13

Updated trial balance report

Wild Water Sports - Student Name (ID Number)

Trial Balance
As of January 1, 2027

	DEBIT	CREDIT
Checking	25,000.00	
Accounts receivable (A/R)	70,000.00	
Inventory	172,800.00	
Prepaid expenses	15,000.00	
Accounts Payable (A/P)		56,000.00
Long-term business loans		50,000.00
Common stock		1,000.00
Opening balance equity		175,800.00
TOTAL	$282,800.00	$282,800.00

So far, we have added a $175,800 (Checking $25,000 + Accounts Receivable $70,000 + Inventory $172,800 + Prepaid expenses $15,000 − Accounts Payable $56,000 − Long-term business loans $50,000 − Common stock $1,000) net increase to the Wild Water Sports company as of 1/1/27. The Opening Balance Equity account has increased as a result of this adjustment.

Finally, let's add some fixed asset accounts. The company had equipment it had purchased and partially depreciated in 2026. Thus, as of 1/1/2027, we need to set up some fixed asset accounts related to equipment. These assets will continue to be depreciated over their estimated useful lives so it will be necessary to create an equipment account and two subaccounts: original cost and accumulated depreciation.

To create the equipment, original cost, and accumulated depreciation accounts:

1 Click the **Gear** icon.
2 Click **Chart of Accounts**.
3 From the Chart of accounts click **New**.
4 Select **Assets** from the top of the New account window.
5 Select **Fixed Assets** from the drop-down list in the Save account under text box.
6 Select **Fixed Asset Other Tools Equipment** from the drop-down list in the Tax form section text box.
7 Type **Equipment** in the Account name text box.
8 Click **Save** to save this account.
9 From the Chart of accounts click **New**.
10 Select **Assets** from the top of the New account window.
11 Select **Equipment** from the drop-down list in the Save account under text box.
12 Select **Fixed Asset Other Tools Equipment** from the drop-down list in the Tax form section text box.
13 Type **Original Cost** in the Account name text box.
14 Click **Starting date and opening balance**.
15 Select **Other Date** from the drop-down list in the Select Date text box.
16 Type **12/31/2026** in the Start date text box. (This date will be different for each case.)
17 Type **40000** in the Account balance at the end of day text box. (This amount will be different for each case.)
18 Click **Save** to save this account.
19 From the Chart of accounts click **New**.

20   Select **Assets** from the top of the New account window.

21   Select **Equipment** from the drop-down list in the Save account under text box.

22   Select **Accumulated Depreciation** from the drop-down list in the Tax form section text box.

23   Type **Accumulated depreciation** in the Account name text box.

24   Click **Starting date and opening balance**.

25   Select **Other Date** from the drop-down list in the Select Date text box.

26   Type **12/31/26** in the Start date text box. (This date will be different for each case.)

27   Type **10000** in the Account balance at the end of day text box. (This amount will be different for each case.) Your window should look like Figure 3.14.

Figure 3.14

Adding a new accumulated depreciation account

28   Click **Save**.

Close Opening Balance Equity and Create a Balance Sheet

The final step in establishing beginning balances in QBO is to close out the Opening Balance Equity account as of 1/1/27 of $205,800. As we established a common stock account, the only account left in a corporation's equity accounts is retained earnings. Retained earnings are the earnings generated from prior years less dividends. You will need to create a trial balance, which lists the debit or credit balance in all accounts as of a specific date. Your instructor may ask you to customize, print, or export the trial balance to Excel, so you may do that as well.

To close opening balance equity and create, customize, save, print, and export a balance sheet, do the following:

1 Click the ⟨ + New ⟩ icon, and click on **Journal Entry** from the Other column.

2 Type **12/31/2026** in the Journal date text box.

3 Select **Opening Balance Equity** as the first account, and type **205800** in the Debits column.

4 Select **Retained Earnings** as the second account, and type **205800** in the Credits column. Note: Retained Earnings was used since this company is a corporation. If this company was a sole proprietorship, you would use Owner's Equity. Your journal entry should look like Figure 3.15.

5 Click **Save and Close**.

6 Click **Reports** in the navigation bar.

7 Type **Balance Sheet** into the Find report by name search text box and then select **Balance Sheet** from the list provided from your search.

8 Scroll to the top of the Balance Sheet report and then select **Custom** from the drop-down list in the Report period text box.

9 Press **[Tab]** and then type **1/1/27** in the from text box, and press **[Tab]**.

10 Type **1/1/27** in the to text box, and press **[Tab]**.

Figure 3.15

Journal Entry #4 (for closing Opening Balance Equity)

Navigate your browser to the Video Tutorials provided by Intuit (see website address specified in the Preface to this text) and then search on understanding the balance sheet.

11 Click the **Run Report** button. Scroll to the top of the Balance Sheet report, and your screen should look like Figure 3.16.

12 Click the **Printer** icon at the top of the report, and follow instructions to print your report as either a PDF file or a printed document and then close the Print window.

Figure 3.16

Balance Sheet
(partial view as of 1/1/27)

Wild Water Sports - Student Name (ID Number)	
Balance Sheet As of January 1, 2027	
	TOTAL
▾ ASSETS	
▾ Current Assets	
▾ Bank Accounts	
Checking	25,000.00
Total Bank Accounts	**$25,000.00**
▾ Accounts Receivable	
Accounts receivable (A/R)	70,000.00
Total Accounts Receivable	**$70,000.00**
▾ Other Current Assets	
Inventory	172,800.00
Prepaid expenses	15,000.00
Total Other Current Assets	**$187,800.00**
Total Current Assets	**$282,800.00**
▾ Fixed Assets	
▾ Equipment	
Accumulated depreciation	-10,000.00
Original Cost	40,000.00
Total Equipment	**30,000.00**
Total Fixed Assets	**$30,000.00**
TOTAL ASSETS	**$312,800.00**
▾ LIABILITIES AND EQUITY	
▾ Liabilities	
▾ Current Liabilities	
▾ Accounts Payable	
Accounts Payable (A/P)	56,000.00
Total Accounts Payable	**$56,000.00**
Total Current Liabilities	**$56,000.00**
▾ Long-Term Liabilities	
Long-term business loans	50,000.00
Total Long-Term Liabilities	**$50,000.00**
Total Liabilities	**$106,000.00**
▾ Equity	
Common stock	1,000.00
Opening balance equity	0.00
Retained Earnings	205,800.00
Net Income	
Total Equity	**$206,800.00**
TOTAL LIABILITIES AND EQUITY	**$312,800.00**

Navigate your browser to the Video Tutorials provided by Intuit (see website address specified in the Preface to this text) and then search on how to customize reports.

13 Click the **Save customization** button.

14 Type **Balance Sheet as of 1/1/27** in the Custom report name text box as shown in Figure 3.17.

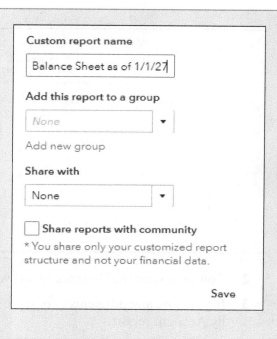

Figure 3.17

Save report customizations

Navigate your browser to the Video Tutorials provided by Intuit (see website address specified in the Preface to this text) and then search on how to save customized reports.

15 Click **Save**.

16 Click the **Export** icon shown next to the Printer icon at the top of the report and then select **Export to Excel** from the drop-down list to begin the export to Excel process.

17 Click **Save** after you have navigated to a place on your computer to save this file.

18 Open Excel and then open the file you just saved.

19 After viewing your newly created Excel file, close Excel.

Trial Balance

The work you completed in this chapter influenced the company's trial balance. You decided to create a Trial Balance report after entering all business events described in this chapter and investigate any differences between your report and that shown in Figure 3.18.

To create a trial balance:

1 Click **Reports**, then select the **Custom reports** tab, then select Trial Balance. Change the to date of the report to 1/1/2027 to view the Trial Balance as shown in Figure 3.18.

Figure 3.18

Trial Balance

	DEBIT	CREDIT
Wild Water Sports - Student Name (ID Number)		
Trial Balance As of January 1, 2027		
Checking	25,000.00	
Accounts receivable (A/R)	70,000.00	
Inventory	172,800.00	
Prepaid expenses	15,000.00	
Equipment:Accumulated depreciation		10,000.00
Equipment:Original Cost	40,000.00	
Accounts Payable (A/P)		56,000.00
Long-term business loans		50,000.00
Common stock		1,000.00
Opening balance equity		0.00
Retained Earnings		205,800.00
TOTAL	$322,800.00	$322,800.00

2 Compare your trial balance report with Figure 3.18.

3 If you note any differences continue below to create a Transaction Detail by Account report.

Create, Print, and Export a Transaction Detail by Account

Often, you will want to investigate a detailed list of transactions you have recorded for a specific period. In your end-of-chapter cases, a usual explanation for an incorrect report is recording a transaction in the incorrect period. To explore this option, you will create a transaction detail by account report for a specific period. You can create such a report for a large period to see if your transactions were recorded in the proper period and to see where you may have entered a wrong amount or account.

To create, print, and export a transaction detail by account report for the period 1/1/30 to 12/31/30, do the following:

1 Click **Reports** from the navigation bar.

2 Type **Transaction** in the Find a report by name text box.

3 Select **Transaction Detail by Account**.

4 Scroll to the top of the report window and then select **Custom** from the Report period drop-down text box and then press [**Tab**].

5 Type **01/01/2020** in the text box and then press [**Tab**].

6 Type **12/31/2030** in the text box and then press [**Tab**].

7 Click **Run report**. Even though the transactions shown in this report should match yours, the dates will be different. The top of the report is shown in Figure 3.19.

DATE	TRANSACTION TYPE	NUM	NAME	MEMO/DESCRIPTION	SPLIT	AMOUNT	BALANCE
▾ Checking							
12/31/2026	Deposit			Opening Balance	Opening balance equity	25,000.00	25,000.00
Total for Checking						$25,000.00	
▾ Accounts receivable (A/R)							
12/31/2026	Journal Entry	3			-Split-	70,000.00	70,000.00
Total for Accounts receivable (A/R)						$70,000.00	
▾ Inventory							
12/31/2026	Inventory Starting Value	START		Malibu Sportster LX - Openi...	Opening balance equity	124,800.00	124,800.00
12/31/2026	Inventory Starting Value	START		Malibu Sunset LX - Opening...	Opening balance equity	48,000.00	172,800.00
12/31/2026	Inventory Starting Value	START		Malibu Sunset - Opening in...	Opening balance equity	0.00	172,800.00
Total for Inventory						$172,800.00	
▾ Prepaid expenses							
12/31/2026	Deposit		Allstate Insurance		Opening balance equity	15,000.00	15,000.00
Total for Prepaid expenses						$15,000.00	
▾ Equipment							
▾ Accumulated depreciation							
12/31/2026	Journal Entry			Opening Balance	-Split-	-10,000.00	-10,000.00
Total for Accumulated depreciation						$ -10,000.00	
▾ Original Cost							
12/31/2026	Journal Entry			Opening Balance	-Split-	40,000.00	40,000.00
Total for Original Cost						$40,000.00	
Total for Equipment						$30,000.00	

Wild Water Sports - Student Name (ID Number)
Transaction Detail by Account
January 2020 - December 2030

Figure 3.19

Transaction Detail by Account Report (top section)

8 Click **Deposit** in the Prepaid expenses section.

9 Close this window, scroll down the report, and investigate other transactions.

10 Scroll back to the top of this report, and click **Save customization**.

11 Leave Transaction Detail by Account as the custom report name and then click **Save**. Export this report like you exported the Balance Sheet earlier in this chapter.

12 Click the **Print** button to set this report up for printing; however, do not print this report as it is too long and unnecessary. Click **Cancel**.

13 Click the **Account** icon (in this case **S** for the owner Sample Student) and then click **Sign Out**.

End Note

In this chapter, using the Wild Water Sports company you have modified company settings, added new accounts to the chart of accounts, and added beginning balances where appropriate. You have added customers, vendors, products, and services and closed the Opening Balance Equity account. You are ready to add operating activities like sales receipts, invoices, and cash receipts.

Chapter 3 Questions

1 How do you access company settings?

2 When is it appropriate to add beginning balances to accounts?

3 What steps need to be followed to add an account to the chart of accounts?

4 When you add a beginning balance to an account, what other account is affected?

5 What information is required when adding a new product to QBO?

6 What additional information is required when you add beginning balance amounts to the accounts receivable account?

7 What additional information is required when you add beginning balance amounts to the accounts payable account?

8 Which additional account is used when you close Opening Balance Equity?

9 How do you access the Balance Sheet report?

10 How can you review a Transactions Report for any account when you are viewing the Balance Sheet?

Chapter 3 Matching

a. Transactions report

b. Trial balance

c. Journal entry

d. Opening Balance Equity

e. Customer

f. Vendor

g. Product

h. Service

i. Account type

j. Detailed type example

_____ Entity to whom you sell products/services

_____ Account used to offset beginning balance adjustments

_____ Merchandise a company purchases from a vendor

_____ Efforts made by a company to add value to a customer

_____ A listing of the debit or credit balances as of a specific date

_____ Dictates where an account appears in all reports

_____ Transactions for an account for a specified period

_____ Entity from whom you purchase products/services

_____ Checking

_____ Commonly used to adjust accounts

Chapter 3 Cases

The following cases require you to accept a new invitation from your instructor. Each of the following cases continues throughout the text in a sequential manner. For example, if you are assigned Case 01, you will use the file you modified in this chapter in all of the following chapters. Each of the following cases is similar in concepts assessed but differs in amounts and transactions. See the Preface to this text for a matrix of each student case and its attributes.

To create your company, do the following:

1 Open the email you received from your instructor and click **Accept Invitation**. A new browser window should open a QBO sign up page.

2 Click **Sign In** (as shown in Figure 3.20) to accept your email or user ID and then type your password and click **Continue**.

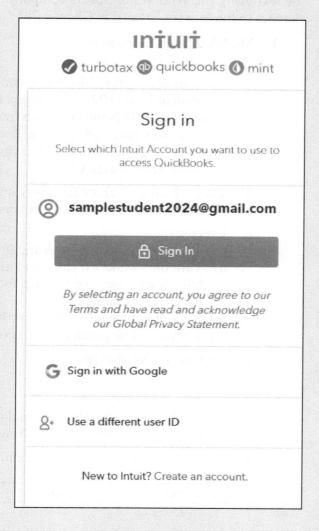

Figure 3.20

Sign In window (for logging in)

3 Once your file is created you should see a welcome screen. Click **Next** to continue.

4 Type **Case # - Student Name** as your business name replacing # with the case number your instructor assigned and Student Name with your name. (Note: in figures provided below Case 1 - Student Name is used.)

5 Click **Next** then click **Nothing, I'm just getting started** then click **Next**.

6 Click **Bookkeeper or accountant** when asked What your main role is, then click **Next**.

7 Click **Let's go**.

Case 1

Your company is a distributor of surfboards located in La Jolla, California. The company does not collect sales tax as all of its customers are resellers. Leave Industry text box blank. You began business in 2023 and want to use QBO starting January 1, 2024. Beginning balances as of 12/31/23 have been provided below.

You must make changes to your company. Based on what you learned in the text using the Wild Water Sports company, you are to make the following changes to the case you created in Chapter 2:

1   Modify settings as follows:

a. Company
   i)   Company name—Modify the company name to Case 01 – Student Name (ID Number) replacing Student Name with your name and ID Number with the number your instructor indicated.
   ii) Company type—Modify the Tax form by selecting **Form 1120** from the drop-down list of forms. Leave Industry text box blank and then click **Save**.

b. Sales—Turn on – Track inventory quantity on hand. (This will automatically show items table on expense and purchase forms.)

c. Expenses
   i)   Turn on – Track expenses and items by customer.
   ii) Turn on – Make expenses and items billable (no markup, track billable expenses and items as income in a single account, and no sales tax charged).
   iii) Default bill payment terms net 30.
   iv) Turn on – Use purchase orders (no custom fields).

d. Payments—No changes

e. Advanced
   i)   Time tracking
       (1) Turn on – Add Service field to timesheets.
       (2) Turn on – Make Single-Time Activity Billable to Customer.

2   Create new accounts and related beginning balances as follows:

Account Type	Detail Type	Name	Balance	As of
Bank	Checking	Checking	25,000.00	12/31/23
Fixed Assets*	Furniture & Fixtures	Original cost	40,000.00	12/31/23
Fixed Assets*	Furniture & Fixtures	Depreciation	10,000.00	12/31/23
Long-Term Liabilities	Notes Payable	Notes Payable	60,000.00	12/31/23
Equity	Common Stock	Common Stock	1,000.00	12/31/23

*When entering a new fixed asset, place a check in the **Track depreciation of this asset** check box to reveal Original cost and Depreciation text boxes. Enter amounts from above as positive numbers.

3   Create two new products and one new service item as follows:

a.   Products

   i)   Name/Description – Rook 15, initial quantity 12/31/23 – 10, inventory asset account – Inventory Asset (this account will automatically be created in the chart of accounts when you add this product), price – $650, cost – $400, income account – Sales, expense account – Cost of Goods Sold

   ii)   Name/Description – The Water Hog, track quantity, initial quantity 12/31/23 – 8, inventory asset account – Inventory Asset, price – $860, cost — $500, income account – Sales, expense account – Cost of Goods Sold

b.   Service—Name/Description – Consulting, rate – $25, income account – Services. Click **+ Add new**, Account Type: Income, Detail Type: Service/Fee Income, Name: Services

c.   Make changes to the following accounts via journal entry 1 as of 12/31/23 with an offset to Opening Balance Equity. Note: You'll have to add these accounts first.

Account	Amount	Name
Accounts Receivable	5,000.00	Blondie's Boards (new customer)
Prepaid Expenses	3,000.00	
Accounts Payable	4,500.00	Channel Islands (new vendor)

4   Close the Opening Balance Equity account to Retained Earnings via journal entry 2 as of 12/31/23.

5   Prepare and print a Trial Balance report as of 12/31/23, save it as a customized report named Trial Balance 12/31/23, and share it with all users. Click **Reports**, then scroll down the page to the For my accountant section, and click **Trial Balance**. Then select **Custom** as the report period and type **1/1/23** and **12/31/23** as the from–to dates. Your report should look like Figure 3.21.

6   If your trial balance differs from what is shown in Figure 3.21, do the following:

a.   Make sure all of your changes were dated 12/31/23.

b.   Click on the debit or credit balance to view a transactions report for each account, and investigate why your answer is different.

c.   Ask your instructor for assistance.

d.   Be sure your company matches the above as you will be adding additional business events in Chapter 4.

Figure 3.21

Trial Balance (as of 12/31/23)

Case 1 TRIAL BALANCE As of December 31, 2023		
	DEBIT	CREDIT
Checking	25,000.00	
Accounts Receivable	5,000.00	
Inventory Asset	8,000.00	
Prepaid Expenses	3,000.00	
Furniture & Fixtures:Depreciation		10,000.00
Furniture & Fixtures:Original cost	40,000.00	
Accounts Payable		4,500.00
Notes Payable		60,000.00
Common Stock		1,000.00
Opening Balance Equity		0.00
Retained Earnings		5,500.00
TOTAL	$81,000.00	$81,000.00

7   Export your Trial Balance report to Excel, and save it with the file name Student Name (replace with your name) Ch 03 Case 01 Trial Balance.xlsx.

8   Prepare and print a Transaction Detail by Account report for transactions between 1/1/24 and 12/31/24, save it as a customized report named Transaction Detail by Account, and share it with all users. If asked, indicate that your business is accrual based.

9   Use your Transaction Detail by Account report to locate any differences in your Trial Balance report created above.

   a.   Make sure that all of your changes were dated 12/31/23.

   b.   Click on the line that does not match to view the transaction for that account, and investigate why your answer differs.

   c.   Ask your instructor for assistance.

   d.   Be sure your company matches the above as you will be adding additional business events in Chapter 4.

10   Export your Transactions Detail by Account report to Excel, and save it with the file name Student Name (replace with your name) Ch 03 Case 01 Transaction Detail by Account.xlsx.

11   Sign out of your company.

Case 2

Your company is a distributor of remote control toys located in La Jolla, California. The company does not collect sales tax as all of its customers are resellers. You began business in 2024 and want to use QBO starting January 1, 2025. Beginning balances as of 12/31/24 have been provided below.

You must make changes to your company. Based on what you learned in the text using the Wild Water Sports company, you are to make the following changes to the case you created in Chapter 2:

1   Modify settings as follows:

a.   Company—Company name – Modify the company name to Case 02 – Student Name (ID Number) replacing Student Name with your name and ID Number with the number your instructor indicated.

b.   Sales—Turn on – Track quantity on hand. (This will automatically show items table on expense and purchase forms.)

c.   Expenses
   i)   Turn on – Track expenses and items by customer.
   ii)   Turn on – Make expenses and items billable (no markup, track billable expenses and items as income in a single account, no sales tax charged).
   iii)   Default bill payment terms net 30.
   iv)   Turn on – Use purchase orders (no custom fields).

d.   Payments—No changes

e.   Advanced
   i)   Time tracking
      (1)   Turn on – Add Service field to timesheets.
      (2)   Turn on – Make Single-Time Activity Billable to Customer.

2   Create new accounts and related beginning balances as follows:

Account Type	Detail Type	Name	Balance	As of
Bank	Checking	Checking	5,000.00	12/31/24
Fixed Assets*	Machinery & Equipment	Original cost	10,000.00	12/31/24
Fixed Assets*	Machinery & Equipment	Depreciation	1,000.00	12/31/24
Long-Term Liabilities	Notes Payable	Notes Payable	12,000.00	12/31/24
Equity	Common Stock	Common Stock	100.00	12/31/24

*When entering a new fixed asset, place a check in the **Track depreciation of this asset** check box to reveal Original cost and Depreciation text boxes. Enter amounts from above as positive numbers.

3   Create two new products and one new service item:

a.   Products
   i)   Name/Description/Purchasing Information – Broon F830 Ride, initial quantity 12/31/24 – 4, inventory asset account – Inventory Asset. Note: This account will automatically be created in the chart of accounts when you add this product. Price – $1,500, cost – $800, income account – Sales, expense account – Cost of Goods Sold.
   ii)   Name/Description/Purchasing Information – Sea Wind Carbon Sailboat, initial quantity 12/31/24 – 3, inventory asset account – Inventory Asset, price – $1,200, cost – $620, income account – Sales, expense account – Cost of Goods Sold.

b. Service—Name/Description – Repairs, rate – $45, income account – Services. Click **+ Add new** in the Income account text box, Account Type: Income, Detail Type: Service/Fee Income, Name: Services.

c. Make changes to the following accounts via journal entry 1 as of 12/31/24 with an offset to Opening Balance Equity. Note: You'll have to add these accounts first.

Account	Amount	Name
Accounts Receivable	925.00	Benson's RC (new customer)
Prepaid Expenses	2,400.00	
Accounts Payable	1,900.00	Kyosho (new vendor)

4 Close the Opening Balance Equity account to Retained Earnings via journal entry 2 as of 12/31/24.

5 Prepare and print a Trial Balance report as of 12/31/24 (Click **Reports**, then scroll down the page to the For my accountant section, and click **Trial Balance**. Then select **Custom** as the report period and type **1/1/24** and **12/31/24** as the from–to dates.), save it as a customized report named Trial Balance 12/31/24, and share it with all users. Your report should look like Figure 3.22.

Figure 3.22

Trial Balance (as of 12/31/24)

Case 2

TRIAL BALANCE

As of December 31, 2024

	DEBIT	CREDIT
Checking	5,000.00	
Accounts Receivable	925.00	
Inventory Asset	5,060.00	
Prepaid Expenses	2,400.00	
Machinery & Equipment:Depreciation		1,000.00
Machinery & Equipment:Original cost	10,000.00	
Accounts Payable		1,900.00
Notes Payable		12,000.00
Common Stock		100.00
Opening Balance Equity		0.00
Retained Earnings		8,385.00
TOTAL	$23,385.00	$23,385.00

6 If your trial balance is different from what is shown in Figure 3.22, do the following:

a. Make sure all of your changes were dated 12/31/24.

b. Click on the debit or credit balance to view a transactions report for each account, and investigate why your answer is different.

c. Ask your instructor for assistance.

d. Be sure your company matches the above as you will be adding additional business events in Chapter 4.

7 Export your Trial Balance report to Excel, and save it with the file name Student Name (replace with your name) Ch 03 Case 02 Trial Balance.xlsx.

8 Prepare and print a Transaction Detail by Account report for all transactions between 1/1/10 and 12/31/28, save it as a customized report named Transaction Detail by Account, and share it with all users. If asked, indicate that your business is accrual based.

9 Use your Transaction Detail by Account report to locate any differences in your Trial Balance report created above.

    a.   Make sure all of your changes were dated 12/31/24.

    b.   Click on the line that does not match to view the transaction for that account, and investigate why your answer differs.

    c.   Ask your instructor for assistance.

    d.   Be sure your company matches the above as you will be adding additional business events in Chapter 4.

10 Export your Transactions Detail by Account report to Excel and save it with the file name Student Name (replace with your name) Ch 03 Case 02 Transaction Detail by Account.xlsx.

11 Sign out of your company.

Case 3

Your company sells and services cell phones. They are a sole proprietor located in La Jolla, California. The company does collect sales tax as all of its customers are consumers. (See Appendix 1 for directions on how to add a sales tax to a company file.) They began business in 2025 and want to use QBO starting January 1, 2026. Beginning balances as of 12/31/25 have been provided below.

    You must make changes to your company. Based on what you learned in the text using the Wild Water Sports company, you are to make the following changes to the case you created in Chapter 2:

1 Modify settings as follows:

    a.   Company—Company name – Modify the company name to Case 03 – Student Name (ID Number) replacing Student Name with your name and ID Number with the number your instructor indicated. Use 3990 La Jolla Shores Drive, La Jolla, CA 92037 as the company's address.

    b.   SSN—Add 987-65-4321 as your business social security number as you are a sole proprietor.

    c.   Sales—Make sure that Track inventory quantity on hand is on. (This will automatically show items table on expense and purchase forms.)

    d.   Expenses
        i)   Turn on – Track expenses and items by customer.
        ii) Turn on – Make expenses and items billable (no markup, track billable expenses and items as income in a single account, and charge sales tax).
        iii) Set default bill payment terms to Due on receipt.
        iv) Turn on – Use purchase orders (no custom fields).

  e. Payments—No changes

  f. Time Timesheet
    i)   Turn on – Show service field to timesheets.
    ii) Turn on – Allow time to be billable.

2 Follow steps provided in Appendix 1 to add sales tax paid annually beginning 1/1/26.

3 Create new accounts and related beginning balances (Account Type, Detail Type, Name, Balance as of 12/31/25) as follows:

  a. Bank, Checking, Checking, $12,000

  b. Fixed Assets, Machinery & Equipment, Original cost, $15,000

    Note: When entering a new fixed asset, place a check in the **Track depreciation of this asset** check box to reveal Original cost and Depreciation text boxes. Enter amounts from above as positive numbers.

    Fixed Assets, Machinery & Equipment, Depreciation, $2,000

  c. Long-Term Liabilities, Notes Payable, Notes Payable, $23,000

  d. Equity, Owner's Equity, Owner's Equity, 0

4 Create two new products (Name/Description, initial quantity 12/31/25, inventory asset account, price, cost, income account, expense account):

  a. Apple iPhone 7, 10, Inventory Asset, $750, $500. Note: This account will automatically be created in the chart of accounts when you add this product. Sales of Product Income, Cost of Goods Sold, taxable.

  b. Pixel, 3, Inventory Asset, $650, $400, Sales of Product Income, Cost of Goods Sold, taxable.

5 Create two new service items (Name/Description, rate, income account):

  a. Apple Repairs, $45, Services, not taxable. (Click + **Add new** in the Income account text box, Account Type: Income, Detail Type: Service/Fee Income, Name: Services.)

  b. Pixel Repairs, $40, Services, not taxable.

6 Make changes to the following accounts via journal entry 1 as of 12/31/25 with an offset to Opening Balance Equity:

Account	Amount	Name
Accounts Receivable (A/R)	4,125.00	GHO Marketing (new customer)
Prepaid Expenses	2,750.00	
Accounts Payable (A/P)	5,000.00	Apple Inc. (new vendor)

7 Close the Opening Balance Equity account (which should have a balance of $10,075) to Owner's Equity via journal entry 2 as of 12/31/25. (Note: Use Owner's Equity as this company is a sole proprietorship. Retained Earnings would have been used if this company had been a corporation.)

8   Prepare and print a Trial Balance report as of 12/31/25, click the **Run report** button, and then save it as a customized report named Trial Balance 12/31/25, and share it with all users. Click **Reports**, then scroll down the page to the For my accountant section, and click **Trial Balance**. Then select **Custom** as the report period and type **1/1/25** and **12/31/25** as the from–to dates. Your report should look like Figure 3.23.

Figure 3.23

Trial Balance

Case 03 - Student Name (ID Number)		
Trial Balance		
As of December 31, 2025		
	DEBIT	**CREDIT**
Checking	12,000.00	
Accounts receivable (A/R)	4,125.00	
Inventory Asset	6,200.00	
Prepaid expenses	2,750.00	
Machinery & Equipment:Depreciation		2,000.00
Machinery & Equipment:Original cost	15,000.00	
Accounts Payable (A/P)		5,000.00
Notes Payable		23,000.00
Opening balance equity		0.00
Owner's Equity		10,075.00
TOTAL	$40,075.00	$40,075.00

9   If your trial balance differs from what is shown in Figure 3.23, do the following:

   a.   Make sure all of your changes were dated 12/31/25.

   b.   Click on the debit or credit balance to view a transactions report for each account, and investigate why your answer is different.

   c.   Ask your instructor for assistance.

   d.   Be sure your company matches the above as you will be adding additional business events in Chapter 4.

10   Export your Trial Balance report to Excel, and save it with the file name Student Name (replace with your name) Ch 03 Case 03 Trial Balance.xlsx.

11   Prepare and print a Transaction Detail by Account report for all transactions between 1/1/10 and 12/31/30, save it as a customized report named Transaction Detail by Account, and share it with all users. If asked, indicate that your business is accrual based.

12 Use your Transaction Detail by Account report to locate any differences in your Trial Balance report created above.

    a. Make sure all of your changes were dated 12/31/25.

    b. Click on the line that does not match to view the transaction for that account, and investigate why your answer differs.

    c. Ask your instructor for assistance.

    d. Be sure your company matches the above as you will be adding additional business events in Chapter 4.

13 Export your Transactions Detail by Account report to Excel and save it with the file name Student Name (replace with your name) Ch 03 Case 03 Transaction Detail by Account.xlsx.

14 Sign out of your company.

Case 4

Your company is a sports gym serving the Hollywood area in California. They sell month-to-month memberships to individuals and businesses as well as T-shirts, yoga pants, and other sports-related accessories. They began their business in 2026 and want to use QBO starting January 1, 2027. Beginning balances as of 12/31/26 have been provided below.

Based on what you learned in the text using the Wild Water Sports company, you are to make the following changes to the case you created in Chapter 2.

1 Modify settings as follows (click the **Gear** icon and then click **Account and Settings**):

    a. Company
        i) Name – Case 04 – Student Name (ID Number)
        ii) EIN – 98-9875461
        iii) Tax form – Form 1120
        iv) Industry – Fitness and Recreational Sports Centers
        v) Email – Your email address
        vi) Address – 6540 Sunset Blvd., Hollywood, CA 90028

    b. Sales (turn the following on, and all others turn off or leave off)
        i) Preferred invoice terms – Net 30
        ii) Custom transaction numbers
        iii) Show Product/Service column on sales form
        iv) Track quantity and price/rate
        v) Track inventory quantity on hand
        vi) Show aging table at the bottom of the statement

    c. Expenses (turn the following on, and all others turn off or leave off)
        i) Show items table on expense and purchase forms
        ii) Use purchase orders

    d. Payments—No changes

    e. Advanced—No changes

2 Add sales tax that is payable to the California State Board of Equalization. (Follow the steps provided in Appendix 1.)

3 Create new accounts and related beginning balances where appropriate. (Click the **Gear** icon and then click **Chart of Accounts**.)

a. First account
- i) Account Type – Banks, Save account under **Bank Accounts**.
- ii) Tax form section – Checking
- iii) Name – Checking
- iv) Start date 12/31/2026, balance as of 12/31/26 – $27,000

b. Second account
- i) Account Type – Assets, Save account under Other Current Assets.
- ii) Tax form section – Prepaid Expenses
- iii) Name – Prepaid rent
- iv) Start date 12/31/2026, balance as of 12/31/26 – $12,000

c. Third, fourth, and fifth accounts
- i) Account Type – Assets, Save account under Fixed Assets
- ii) Tax form section – Fixed Asset Furniture
- iii) Name – Furniture
- iv) Start date 12/31/2026, balance $0
- v) Account Type – Assets, Save account under Furniture
- vi) Tax form section – Fixed Asset Furniture
- vii) Name – Original Cost
- viii) Start date 12/31/2026, balance $65,000
- ix) Account Type – Assets, Save account under Furniture
- x) Tax form section – Accumulated Depreciation
- xi) Name – Accumulated Depreciation
- xii) Start date 12/31/2026, balance – $10,000

d. Sixth, seventh, and eighth accounts
- i) Account Type – Assets, Save account under Fixed Assets
- ii) Tax form section – Vehicles
- iii) Name – Vehicles
- iv) Start date 12/31/2026, balance $0
- v) Account Type – Assets. Save account under Vehicles
- vi) Tax form section – Vehicles
- vii) Name – Original Cost
- viii) Start date 12/31/2026, balance $115,000
- ix) Account Type – Assets, Save account under Vehicles
- x) Tax form section – Accumulated Depreciation
- xi) Name – Accumulated Depreciation
- xii) Start date 12/31/2026, balance – $6,500

e. Ninth account
- i) Account Type – Liabilities, Save account under Long Term Liabilities.
- ii) Tax form section – Other Long Term Liabilities
- iii) Name – Long-term debt
- iv) Start date 12/31/2026, balance $82,000

    f.   Tenth account
       i)   Account Type – Equity, Save account under Equity.
       ii) Tax form section – Common Stock
       iii) Name – Common stock
       iv) Start date 12/31/2026, balance $1,000

4   Create two new Inventory products as follows:

    a.   First product
       i)   Name – T-shirts
       ii)   Initial quantity on hand – 250
       iii) As of date – 12/31/26
       iv) Inventory asset account – Inventory Asset
       v)   Description – T-shirts
       vi) Sales price/rate – $25
       vii) Income account – Sales of Product Income
       viii) Is taxable – Yes
       ix) Purchasing information – T-shirts
       x)   Cost – $12
       xi) Expense account – Cost of Goods Sold

    b.   Second product
       i)   Name – Yoga pants
       ii)   Initial quantity on hand – 125
       iii) As of date – 12/31/26
       iv) Inventory asset account – Inventory Asset
       v)   Description – Yoga pants
       vi) Sales price/rate – $45
       vii) Income account – Sales of Product Income
       viii) Is taxable – Yes
       ix) Purchasing information – Yoga pants
       x)   Cost – $20
       xi) Expense account – Cost of Goods Sold

5   Create two new service items as follows:

    a.   First service
       i)   Name and description – Monthly Fee
       ii)   Sales information – Yes you do sell this service to customers. "Monthly Fee"
       iii) Sales price/rate – $150
       iv) Income account – Sales
       v)   Is taxable – No
       vi) Purchasing information – No you don't purchase this service from a vendor

    b.   Second service
       i)   Name and description – Training
       ii)   Sales information – Yes you do sell this service to customers. "Training"
       iii) Sales price/rate – $75
       iv) Income account – Sales

v) Is taxable – No

vi) Purchasing information – No you don't purchase this service from a vendor

6 Prepare journal entry 1 as of 12/31/26 with an offset to Opening Balance Equity to record the following beginning balances (if your chart of accounts doesn't already have an accounts receivable or accounts payable account you'll need to add them.):

a. Accounts Receivable (A/R) – Debit $8,500 – Disney (new customer)

b. Accounts Payable (A/P) – Credit $18,000 – Precor (new vendor)

7 Prepare journal entry 2 as of 12/31/26 to close the Opening Balance Equity to Retained Earnings ($115,500).

8 Prepare and print a Trial Balance report with a custom reporting period of 12/31/2026 to 12/31/2026 and then save it as a customized report named Trial Balance 12/31/2026. Your report should look like Figure 3.24.

Trial Balance
As of December 31, 2026

	DEBIT	CREDIT
Checking	27,000.00	
Accounts Receivable (A/R)	8,500.00	
Inventory Asset	5,500.00	
Prepaid rent	12,000.00	
Furniture:Accumulated Depreciation		10,000.00
Furniture:Original Cost	65,000.00	
Vehicles:Accumulated Depreciation		6,500.00
Vehicles:Original Cost	115,000.00	
Accounts Payable (A/P)		18,000.00
Long-term debt		82,000.00
Common Stock		1,000.00
Opening Balance Equity		0.00
Retained Earnings		115,500.00
TOTAL	$233,000.00	$233,000.00

Figure 3.24

Trial Balance

9 If necessary, prepare and print a Transaction Detail by Account report for all transactions between 1/1/20 and 12/31/30, and save it as a customized report named Transaction Detail by Account. If asked, indicate that your business is accrual based.

10 Use your Transaction Detail by Account report to locate any differences in your Trial Balance report created above.

a Make sure all your changes were dated 12/31/26.

b. Click on the line that does not match to view the transaction for that account and investigate why your answer differs.

c. Ask your instructor for assistance.

d. Be sure your company matches the above as you will be adding additional business events in Chapter 4.

Case 5

Your company is a software engineering firm in the state of Alabama. They develop training materials and computer workstations for government and commercial enterprises. In addition, they provide program support, training, and technical solutions. They want to use QBO starting January 1, 2022. Beginning balances as of 12/31/21 have been provided below.

Based on what you learned in the text using the Wild Water Sports company, you are to make the following changes to the case you created in Chapter 2.

1   Modify settings as follows (click the **Gear** icon and then click **Account and Settings**):

    a.   Company
        i) Name – Case 05 – Student Name (ID Number)
        ii) SSN – 556-95-7847
        iii) Company type – Sole Proprietor
        iv) Tax form – Form 1040
        v) Industry – Software Publishing
        vi) Email – your email address
        vii) Address – 5100 Bradford Drive, Huntsville, AL 35805

    b.   Sales (turn the following on, and all others turn off or leave off)
        i) Preferred invoice terms – Net 30
        ii) Custom transaction numbers
        iii) Show Product/Service column on sales form
        iv) Track quantity and price/rate
        v) Track inventory quantity on hand
        vi) Show aging table at bottom of statement

    c.   Expenses (turn the following on, and all others turn off or leave off)
        i) Show items table on expense and purchase forms
        ii) Use purchase orders

    d.   Payments—No changes

    e.   Advanced—No changes

2   Add sales tax that is quarterly. (Follow the steps provided in Appendix 1.) Since this company is in Alabama, the instructions and Figure A.1 are different than what's listed for California. There are three agencies that receive tax payments: Alabama Department of Revenue; Alabama, Madison County; and Alabama, Huntsville. Select the filing frequency of quarterly in the three screens. Start date is 01/01/22.

3   Create new accounts and related beginning balances where appropriate (click the **Gear** icon and then click **Chart of Accounts**):

    a.   First account
        i) Account Type – Bank
        ii) Detail Type – Checking
        iii) Name – Checking
        iv) Balance as of 12/31/21 – $30,000

b. Second account
   i) Account Type – Accounts Receivable (A/R)
   ii) Detail Type – Accounts Receivable (A/R)
   iii) Name – Accounts Receivable (A/R)
   iv) Balance as of 12/31/21 – n/a

c. Third account
   i) Account Type – Other Current Assets
   ii) Detail Type – Prepaid Expenses
   iii) Name – Prepaid Expenses
   iv) Balance as of 12/31/21 – $10,000

d. Fourth and fifth accounts (Note: When entering a new fixed asset, place a check in the **Track depreciation of this asset** check box to reveal Original cost and Depreciation text boxes. Enter both amounts as positive numbers.)
   i) Account Type – Fixed Assets
   ii) Detail Type – Fixed Asset Computers
   iii) Name – Fixed Asset Computers
   iv) Original cost – $250,000
   v) Depreciation – $25,000
   vi) Balance as of 12/31/21

e. Sixth and seventh accounts (see note above on depreciation)
   i) Account Type – Fixed Assets
   ii) Detail Type – Fixed Asset Furniture
   iii) Name – Fixed Asset Furniture
   iv) Original cost – $80,000
   v) Depreciation – $8,000
   vi) Balance as of 12/31/21

f. Eighth account
   i) Account Type – Accounts Payable (A/P)
   ii) Detail Type – Accounts Payable (A/P)
   iii) Name – Accounts Payable (A/P)
   iv) Balance as of 12/31/21 – n/a

g. Ninth account
   i) Account Type – Long-Term Liabilities
   ii) Detail Type – Notes Payable
   iii) Name – Notes Payable
   iv) Balance as of 12/31/21 – $45,000

h. Tenth account
   i) Account Type – Equity
   ii) Detail Type – Owner's Equity
   iii) Name – Owner's Equity
   iv) Balance as of 12/31/21 – $10,000

i. Eleventh account
   i) Account Type – Income
   ii) Detail Type – Service/Fee Income
   iii) Name – Consulting

4   Create two new inventory products as follows:

    a.   First product

        i)   Name – Training Materials – Volume 1

        ii)   Initial quantity on hand – 20

        iii)   As of date – 12/31/21

        iv)   Inventory asset account – Inventory

        v)   Description – Training Materials – Volume 1

        vi)   Sales price/rate – $15,000

        vii)   Income account – Sales

        viii)   Taxable – standard rate

        ix)   Purchasing information – Training Materials – Volume 1

        x)   Cost – $8,000

        xi)   Expense account – Cost of Goods Sold

    b.   Second product

        i)   Name – Training Materials – Volume 2

        ii)   Initial quantity on hand – 30

        iii)   As of date – 12/31/21

        iv)   Inventory asset account – Inventory

        v)   Description – Training Materials – Volume 2

        vi)   Sales price/rate – $20,000

        vii)   Income account – Sales

        viii)   Taxable – standard rate

        ix)   Purchasing information – Training Materials – Volume 2

        x)   Cost – $10,000

        xi)   Expense account – Cost of Goods Sold

5   Create two new service items as follows:

    a.   First service

        i)   Name – Program Support

        ii)   Description – Yes you do sell this service to customers. "Program Support"

        iii)   Sales price/rate – $300

        iv)   Income account – Account Type: Income, Detail Type: Service/Fee Income, Name: Consulting Click **+ Add new** in the Income account text box, Account Type: Income, Detail Type: Service/Fee Income, Name: Consulting

        v)   Nontaxable

        vi)   Purchasing information – No you don't purchase this service from a vendor

    b.   Second service

        i)   Name – Technical Solutions

        ii)   Description – Yes you do sell this service to customers. "Technical Solutions"

        iii)   Sales price/rate – $400

        iv)   Income account – Consulting

        v)   Nontaxable

        vi)   Purchase information – No you don't purchase this service from a vendor

6   Prepare journal entry 1 as of 12/31/21 with an offset to Opening Balance Equity to record the following beginning balances:

    a.   Accounts Receivable (A/R) – Debit $150,000 – NASA (new customer)

    b.   Accounts Payable (A/P) Credit $20,000 – Wild Research Inc. (new vendor)

    c.   Notes Payable Credit $500,000 – Chase Bank (new vendor)

7   Prepare journal entry 2 as of 12/31/21 to close the Opening Balance Equity to Owner's Equity ($372,000).

8   Prepare and print a Trial Balance report with a custom reporting period of 1/1/21 to 12/31/21 and then save it as a customized report named Trial Balance 12/31/21. Your report should look like Figure 3.25.

Figure 3.25

Trial Balance

Case 05 - Student Name (ID Number)		
TRIAL BALANCE As of December 31, 2021		
	DEBIT	CREDIT
Checking	30,000.00	
Accounts Receivable (A/R)	150,000.00	
Inventory	460,000.00	
Prepaid Expenses	10,000.00	
Fixed Asset Computers:Depreciation		25,000.00
Fixed Asset Computers:Original cost	250,000.00	
Fixed Asset Furniture:Depreciation		8,000.00
Fixed Asset Furniture:Original cost	80,000.00	
Accounts Payable (A/P)		20,000.00
Notes Payable		545,000.00
Opening Balance Equity		0.00
Owner's Equity		382,000.00
TOTAL	$980,000.00	$980,000.00

9   Prepare and print a Transaction Detail by Account report for all transactions between 1/1/10 and 12/31/23, and save it as a customized report named Transaction Detail by Account. If asked, indicate that your business is accrual based.

10   Use your Transaction Detail by Account report to locate any differences in your Trial Balance report created above.

    a.   Make sure all your changes were dated 12/31/21.

    b.   Click on the line that does not match to view the transaction for that account, and investigate why your answer differs.

    c.   Ask your instructor for assistance.

    d.   Be sure your company matches the above as you will be adding additional business events in Chapter 4.

Case 6

Your company is a Recreational Vehicle (RV) dealership in the state of Washington. They sell new RVs and related accessories to individuals and businesses. In addition, they repair and service RVs. They began business in 2021 and want to use QBO starting January 1, 2023. Beginning balances as of 12/31/22 have been provided below.

Based on what you learned in the text using the Wild Water Sports company, you are to make the following changes to the case you created in Chapter 2.

1   Modify settings as follows (click the **Gear** icon and then click **Account and Settings**):

   a. Company
- i) Name – Case 06 – Student Name (ID Number)
- ii) EIN – 99-9811161
- iii) Tax form – Form 1120
- iv) Industry – Automotive Dealers
- v) Email – your email address
- vi) Address – 4309 E Valley Hwy E, Sumner, WA 98390

   b. Sales (turn the following on, all others turn off or leave off)
- i) Preferred invoice terms – Net 30
- ii) Custom transaction numbers
- iii) Show Product/Service column on sales form
- iv) Track quantity and price/rate
- v) Track inventory quantity on hand
- vi) Show aging table at bottom of statement

   c. Expenses (turn the following on, all others turn off or leave off)
- i) Show items table on expense and purchase forms
- ii) Use purchase orders

   d. Payments—No changes

   e. Advanced—No changes

2   Add sales tax that is payable to the Washington State Department of Revenue (follow the steps provided in Appendix 1).

3   Create new accounts and related beginning balances where appropriate (click the **Gear** icon and then click **Chart of Accounts**):

   a. First account
- i) Account Type – Bank
- ii) Detail Type – Checking
- iii) Name – Checking
- iv) Balance as of 12/31/22 – $50,000

   b. Second account
- i) Account Type – Accounts Receivable (A/R)
- ii) Detail Type – Accounts Receivable (A/R)
- iii) Name – Accounts Receivable (A/R)
- iv) Balance as of 12/31/22 – n/a

   c. Third account
- i) Account Type – Other Current Assets
- ii) Detail Type – Loans to Officers
- iii) Name – Loans to Officers
- iv) Balance as of 12/31/22 – $15,000

   d. Fourth and fifth accounts (Note: When entering a new fixed asset, place a check in the **Track depreciation of this asset** check box to reveal Original cost and Depreciation text boxes. Enter both amounts from above as positive numbers.)
- i) Account Type – Fixed Asset
- ii) Detail Type – Buildings
- iii) Name – Buildings
- iv) Original cost $150,000
- v) Depreciation $15,000
- vi) Balance as of 12/31/22

   e. Sixth and seventh accounts (see note above)
- i) Account Type – Fixed Asset
- ii) Detail Type – Machinery & Equipment
- iii) Name – Machinery & Equipment
- iv) Original cost $100,000
- v) Depreciation $10,000
- vi) Balance as of 12/31/22

   f. Eighth account
- i) Account Type – Accounts Payable (A/P)
- ii) Detail Type – Accounts Payable (A/P)
- iii) Name – Accounts Payable (A/P)
- iv) Balance as of 12/31/22 – n/a

   g. Ninth account
- i) Account Type – Long-Term Liabilities
- ii) Detail Type – Notes Payable
- iii) Name – Notes Payable
- iv) Balance as of 12/31/22 – n/a

   h. Tenth account
- i) Account Type – Equity
- ii) Detail Type – Common Stock
- iii) Name – Common Stock
- iv) Balance as of 12/31/22 – n/a

   i. Eleventh account
- i) Account Type – Equity
- ii) Detail Type – Paid-In Capital or Surplus
- iii) Name – Paid-In Capital
- iv) Balance as of 12/31/22 – n/a

4 Create two new Inventory products as follows:

   a. First product
- i) Name – 2022 Winnebago Revel 44E
- ii) Initial quantity on hand – 2

        iii) As of date – 12/31/22

        iv) Inventory asset account – Inventory Asset

        v) Description – 2022 Winnebago Revel 44E

        vi) Sales price/rate – $150,000

        vii) Income account – Sales of Product Income

        viii) Sales Tax Category – Taxable-Standard rate

        ix) Purchasing information – 2022 Winnebago Revel 44E

        x) Cost – $120,000

        xi) Expense account – Cost of Goods Sold

    b. Second product

        i) Name – 2022 Winnebago View 24G

        ii) Initial quantity on hand – 3

        iii) As of date – 12/31/22

        iv) Inventory asset account – Inventory Asset

        v) Description – 2022 Winnebago View 24G

        vi) Sales price/rate – $140,000

        vii) Income account – Sales of Product Income

        viii) Sales Tax Category – Taxable-Standard rate

        ix) Purchasing information – 2022 Winnebago View 24G

        x) Cost – $112,000

        xi) Expense account – Cost of Goods Sold

5 Create two new service items as follows:

    a. First service

        i) Name – Lube, Oil, Filter

        ii) Description – Yes you do sell this service to customers. "Lube, Oil, Filter"

        iii) Sales price/rate – $300

        iv) Income account – Sales

        v) Sales Tax Category – Nontaxable

        vi) Purchasing information – No you don't purchase this service from a vendor

    b. Second service

        i) Name – Transmission Service

        ii) Description – Yes you do sell this service to customers. "Transmission Service"

        iii) Sales price/rate – $350

        iv) Income account – Sales

        v) Sales Tax Category – Nontaxable

        vi) Purchasing information – No you don't purchase this service from a vendor

6 Prepare journal entry 1 as of 12/31/22 with an offset to Opening Balance Equity to record the following beginning balances:

    a. Accounts Receivable (A/R) – Debit $10,000 – Sam Ski (new customer)

    b. Accounts Payable (A/P) Credit $464,000 – Winnebago (new vendor)

    c. Notes Payable Credit $100,000 – Chase Bank (new vendor)

    d. Common Stock Credit $1,000

   e. Paid-In Capital Credit $250,000

   f. Opening Balance Equity Debit $805,000

7 Prepare journal entry 2 as of 12/31/22 to close the Opening Balance Equity to Retained Earnings ($61,000).

8 Prepare and print a Trial Balance report with a custom reporting period of 1/1/22 to 12/31/22 and then save it as a customized report named Trial Balance 12/31/22. Your report should look like Figure 3.26.

Figure 3.26

Trial Balance

Case 06 - Student Name (ID Number)

TRIAL BALANCE
As of December 31, 2022

	DEBIT	CREDIT
Checking	50,000.00	
Accounts Receivable (A/R)	10,000.00	
Inventory Asset	576,000.00	
Loans To Officers	15,000.00	
Buildings:Depreciation		15,000.00
Buildings:Original cost	150,000.00	
Machinery & Equipment:Depreciation		10,000.00
Machinery & Equipment:Original cost	100,000.00	
Accounts Payable (A/P)		464,000.00
Notes Payable		100,000.00
Common Stock		1,000.00
Opening Balance Equity		0.00
Paid-In Capital		250,000.00
Retained Earnings		61,000.00
TOTAL	$901,000.00	$901,000.00

9 Prepare and print a Transaction Detail by Account report for all transactions between 1/1/10 and 12/31/25 and then save it as a customized report named Transaction Detail by Account. If asked, indicate that your business is accrual based.

10 Use your Transaction Detail by Account report to locate any differences in your Trial Balance report created above.

   a. Make sure all your changes were dated 12/31/22.

   b. Click on the line that does not match to view the transaction for that account and investigate why your answer differs.

   c. Ask your instructor for assistance.

   d. Be sure your company matches the above as you will be adding additional business events in Chapter 4.

Recording Operating Activities: Sales and Cash Receipts

Upon completion of this chapter, the student will be able to do the following:

- Add a new service, product, and customer
- Record a sales receipt
- Record an invoice for services rendered on account
- Record an invoice for products sold on account
- Record cash receipts (payments received on account)
- Deposit payments received on account
- Prepare Trial Balance and Transaction Detail by Account reports

Overview

In Chapter 3 you modified company settings, added new accounts to the chart of accounts, and added beginning balances where appropriate. You added customers, vendors, products, and services and closed the Opening Balance Equity account. In this chapter you will add operating activities like sales receipts, invoices, and cash receipts. Specifically you will be recording operating activities, such as adding new services, new products, new customers, new sales receipts, new invoices, and new cash receipts to the Wild Water Sports company. At the end of the chapter, you will perform the same tasks completed on the Wild Water Sports company on a case assigned by your instructor.

Services, Products, and Customers

In this section, you will add new services, products, and customers. To add new services and products, you will access the Product and Services section using the Gear icon. To add customers, you will use the Customers menu item in the navigation bar, but first we'll verify your starting numbers are correct.

To add new services, products, and customers to the Wild Water Sports company, do the following:

1 Sign into your QBO account, then open the Wild Water Sports company you used in Chapter 3.

2 Click **Reports** then click the **Custom reports** tab, then click **Trial Balance** to open the Trial Balance report. Set the to and from dates to **01/01/2027**. Compare your report to Figure 4.1. If your report doesn't match Figure 4.1, go back to your work in Chapter 3 to fix your errors. Otherwise close your Trial Balance report.

Navigate your browser to the Video Tutorials provided by Intuit (see website address specified in the Preface to this text) and then search on How to Set Up Service Items.

Figure 4.1

Wild Water Sports trial balance as of 1/1/27

Wild Water Sports - Student Name (ID Number)

Trial Balance
As of January 1, 2027

	DEBIT	CREDIT
Checking	25,000.00	
Accounts receivable (A/R)	70,000.00	
Inventory	172,800.00	
Prepaid expenses	15,000.00	
Equipment:Accumulated depreciation		10,000.00
Equipment:Original Cost	40,000.00	
Accounts Payable (A/P)		56,000.00
Long-term business loans		50,000.00
Common stock		1,000.00
Opening balance equity		0.00
Retained Earnings		205,800.00
TOTAL	$322,800.00	$322,800.00

3 Click the **Gear** icon, and click **Products and services**.

4 Click **New** in the upper-right corner of the Products and Services list.

5 Click **Service**.

6 Type **Cleaning** in the Name text box and the Description text boxes.

7 Select **Services** from the Category drop-down text box, then check the I sell this product/service to my customers check box, and then type **500** in the Sales price/rate text box.

8 Scroll down the window and accept Service Revenue as the Income account and then click **Edit sales tax**, then click **Nontaxable,** and then click **Done**. Your window should now look like Figure 4.2.

Figure 4.2

Adding a new service

Navigate your browser to the Video Tutorials provided by Intuit (see website address specified in the Preface to this text) and then search on How to Create an Inventory Product.

9   Click on the drop-down arrow to the right of the Save and close button, and select **Save and new**.

10 Click **Change type** and then select **Inventory**.

11 Type **Tige 25 zx** in the Name text box and then click the drop-down arrow in the Category text box and select **Boats**.

12 Type **0** in the Initial Quantity On Hand text box and type 1/1/2027 in the As Of Date text box.

13 Select **Inventory** as the Inventory asset account.

14 Type **Tige 25 zx** in the Description and in Purchasing information text boxes.

15 Type **225000** in the Sales price/rate text box, then type **01/01/2027** in the As of date text box, and then type **180000** in the Cost text box.

16 Select **Sales of Product Income** from the Income account drop-down list and **Cost of Goods Sold** from the Expense account drop-down list.

17 Click **Edit sales tax**, then click **Taxable**, and then click **Done**. A partial view of the Product or Service Information window should look like Figure 4.3. Note that the Wild Water Sports company had already set up Sales Taxes. To learn more about setting up Sales Taxes read Appendix 1—Sales Taxes.

Figure 4.3

Adding a new product (partial view)

Navigate your browser to the Video Tutorials provided by Intuit (see website address specified in the Preface to this text) and then search on How to Set Up Sales Tax.

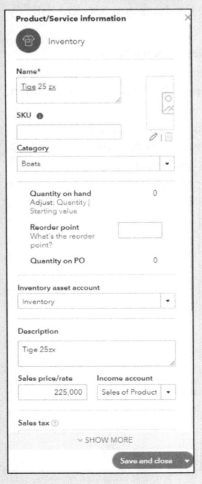

18   Click on the drop-down arrow to the right of the **Save and new button**, and select **Save and close**.

19   Scroll down the revised list of Products and Services to see the service and product you entered as shown in Figure 4.4.

Figure 4.4

Updated list of Products and Services (partial view)

Navigate your browser to the Video Tutorials provided by Intuit (see website address specified in the Preface to this text) and then search on How to Manage Customers.

20   Click **Sales** from the navigation bar, then click **Customers**, and then click the **New customer** button.

21   Type **James** in the First name text box and **Rogers** in the Last name text box. Type **j.rogers@gmail.com** in the Email text box and then type **805 588 1234** in the Mobile number text box.

22   Type **Performance Rentals** in the Company name, Customer display name, and Name to print on checks text boxes.

23   Type **15 Hwy 22, Orlando, FL 32807 United States** in the appropriate text boxes. Click **Save** to view the data you just entered. A partial view of the Customer information window is shown in Figure 4.5.

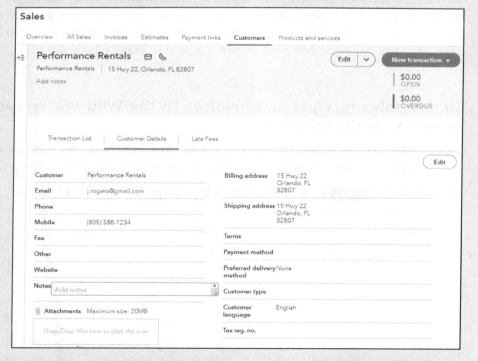

Figure 4.5

Customer information window (partial view)

24   Scroll down the page to the Payments section and select **Net 30** from the Terms text box, then click **Save**.

25   The Performance Rentals customer window appears as shown in Figure 4.6.

Figure 4.6

Performance Rentals customer window

26   Click **Dashboard.**

Navigate your browser to the Video Tutorials provided by Intuit (see website address specified in the Preface to this text) and then search on Sales Receipt versus Invoice.

You have now added a new service, a new product, and a new customer. Next up, adding sales receipts to record cash sales and invoices to record credit sales.

Sales Receipts and Invoices

A business uses sales receipts to record sales transactions on a daily basis when payment is received at the same time as a product or service is delivered. Sales invoices are used to record sales transactions when customers are granted credit terms and given some time to pay after a product or service is delivered. In either case, sales are recorded when the product is sold or service is rendered.

To add sales receipts and invoices to the Wild Water Sports company, do the following:

1   Continue from where you left off. If you closed the Wild Water Sports company, follow the steps at the beginning of this chapter to reopen it.

2   Click the `+ New` icon, and select **Sales receipt** as shown in Figure 4.7.

Figure 4.7

Create window (adding a sales receipt)

Navigate your browser to the Video Tutorials provided by Intuit (see website address specified in the Preface to this text) and then search on How to Record a Sales Receipt.

CUSTOMERS	VENDORS	EMPLOYEES	OTHER
Invoice	Expense	Payroll 🔔	Bank deposit
Receive payment	Check	Time entry	Transfer
Estimate	Bill		Journal entry
Credit memo	Pay bills		Statement
Sales receipt	Purchase order		Inventory qty adjustment
Refund receipt	Vendor credit		Pay down credit card
Delayed credit	Credit card credit		
Delayed charge	Print checks		

3 Click ⟨ + New ⟩ from the Customer drop-down list, then type **Southtown Watersports** as the new customer's company name, then select **Due on receipt** from the Terms text box, and then type **3333 Scott Futrell Dr. Charlotte NC 28208** as their address. Click **Save**.

4 Change the Sales Receipt date to **01/04/2027**.

5 Select **Check** from the drop-down list of Payment methods and **6985** as the Reference no.

6 Select **Payments to Deposit** from the Deposit to drop-down text box. The check will be recorded in the Payments to deposit account as deposits for this company are made every other day.

7 On line 1 of the sales receipt, select **Malibu Sportster LX** in the Product/Service column.

8 Type **1** in the QTY (Quantity) column and then press [**Tab**]. The sales receipt should look like Figure 4.8. Note: you may have to click **See the math** in the sales tax section to apply sales tax.

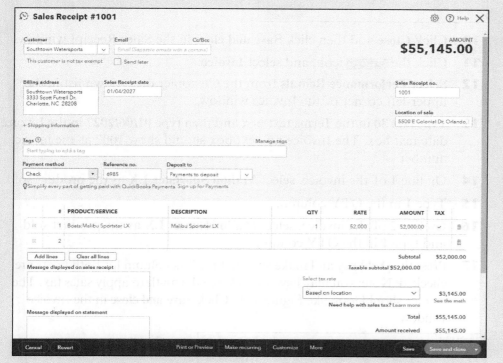

Figure 4.8

Sales Receipt

9 Click **See the math** to view Figure 4.9 which shows how sales tax was calculated.

Figure 4.9

Sales tax calculations

10   Click **Close** and then click **Save and close** in the Sales Receipt window.

11   Click the ⟨ + New ⟩ icon, and select **Invoice**.

12   Select **Performance Rentals** from the Customer drop-down list in the upper-left corner of the Invoice window.

13   Type **Net 30** in the Terms text box and then type **01/06/2027** in the Invoice date text box. The Invoice no. text box should show 1002 as the invoice number.

14   On line 1 of the invoice, select **Malibu Sportster LX** as the product sold.

15   Type **1** in the QTY column.

16   On line 2 of the invoice, select **Malibu Sunset LX** as the product sold and type **1** in the QTY column.

17   Press the [**Tab**] key and make sure that the Tax column for both boats are checked. Note: you may have to click See the math to apply sales tax. The invoice should look like Figure 4.10. Click **Save and close** in the Invoice window.

Figure 4.10

Invoice

18   To record an invoice for services rendered, click the [+ New] and then click Invoice like you did in the previous example.

19   Click **+ Add new** in the Customer drop-down text.

20   Type **Florida Ski School** in the Company name text box and then type **Net 30** as their terms.

21   Type **10900 Chase Road Windermere FL 34786** as their address and then click **Save**.

22   Type **01/10/2027** as the Invoice date.

23   Select **Diagnostic Service** from the Select a product/service text box, then type **4** as the quantity, then press [Tab] to view invoice 1003 shown in Figure 4.11.

Figure 4.11

Invoice for services rendered

24   Click **Save and close**.

25   Click **Sales** and then select All Sales. Click on the column title **Date** to sort the report by date. A listing of recent transactions is shown in Figure 4.12.

Figure 4.12

All Sales

Cash Receipts

In QBO, the concept of cash receipts is referred to as receiving payments. Thus, to record the receipt of payment from a customer, you can use the Receive Payment item in the Create menu to record the transaction, or you can use Receive Payment from the Action column in a customer's list of transactions. Once a payment is received, it must be deposited into your bank account. This is a separate but important process in QBO.

To record the receipt of a payment from a customer, do the following:

1   Continue from where you left off. If you closed the Wild Water Sports company, follow the steps at the beginning of this chapter to reopen it.

2   Click the icon, and select **Receive payment** as shown in Figure 4.13.

Figure 4.13

Receive Payment (recording the receipt of a customer payment)

CUSTOMERS

Invoice

Receive payment

Estimate

Credit memo

Sales receipt

Refund receipt

Delayed credit

Delayed charge

VIDEO LINK

Navigate your browser to the Video Tutorials provided by Intuit (see website address specified in the Preface to this text) and then search on How to Record the Receipt of Payment on an Invoice.

3   Select **Refugio** from the Customer drop-down list in the upper-left corner of the Receive Payment window.

4   Type **1/12/2027** as the Payment date.

5   Select **Check** as the Payment method. Select **Payments to deposit** from the Deposit to text box.

6   Place a check in the **Journal Entry #3** check box as shown in Figure 4.14. This was the accounts receivable balance recorded when you set up your company's accounts. Click **Save and close**.

Figure 4.14

Receive Payment window

7 Recall that when the two payments above were received they were recorded to an account titled Payments to deposit. Now it's time to deposit one of those payments to our bank and record that deposit into our checking account. Click the ⊕ New icon, and select **Bank deposit** from the Other column as shown in Figure 4.15.

Figure 4.15

Create window (inputting a bank deposit)

Navigate your browser to the Video Tutorials provided by Intuit (see website address specified in the Preface to this text) and then search on How to Record a Bank Deposit.

8 Select **Checking** as the account you're depositing to then select **1/12/2027** as the date of deposit. Select the payment received from **Southtown Watersports** from the list of existing payments as shown in Figure 4.16.

Figure 4.16

Deposit window

9 Click **Save and close**.

Trial Balance and Transaction Detail by Account

In the Wild Water Sports and the cases found at the end of each chapter, you will be asked to create a Trial Balance report as of a certain date. You will compare your Trial Balance report with the one provided in the case to see if you have correctly recorded various business events. If your Trial Balance differs, you will need to fix your errors.

A usual explanation for an incorrect Trial Balance report is recording a transaction in an incorrect period, not recording it at all, or recording it incorrectly. To investigate, you will need to create a transaction detail by account report for a specific period. You can create such a report for all transactions to see if yours were recorded in the proper period and to see where you may have entered a wrong amount or account.

To create, print, and export a trial balance and transaction detail by account report:

1   Continue from your work earlier.

2   Click **Reports** from the navigation bar.

3   Click the **Custom reports tab**.

4   Select **Trial Balance**.

5   Type **01/01/2027** and **01/13/2027** as the from and to dates. You may have to scroll to the top of this report to see the Report period date text boxes.

6   Click **Run report**. The report is shown in Figure 4.17.

Figure 4.17

Trial balance report as of 1/13/2027

Wild Water Sports - Student Name (ID Number)		
Trial Balance		
As of January 13, 2027		
	DEBIT	**CREDIT**
Checking	80,145.00	
Accounts receivable (A/R)	120,770.00	
Inventory	41,600.00	
Payments to deposit	70,000.00	
Prepaid expenses	15,000.00	
Equipment:Accumulated depreciation		10,000.00
Equipment:Original Cost	40,000.00	
Accounts Payable (A/P)		56,000.00
Florida Department of Revenue Payable		9,915.00
Long-term business loans		50,000.00
Common stock		1,000.00
Opening balance equity		0.00
Retained Earnings		205,800.00
Sales		164,000.00
Service Revenue		2,000.00
Cost of goods sold	131,200.00	
TOTAL	$498,715.00	$498,715.00

7 Click **Reports**, then click the **Custom Reports** tab, then click **Transaction Detail by Account**.

8 Click in the Report Period text box and select **All Dates** to view the report shown in Figure 4.18.

Figure 4.18

Transaction Detail by Account Report (partial view)

Wild Water Sports - Student Name (ID Number)

Transaction Detail by Account
All Dates

DATE	TRANSACTION TYPE	NUM	NAME	MEMO/DESCRIPTION	SPLIT	AMOUNT	BALANCE
▾ Checking							
12/31/2026	Deposit			Opening Balance	Opening balance equity	25,000.00	25,000.00
01/13/2027	Deposit		Southtown Watersports		Payments to deposit	55,145.00	80,145.00
Total for Checking						**$80,145.00**	
▾ Accounts receivable (A/R)							
12/31/2026	Journal Entry	3			-Split-	70,000.00	70,000.00
01/06/2027	Invoice	1002	Performance Rentals		-Split-	118,770.00	188,770.00
01/10/2027	Invoice	1003	Florida Ski School		Service Revenue	2,000.00	190,770.00
01/12/2027	Payment		Refugio		Payments to deposit	-70,000.00	120,770.00
Total for Accounts receivable (A/R)						**$120,770.00**	
▾ Inventory							
12/31/2026	Inventory Starting Value	START		Tige 25 zx - Opening invent...	Opening balance equity	0.00	0.00
12/31/2026	Inventory Starting Value	START		Malibu Sunset - Opening in...	Opening balance equity	0.00	0.00
12/31/2026	Inventory Starting Value	START		Malibu Sunset LX - Opening...	Opening balance equity	48,000.00	48,000.00
12/31/2026	Inventory Starting Value	START		Malibu Sportster LX - Openi...	Opening balance equity	124,800.00	172,800.00
01/04/2027	Sales Receipt	1001	Southtown Watersports	Malibu Sportster LX	Payments to deposit	-41,600.00	131,200.00
01/06/2027	Invoice	1002	Performance Rentals	Malibu Sunset LX	Accounts receivable (A/R)	-48,000.00	83,200.00
01/06/2027	Invoice	1002	Performance Rentals	Malibu Sportster LX	Accounts receivable (A/R)	-41,600.00	41,600.00
Total for Inventory						**$41,600.00**	
▾ Payments to deposit							
01/04/2027	Sales Receipt	1001	Southtown Watersports		Sales	55,145.00	55,145.00
01/12/2027	Payment		Refugio		Accounts receivable (A/R)	70,000.00	125,145.00
01/13/2027	Deposit		Southtown Watersports		Checking	-55,145.00	70,000.00
Total for Payments to deposit						**$70,000.00**	
▾ Prepaid expenses							
12/31/2026	Deposit		Allstate Insurance		Opening balance equity	15,000.00	15,000.00
Total for Prepaid expenses						**$15,000.00**	

9 Click **Save customization**, then type **Transaction Detail by Account All Dates** as the report name, then click **Save**.

10 Click the **Print** icon to print this report.

11 Sign out of this company.

Be sure to verify that your Trial Balance and Transaction Detail by Account reports match those shown above. This report can help in identifying and correcting errors.

End Note

You have now added a customer, product, and service. You have recorded a sales receipt, invoice, payment received from a customer, and deposit to a bank account. These are operating activities. Additional operating activities related to purchases and cash payments follow in Chapter 5.

Chapter 4 Questions

1 What steps need to be followed to add a new product or service?

2 What steps need to be followed to record a new sales receipt?

3 What steps need to be followed to record a new invoice?

4 What steps need to be followed to record a new payment from a customer?

5 What steps need to be followed to record a new deposit to the bank?

6 What are the differences between adding a new product and adding a new service?

7 What is the difference between a sales receipt and a sales invoice?

Chapter 4 Matching

a. Invoice   _____   A service in the Wild Water Sports company

b. Sales receipt   _____   Providing the bank a payment from a customer

c. Product   _____   Used when recording a sale on account

d. Service   _____   Used to add invoices, sales receipts, or bank deposits

e. `+ New` icon   _____   A customer in the Wild Water Sports company

f. Payment from a customer   _____   Quantities of this are not tracked

g. Deposit   _____   Used when cash is collected at the time of a sale

h. Cleaning   _____   Cash receipts received from a sale

i. Tige 25 zx   _____   Quantities of this are tracked

j. Performance Rentals   _____   A product that is added in the Wild Water Sports company

Chapter 4 Cases

The following cases require you to open the company you updated in Chapter 3. Each of the following cases continues throughout the text in a sequential manner. For example, if you are assigned Case 01, you will use the file you modified in this chapter in all of the following chapters. Each of the following cases is similar in concepts assessed but differs in amounts and transactions. See the Preface to this text for a matrix of each student case and its attributes.

To reopen your company, do the following:

1 Open your Internet browser.

2 Type **https://qbo.intuit.com** into your browser's address text box.

3 Type your user ID and password into the text boxes as you have done before.

Case 1

Add some operating activities (sales and cash receipts) to your company. Based on what you learned in the text using the Wild Water Sports company, you are to make the following changes to the Case 1 company you modified in Chapter 3:

1 Add a new customer – Name: Sarah Hay, Company: Hey Hays Surf, Display name as: Sarah Hay, Address: 230 Beach Way, La Jolla, CA, 92039.

2 Add a new service – Tune-Up, rate: $85.00, income account: Services.

3 Add a new product – Fred Rubble, initial quantity on hand: 0, as of date: 1/1/24, Inventory asset account: Inventory Asset, price: $950.00, cost: $600.00, income account: Sales, expense account: Cost of Goods Sold.

4 Record a new sales receipt on 1/3/24 – Customer: Blondie's Boards, payment method: Check, reference no.: 893, deposit to: Undeposited Funds (add this new current asset account), product: Rook 15, quantity: 2.

5 Record a new invoice on 1/4/24 – Customer: Sarah Hay, terms: Net 30, service: Tune-Up, quantity: 2, product: The Water Hog, quantity: 1.

6 Record a new cash payment received on 1/5/24 – Customer: Blondie's Boards, payment method: Check, reference no.: 984, deposit to: Undeposited Funds, amount received: $5,000.00. (Be sure to place a check in the Journal Entry #1 check box.)

7 Record a deposit made on 1/8/24 to the checking account – Received from: Blondie's Boards, amount received: $1,300.00, related to: Sales Receipt.

8 Prepare a Trial Balance report with a From date of 1/1/24 and a To date of 1/31/24, save it as a customized report named Trial Balance 1/31/24, and share it with all users. Your report should look like Figure 4.19. If asked, indicate that your business is accrual based.

Figure 4.19

Trial Balance (as of 1/31/24)

Case 1
TRIAL BALANCE
As of January 31, 2024

	DEBIT	CREDIT
Checking	26,300.00	
Accounts Receivable	1,030.00	
Inventory Asset	6,700.00	
Prepaid Expenses	3,000.00	
Undeposited Funds	5,000.00	
Furniture & Fixtures:Depreciation		10,000.00
Furniture & Fixtures:Original cost	40,000.00	
Accounts Payable		4,500.00
Notes Payable		60,000.00
Common Stock		1,000.00
Opening Balance Equity		0.00
Retained Earnings		5,500.00
Sales		2,160.00
Services		170.00
Cost of Goods Sold	1,300.00	
TOTAL	**$83,330.00**	**$83,330.00**

9 If your trial balance differs from what is shown in Figure 4.19, do the following:

   a. Make sure that all of your changes were dated in January 2024.

   b. Click on the debit or credit balance to view a transactions report for each account, and investigate why your answer differs.

   c. Ask your instructor for assistance.

   d. Be sure your company matches the above as you will be adding additional business events in Chapter 5.

10 Export your Trial Balance report to Excel, and save it with the file name Student Name (replace with your name) Ch 04 Case 01 Trial Balance. xlsx.

11 Open and print the custom report you created in Chapter 3 called Transaction Detail by Account.

12 Use your Transaction Detail by Account report to locate any differences in your Trial Balance report created above.

   a. Make sure all of your changes were dated in January 2024.

   b. Click on the line that does not match to view the transaction for that account, and investigate why your answer differs.

   c. Ask your instructor for assistance.

   d. Be sure your company matches the above as you will be adding additional business events in Chapter 5.

13 Export your Transactions Detail by Account report to Excel and save it with the file name Student Name (replace with your name) Ch 04 Case 01 Transaction Detail by Account.xlsx.

14 Sign out of your company.

Case 2

Add some operating activities (sales and cash receipts) to your company. Based on what you learned in the text using the Wild Water Sports company, you are to make the following changes to the Case 2 company you modified in Chapter 3:

1 Add a new customer – Hagen's Toys, 3983 Torrey Pines, La Jolla, CA, 92039.

2 Add a new service – Custom Painting, rate: $45.00, income account: Services.

3 Add two new products – GO Aircraft Radio, initial quantity on hand: 0, as of date: 1/1/25, Inventory asset account: Inventory Asset, price: $4,999.00, cost: $2,500.00, income account: Sales, expense account: Cost of Goods Sold and Taylor 22cc, initial quantity on hand: 0, as of date: 1/1/25, Inventory asset account: Inventory Asset, price: $2,999.00, cost: $1,500.00, income account: Sales, expense account: Cost of Goods Sold.

4 Record a new sales receipt on 1/3/25 – Customer: Benson's RC, payment method: Credit Card, reference no.: 16756, deposit to: Undeposited Funds, product: Broon F830 Ride, quantity: 3.

5 Record a new invoice on 1/4/25 – Customer: Hagen's Toys, terms: Net 30, service: Custom Painting, quantity: 5, product: Seawind Carbon Sailboat, quantity: 1.

6 Record a new cash payment received on 1/7/25 – Customer: Benson's RC, payment method: Check, reference no.: 9847, deposit to: Undeposited Funds, amount received: $925.00. (Be sure to place a check in the Journal Entry #1 check box.)

7 Record a deposit made on 1/7/25 to the checking account – Received from: Benson's RC, amount received: $4,500.00, related to: Sales Receipt.

8 Prepare a Trial Balance report with a From date of 1/1/25 and a To date of 1/31/25, save it as a customized report named Trial Balance 1/31/25, and share it with all users. Your report should look like Figure 4.20. If asked, indicate that your business is accrual based.

Figure 4.20

Trial Balance (as of 1/31/25)

Case 2
TRIAL BALANCE
As of January 31, 2025

	DEBIT	CREDIT
Checking	9,500.00	
Accounts Receivable	1,425.00	
Inventory Asset	2,040.00	
Prepaid Expenses	2,400.00	
Undeposited Funds	925.00	
Machinery & Equipment:Depreciation		1,000.00
Machinery & Equipment:Original cost	10,000.00	
Accounts Payable		1,900.00
Notes Payable		12,000.00
Common Stock		100.00
Opening Balance Equity		0.00
Retained Earnings		8,385.00
Sales		5,700.00
Services		225.00
Cost of Goods Sold	3,020.00	
TOTAL	$29,310.00	$29,310.00

9 If your trial balance differs from what is shown in Figure 4.20, do the following:

   a. Make sure that all of your changes were dated in January 2025.

   b. Click on the debit or credit balance to view a transactions report for each account, and investigate why your answer differs.

   c. Ask your instructor for assistance.

   d. Be sure your company matches the above as you will be adding additional business events in Chapter 5.

10 Export your Trial Balance report to Excel, and save it with the file name Student Name (replace with your name) Ch 04 Case 02 Trial Balance. xlsx.

11 Open and print the custom report you created in Chapter 3, which is called Transaction Detail by Account.

12 Use your Transaction Detail by Account report to locate any differences in your Trial Balance report created above.

   a. Make sure that all of your changes were dated in January 2025.

   b. Click on the line that does not match to view the transaction for that account, and investigate why your answer differs.

   c. Ask your instructor for assistance.

   d. Be sure your company matches the above as you will be adding additional business events in Chapter 5.

13 Export your Transactions Detail by Account report to Excel, and save it with the file name Student Name (replace with your name) Ch 04 Case 02 Transaction Detail by Account.xlsx.

14 Sign out of your company.

Case 3

Now it's time for you to add some operating activities (sales and cash receipts) to your company. Based on what you learned in the text using the Wild Water Sports company, you are to make the following changes to the Case 3 company you modified in Chapter 3:

1 Add a new customer – Surfer Sales, 3983 Torrey Pines, La Jolla, CA, 92039.

2 Add a new service – Phone Consulting, rate: $35.00, income account: Services, not taxable.

3 Add two new products – Apple iPhone 6s, initial quantity on hand: 0, inventory asset account: Inventory Asset, price: $549.00, cost: $349.00, income account: Sales of Product Income, expense account: Cost of Goods Sold, taxable and Apple iPhone 7 Plus, initial quantity on hand: 0, inventory asset account: Inventory Asset, price: $800, cost: $600.00, income account: Sales of Product Income, expense account: Cost of Goods Sold, taxable. Use 12/31/25 for the as of date.

4 Record a new sales receipt on 1/3/26 – customer: Surfer Sales, payment method: Credit Card, reference no.: 16756, deposit to: Payments to deposit product: Apple iPhone 7, quantity: 6, and 3 hours of Phone Consulting. Click **See the math** to update amounts.

5 Record a new invoice on 1/6/26 – customer: GHO Marketing, terms: Net 30, 3 hours of Apple Repairs, product: Apple iPhone 7, quantity: 3. Click **See the math** to update amounts.

6 Record a new cash payment received on 1/7/26 – customer: GHO Marketing, payment method: Check, reference no.: 9847, deposit to: Payments to deposit, amount received: $4,125.00. (Be sure to place a check in the Journal Entry #1 check box.)

7 Record a deposit made on 1/9/26 to the checking account of $9,078.75, which was received from Surfer Sales, amount $4,953.75, and related to Sales Receipt and GHO Marketing, amount $4,125.00, related to Payment.

8 Prepare a Trial Balance report with a From date of 1/1/26 and a To date of 1/31/26 and then save it as a customized report named Trial Balance 1/31/26 and share it with all users. Your report should look like Figure 4.21.

Figure 4.21

Trial Balance as of 1/31/26

Case 03 - Student Name (ID Number)

Trial Balance
As of January 31, 2026

	DEBIT	CREDIT
Checking	21,078.75	
Accounts receivable (A/R)	2,559.38	
Inventory Asset	1,700.00	
Payments to deposit	0.00	
Prepaid expenses	2,750.00	
Machinery & Equipment:Depreciation		2,000.00
Machinery & Equipment:Original cost	15,000.00	
Accounts Payable (A/P)		5,000.00
California Department of Tax and Fee Administration …		523.13
Notes Payable		23,000.00
Opening balance equity		0.00
Owner's Equity		10,075.00
Sales of Product Income		6,750.00
Services		240.00
Cost of goods sold	4,500.00	
TOTAL	$47,588.13	$47,588.13

9   If your trial balance is different than Figure 4.21, do the following:

    a.   Make sure that all of your changes were dated in January 2026.

    b.   Click on the debit or credit balance to view a transactions report for each account, and investigate why your answer is different.

    c.   Ask your instructor for assistance.

    d.   Be sure your company matches the above as you will be adding additional business events in Chapter 5.

10   Export your Trial Balance report to Excel, and save it with the file name Student Name (replace with your name) Ch 04 Case 03 Trial Balance. xlsx.

11   Open and print the custom report you created in Chapter 3, which is called Transaction Detail by Account.

12   Use your Transaction Detail by Account report to locate any differences in your Trial Balance report created above.

    a.   Make sure that all of your changes were dated in January 2026.

    b.   Click on the line that doesn't match to view the transaction for that account, and investigate why your answer is different.

    c.   Ask your instructor for assistance.

    d.   Be sure your company matches the above as you will be adding additional business events in Chapter 5.

13 Export your Transactions Detail by Account report to MS Excel and save it with the file name Student Name (replace with your name) Ch 04 Case 03 Transaction Detail by Account.xlsx.

14 Sign out of your company.

Case 4

Now it's time for you to add some operating activities (sales and cash receipts) to your company. Based on what you learned in the text using the Wild Water Sports company, you are to make the following changes to the Case 4 company you modified in Chapter 3:

1 Add two new accounts.

   a. First account

      i) Account type: Assets

      ii) Save account under: Other Current Assets

      iii) Tax form section: Other Current Assets

      iv) Account name: Prepaid insurance

   b. Second account

      i) Account type: Expenses

      ii) Save account under: Other business expenses

      iii) Tax form section: Other Business Expenses

      iv) Account name: Laundry services

2 Add three new customers.

   a. Flyer Corporation, 32 Wilshire Blvd., Hollywood, CA 90028, terms: Net 30

   b. ABC Studios, 2300 W Riverside Dr., Burbank, CA 91506, terms: Net 30

   c. Shepard Inc., 10 Hollywood Blvd., Hollywood, CA 90028, terms: Due on receipt

3 Modify an existing customer (use Help to learn how to do this).

   a. Company – Disney

   b. Address – 500 South Buena Vista Street, Burbank, CA 91505, terms: Net 30

4 Add three new vendors.

   a. Bowflex Inc., 3393 Main St., Vancouver, WA 98607, terms: Net 30

   b. NordicTrack Inc., 23 First St., Logan, UT 84321, terms: Net 30

   c. Laundry Service Inc., 432 Sunset Blvd., Hollywood, CA, 90028, terms: Due on receipt

5   Modify an existing vendor (use Help to learn how to do this).

   a.   Company – Precor

   b.   Address – 20031 142nd Avenue NE, Woodinville, WA 98072, terms: Net 30

6   Create a new service item as follows:

   a.   Name/Description – Monthly Fee – Corporate Membership 50 Employees

   b.   Description – Yes you do sell this service to customers

   c.   Sales price/rate – $6,000

   d.   Income account – Sales

   e.   Is taxable – No

   f.   Purchasing information – No you don't purchase this service from a vendor

7   Modify two existing service items (use Help to learn how to do this).

   a.   Old Name/Description – Monthly Fee – New Name/Description – Monthly Fee – Individual

   b.   Old Name/Description – Training – New Name/Description – Training – Individual

8   Add two new products.

   a.   First product

       i)   Name – Bowflex Dumbbells

       ii)   Initial quantity on hand – 0

       iii)   As of date – 12/31/26

       iv)   Inventory asset account – Inventory Asset

       v)   Description – Bowflex Dumbbells

       vi)   Sales price/rate – $249

       vii)   Income account – Sales of Product Income

       viii)   Is taxable – Yes

       ix)   Purchasing information – Bowflex Dumbbells

       x)   Cost – $200

       xi)   Expense account – Cost of Goods Sold

   b.   Second product

       i)   Name – Power Block Elite Dumbbells

       ii)   Initial quantity on hand – 0

       iii)   As of date – 12/31/26

       iv)   Inventory asset account – Inventory Asset

       v)   Description – Power Block Elite Dumbbells

       vi)   Sales price/rate – $299

       vii)   Income account – Sales of Product Income

viii)   Is taxable – Yes

ix)   Purchasing information – Power Block Elite Dumbbells

x)   Cost – $199

xi)   Expense account – Cost of Goods Sold

9   Record a new sales receipt to Shepard Inc. on 1/5/27 for 6 months of Monthly Fee – Individual, 10 hours of Training – Individual, 1 T-shirt, and 1 pair of Yoga pants. Total $1,726.65 (including sales tax) received via check number 6571 and deposited to the Payments to deposit account. If Payments to deposit account is not shown in the drop-down list you'll need to add it as a new other current asset. (Alternatively, if an Undeposited Funds account is shown use that account.)

10   Record a new ABC Studios invoice 1002 on 1/6/27 for 1 Monthly Fee – Corporate Membership 50 Employees and 50 T-shirts for a total amount of $7,368.75 (including sales tax).

11   Record a new Flyer Corporation invoice 1003 on 1/6/27 for 1 Monthly Fee – Corporate Membership 50 Employees and 50 hours of Training – Individual and 50 pairs of Yoga pants for a total amount of $12,213.75 (including sales tax).

12   Record a partial cash payment of $6,000.00 received on 1/7/2027 from Disney using check 9744 recorded to the Payments to deposit account. (Be sure to place a check in the Journal Entry #1 check box.)

13   Record a bank deposit of $7,726.65 made on 1/8/27 from Disney and Shepard Inc.

14   Prepare and print a Trial Balance report with a custom reporting period of 1/1/27 to 1/8/27 and then save it as a customized report named Trial Balance 1/8/27. Your report should look like Figure 4.22.

Trial Balance As of January 8, 2027	DEBIT	CREDIT
Checking	34,726.65	
Accounts Receivable (A/R)	22,082.50	
Inventory Asset	3,868.00	
Payments to deposit	0.00	
Prepaid rent	12,000.00	
Furniture:Accumulated Depreciation		10,000.00
Furniture:Original Cost	65,000.00	
Vehicles:Accumulated Depreciation		6,500.00
Vehicles:Original Cost	115,000.00	
Accounts Payable (A/P)		18,000.00
California Department of Tax and Fee Administration Payable		339.15
Long-term debt		82,000.00
Common Stock		1,000.00
Opening Balance Equity		0.00
Retained Earnings		115,500.00
Sales		17,400.00
Sales of Product Income		3,570.00
Cost of Goods Sold	1,632.00	
TOTAL	$254,309.15	$254,309.15

Figure 4.22

Trial Balance as of 1/8/27

15 If necessary, prepare and print a Transaction Detail by Account report you previously saved.

16 Use your Transaction Detail by Account report to locate any differences in your Trial Balance report created above.

    a. Make sure all your changes were dated in January 2027.

    b. Click on the line that does not match to view the transaction for that account, and investigate why your answer differs.

    c. Ask your instructor for assistance.

    d. Be sure your company matches the above as you will be adding additional business events in Chapter 5.

Case 5

Now it's time for you to add some operating activities (sales and cash receipts) to your company. Based on using what you learned in the text using the Wild Water Sports company, you are to make the following changes to the Case 4 company you modified in Chapter 3:

1 Add three new accounts.

    a. First account
        i) Account Type – Other Current Assets
        ii) Detail Type/Name – Undeposited Funds

    b. Second account
        i) Account Type – Expenses
        ii) Detail Type – Equipment Rental
        iii) Name – Equipment Rental

    c. Third account
        i) Account Type – Expenses
        ii) Detail Type – Legal & Professional Fees
        iii) Name – Recruiting

2 Add two new customers.

    a. US Department of Defense, 25203 Baneberry, San Antonio, TX, 78260, terms: Net 15

    b. Boeing, 3365 160th Ave SE 3307, Bellevue, WA, 98008, terms: Net 30

3 Modify an existing customer (use help to learn how to do this).

    a. Company – Boeing

    b. Address – 4800 Oak Grove Dr, Pasadena, CA, 91109, terms: Net 30

4 Add three new vendors.

    a. United Rentals, 376 Dan Tibbs Rd, Huntsville, AL 35806, terms: Net 30

    b. Indeed, 6433 Champion Grandview Way, Austin, TX, 78750, terms: Net 30

    c. HP Computers, 1501 Page Mill Rd, Palo Alto, CA, 94020, terms: Net 30

5 Modify an existing vendor (use Help to learn how to do this).

a. Company – Chase Bank

b. Address – 416 West Jefferson, Louisville, KY, 40202, terms: Due on receipt

6 Create a new service item as follows:

a. Name/Description – Consulting

b. Description – You sell this product/service to my customers

c. Sales price/rate – $350

d. Income account – Consulting

e. Nontaxable

f. Purchasing information – No you don't purchase this service from a vendor

7 Modify two existing service items (use Help to learn how to do this).

a. Old name/Description – Technical Solutions – New name/Description – Technical Solutions – Commercial

b. Old name/Description – Program Support – New name/Description – Program Support – Government

8 Add two new inventory products.

a. First product
    i) Name – Computer Workstation 100
    ii) Initial quantity on hand – 0
    iii) As of date – 12/31/21
    iv) Inventory asset account – Inventory
    v) Description – Computer Workstation 100
    vi) Sales price/rate – $15,000
    vii) Income account – Sales
    viii) Taxable – standard rate
    ix) Purchasing Information – Computer Workstation 100
    x) Cost – $7,000
    xi) Expense account – Cost of Goods Sold

b. Second product
    i) Name – Computer Workstation 500
    ii) Initial quantity on hand – 0
    iii) As of date – 12/31/21
    iv) Inventory asset account – Inventory
    v) Description – Computer Workstation 500
    vi) Sales price/rate – $35,000
    vii) Income account – Sales
    viii) Taxable – standard rate
    ix) Purchasing Information – Computer Workstation 500
    x) Cost – $17,000
    xi) Expense account – Cost of Goods Sold

9 Record a new sales receipt 1001 to a new customer Blue Origin on 1/4/22 for 50 hours of consulting and received payment via check number 1687 and deposited to the Undeposited Funds account.

10   Record a new invoice 1002 on 1/6/22 to the US Department of Defense for 100 hours of Program Support – Government. If asked, select **I'll create invoice for my accounting, but won't send any**. If asked how I want to get paid, select **Check**.

11   Record a new invoice 1003 on 1/7/22 to Boeing for 80 hours of Technical Solutions – Commercial and 1 Training Materials – Volume 1 for a total invoice of $48,350.00 including sales tax. Click **See the math** to update amounts.

12   Record a cash payment of $70,000.00 received on 1/10/22 from NASA using check 18842 recorded to the Undeposited Funds account. Select **Journal Entry #1** in Outstanding Transactions section.

13   Record a bank deposit of $87,500.00 made on 1/12/22 from Blue Origin and NASA.

14   Prepare and print a Trial Balance report with a custom reporting period of 1/1/22 to 1/31/22 and then save it as a customized report named Trial Balance 1/31/22. Your report should look like Figure 4.23.

Figure 4.23

Trial Balance

Case 05 - Student Name (ID Number)

TRIAL BALANCE

As of January 31, 2022

	DEBIT	CREDIT
Checking	117,500.00	
Accounts Receivable (A/R)	158,350.00	
Inventory	452,000.00	
Prepaid Expenses	10,000.00	
Undeposited Funds	0.00	
Fixed Asset Computers:Depreciation		25,000.00
Fixed Asset Computers:Original cost	250,000.00	
Fixed Asset Furniture:Depreciation		8,000.00
Fixed Asset Furniture:Original cost	80,000.00	
Accounts Payable (A/P)		20,000.00
Alabama Department of Revenue Payable		600.00
Alabama, Huntsville Payable		675.00
Alabama, Madison County Payable		75.00
Notes Payable		545,000.00
Opening Balance Equity		0.00
Owner's Equity		382,000.00
Consulting		79,500.00
Sales		15,000.00
Cost of Goods Sold	8,000.00	
TOTAL	$1,075,850.00	$1,075,850.00

15   Open and print your previously saved report Transaction Detail by Account.

16   Use your Transaction Detail by Account report to locate any differences in your Trial Balance report created above.

a.   Make sure all your changes were dated in January 2022.

b.   Click on the line that does not match to view the transaction for that account, and investigate why your answer differs.

c.   Ask your instructor for assistance.

d.   Be sure your company matches the above as you will be adding additional business events in Chapter 5.

Case 6

Now it's time for you to add some operating activities (sales and cash receipts) to your company. Based on using what you learned in the text using the Wild Water Sports company, you are to make the following changes to the Case 6 company you modified in Chapter 3:

1 Add two new accounts.

   a. First account
- i)   Account Type – Other Current Assets
- ii)   Detail Type/Name – Prepaid Expenses

   b. Second account
- i)   Account Type – Other Current Assets
- ii)   Detail Type – Inventory
- iii)   Name – Inventory Parts

2 Change the name of expense account Repairs & Maintenance to Repairs.

3 Add two new customers.

   a. Ebony Williams, 4101 S Sheridan Ave., Tacoma, WA, 98418, terms: Net 30

   b. Deja Smith, 4648 N Defiance St., Tacoma, WA, 98407, terms: Net 30

4 Modify an existing customer.

   a. Company – Sam Ski

   b. Address – 5633 89th Ave SE, Mercer Island, WA, 98040, terms: Net 30

5 Add two new vendors.

   a. Airstream, Inc., 419 West Pike Street, Jackson Center, OH 45334, terms: Net 30

   b. Thor Motor Coach, 701 County Road 15 Elkhart, Indiana 46516, terms: Net 30

6 Modify an existing vendor.

   a. Company – Winnebago (change Company and Display name to Winnebago, Inc.)

   b. Address – 605 West Crystal Lake Road, Forest City, IA, 50436, terms: Net 30

7 Create two new service items as follows:

   a. First service
- i)   Name – Basic 6,000-mile service
- ii)   Description – Yes you do sell this service to customers
- iii)   Sales price/rate – $450
- iv)   Income account – Sales
- v)   Sales Tax Category – Nontaxable
- vi)   Purchasing information – No you don't purchase this service from a vendor

  b. Second service
   i) Name – Roof inspection and repair
   ii) Description – Yes you do sell this service to customers
   iii) Sales price/rate – $500
   iv) Income account – Sales
   v) Sales Tax Category – Nontaxable
   vi) Purchasing information – No you don't purchase this service from a vendor

  c. Third service
   i) Name – Sewer system inspection and repair
   ii) Description – Yes you do sell this service to customers
   iii) Sales price/rate – $600
   iv) Income account – Sales
   v) Sales Tax Category – Nontaxable
   vi) Purchasing information – No you don't purchase this service from a vendor

8 Add two new inventory products.

  a. First product
   i) Name – 2023 Thor Motor Coach Palazzo 33.2
   ii) Inventory asset account – Inventory Asset
   iii) Description – 2023 Thor Motor Coach Palazzo 33.2
   iv) Sales price/rate – $180,000
   v) Income account – Sales of Product Income
   vi) Sales Tax Category – Taxable - Standard rate
   vii) Purchasing information – 2023 Thor Motor Coach Palazzo 33.2
   viii) Cost – $144,000
   ix) Expense account – Cost of Goods Sold
   x) Preferred Vendor – Thor Motor Coach
   xi) Initial quantity on hand – 0
   xii) As of date – 12/31/22

  b. Second product
   i) Name – 2023 Airstream Flying Cloud 27FB TWIN
   ii) Inventory asset account – Inventory Asset
   iii) Description – 2023 Airstream Flying Cloud 27FB TWIN
   iv) Sales price/rate – $99,000
   v) Income account – Sales of Product Income
   vi) Sales Tax Category – Taxable - Standard rate
   vii) Purchasing information – 2023 Airstream Flying Cloud 27FB TWIN
   viii) Cost – $80,000
   ix) Expense account – Cost of Goods Sold
   x) Preferred Vendor – Airstream, Inc.
   xi) Initial quantity on hand – 0
   xii) As of date – 12/31/22

9 Record a new sales receipt 1001 on 01/05/23 to a new customer Donald Biden for the sale of a 2022 Winnebago Revel 44E for $150,000 plus sales tax of $13,950 with payment method credit card for a total of $163,950.

10 Record a new invoice 1002 on 01/09/23 to Deja Smith for the sale of a 2022 Winnebago View 24G for $140,000 plus sales tax of $13,020 on account for a total of $153,020.

11 Record a new cash payment received on 1/11/23 – Customer: Sam Ski, payment method: Check, deposit to: Undeposited Funds, amount received: $10,000.

12 Record a deposit made on 1/12/23 to the checking account of $10,000 which was received from: Sam Ski.

13 Prepare and print a Trial Balance report with a custom reporting period of 1/1/23 to 1/31/23 and then save it as a customized report named Trial Balance 1/31/23. Your report should look like Figure 4.24.

Figure 4.24

Trial Balance

Case 06 - Student Name (ID Number)
TRIAL BALANCE
As of January 31, 2023

	DEBIT	CREDIT
Checking	223,950.00	
Accounts Receivable (A/R)	153,020.00	
Inventory Asset	344,000.00	
Loans To Officers	15,000.00	
Undeposited Funds	0.00	
Buildings:Depreciation		15,000.00
Buildings:Original cost	150,000.00	
Machinery & Equipment:Depreciation		10,000.00
Machinery & Equipment:Original cost	100,000.00	
Accounts Payable (A/P)		464,000.00
Washington State Department of Revenue Payable		26,970.00
Notes Payable		100,000.00
Common Stock		1,000.00
Opening Balance Equity		0.00
Paid-In Capital		250,000.00
Retained Earnings		61,000.00
Sales of Product Income		290,000.00
Cost of Goods Sold	232,000.00	
TOTAL	$1,217,970.00	$1,217,970.00

14 Prepare and print a Transaction Detail by Account report for all dates and then save it as a customized report named Transaction Detail by Account All Dates. If asked, indicate that your business is accrual based.

15 Use your Transaction Detail by Account report to locate any differences in your Trial Balance report created above.

   a. Make sure all your changes were dated in January 2023.

   b. Click on the line that does not match to view the transaction for that account and investigate why your answer differs.

   c. Ask your instructor for assistance.

   d. Be sure your company matches the above as you will be adding additional business events in Chapter 5.

Recording Operating Activities: Purchases and Cash Payments

Upon completion of this chapter, the student will be able to do the following:

- Add a vendor
- Record a purchase order
- Record a bill for the receipt of products/services on account
- Record the payment of bills
- Record credit card charges
- Record checks
- Prepare a Trial Balance

Overview

In Chapter 4 you added new accounts, new customers, new vendors, new products, and new services to your Wild Water Sports company. In addition, you recorded operating activities like sales receipts, invoices, cash receipts, and bank deposits. In this chapter you will add additional operating activities to the Wild Water Sports company like purchase orders, bills, payment of bills, credit card charges, and checks. At the end of this chapter you will perform similar tasks on the case assigned by your instructor.

To verify the accuracy of you Wild Water Sports company:

1   Sign into your QBO account then open the Wild Water Sports company you used in Chapter 4.

2   Click **Reports**, then click the **Custom reports** tab, then double-click **Trial Balance** to open the Trial Balance report. Set the from and to dates to **1/1/27** and **1/13/27**, respectively. Compare your report to Figure 5.1. If your report doesn't match Figure 5.1 go back to your work in Chapter 4 to fix your errors. Otherwise, close your Trial Balance report.

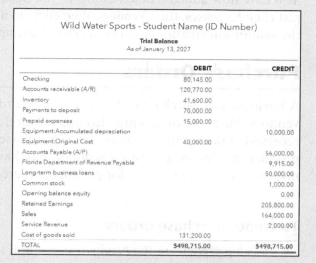

Figure 5.1

Wild Water Sports trial balance as of 1/13/27

Vendors

In this section, you will be adding new vendors. Recall that vendors are your company's suppliers of products and services. To add vendors, you will use the Expenses menu item in the navigation bar.

Navigate your browser to the Video Tutorials provided by Intuit (see website address specified in the Preface to this text) and then search on How to Manage Vendors.

To add new vendors to the Wild Water Sports company:

1   Click **Expenses**, then click **Vendors** in the navigation bar, and then click the **New vendor** button.

2   Type **Tige** in the Company name text box.

3   Type the address **1801 TX Hwy 36 Abilene, TX 79602** in the appropriate text boxes.

4   Select **Net 30** from the Terms text box to view Figure 5.2.

Figure 5.2

Vendor Information window (partial view)

5   Click **Save**.

You have now added a new vendor. If you need to edit a vendor's information, just click **Expenses**, then **Vendors**, then click on a vendor, then click **Edit**. Update the vendor information, then click **Save**. Next up is adding purchase orders.

Purchase Orders

Navigate your browser to the Video Tutorials provided by Intuit (see website address specified in the Preface to this text) and then search on How to Enter Purchase Orders.

A business uses purchase orders to formally order products or services from its vendors. Purchase orders are also used as a reference and control for products received. During the creation of a purchase order, you can create a new product or refer to an existing product. Purchase orders can be used to acquire inventory for future sale or for products ordered for a specific customer.

To create purchase orders:

1   Click [+ New] from the Navigation bar and then click **Purchase order** under the Vendor column.

2   Select **Tige** from the drop-down list of Vendors.

3   Type **1/14/27** in the Purchase Order date text box.

4   Select **Tige 25 zx** from the Select a product/service text box.

5   Type **1** in the QTY column to view Purchase Order #1001 shown in Figure 5.3.

Figure 5.3

Purchase order to Tige

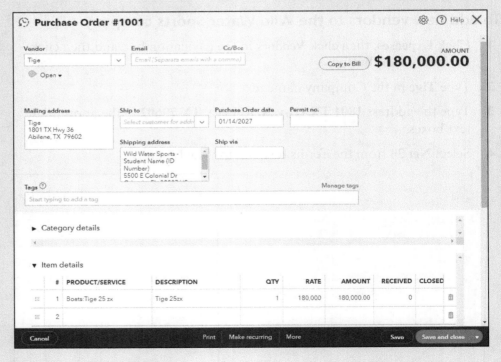

6   Click **Save and new**.

7   Click **+ Add new** from the Vendor text box.

8   Type **Centurion Boats** as the Company name.

9 Add the following address information: **2047 Grogan Avenue, Merced, CA 95341** and set terms to **Net 30**.

10 Click **Save**.

11 Type **1/15/27** in the Purchase Order date text box.

12 Type **2023 Vi22** from the Select a product/service text box and then click **+ Add new 2023 Vi22**.

13 Select **Inventory**, then select **Boats** as the Category.

14 Type **0** as the Initial quantity on hand and **01/05/2027** in the As of date text box.

15 Select **Inventory** as the Inventory asset account.

16 Type **2023 Vi22** in the Description and Purchasing information text boxes.

17 Type **115000** in the sales price text box and **90000** in the cost text box. Select **Sales of Product Income** as the Income account, Cost of goods sold as the Expense account, and Taxable - standard rate as the Sales tax.

18 Click **Save and close**.

19 Type **1** in the QTY column to view Purchase Order #1002 shown in Figure 5.4.

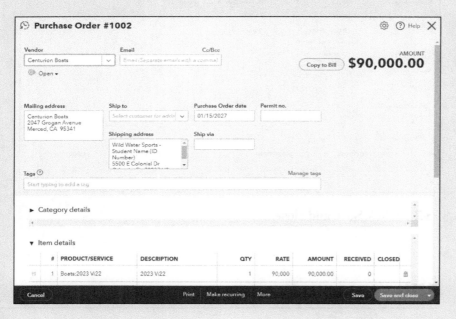

Figure 5.4

Purchase order to Centurion Boats

20 Click **Save and new**.

21 Select **Tige** as the Vendor.

22 Type **1/15/27** in the Purchase Order date text box.

23 Type **Tige Thruster Control Package** in the Product/Service text box and then click **+ Add new Tige Thruster Control Package**.

24 Select **Inventory**, then type **Parts** as the Category, then click **+ Add new Parts**, then click **Save**.

25 Type **0** as the Initial quantity on hand and **01/15/2027** in the As of date text box.

26 Select **Inventory** as the Inventory asset account.

27 Type **Tige Thruster Control Package** in the Description and Purchasing information text boxes.

28 Type **25000** in the sales price text box and **20000** in the cost text box.

29 Type **Sales Parts** in the Income account text box, then click **+ Sales Parts**, then click **Save and close** to accept the new income account.

30 Click **Save and close** to accept the new inventory part.

31 Type **1** in the QTY column to view Purchase Order #1003 shown in Figure 5.5.

Figure 5.5

Purchase order for a new inventory part

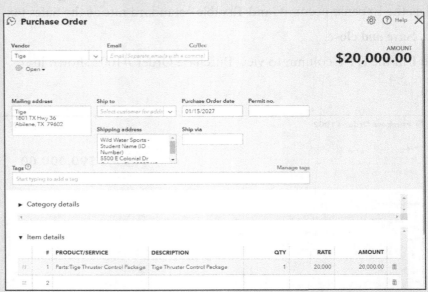

32 Click **Save and close**.

Navigate your browser to the Video Tutorials provided by Intuit (see website address specified in the Preface to this text) and then search on How to Enter Bills.

Bills

In the previous chapter, you created invoices to customers for products or services rendered. That invoice served as a bill to that customer signifying a sales transaction for you and a bill to them. Likewise, when you enter into a business transaction, such as purchasing a product or service from a vendor, you expect them to send you an invoice. In QBO, the invoice you receive from a vendor is called a bill. Bills are recorded in QBO to signify the receipt of a product or service and a related liability, usually accounts payable. The inventory account is affected when the bill represents a product being delivered.

In QBO, the terms of those bills could be one of the following: due on receipt, net 10, net 15, net 30, or net 60. The net reference means the bill is due to be paid within a specified number of days, for example, 10, 15, 30, or 60 days. Other terms, for example, 2/10 net 30, provide for a 2% discount on the invoice if paid within 10 days; otherwise, a payment is required within 30 days. Even though you can set up such terms to appear on invoices to customers and bills from vendors, QBO does not calculate them automatically. To simplify your learning of QBO, discounts have not been implemented in this text.

In this section, you will focus on recording a bill for the receipt of services and products on account, meaning you will have been given terms (usually net 30), so you will not have to pay the bill for 30 days after the bill date. The first bill was for a product received which had been previously ordered using a purchase order. The second bill was for a new product, which had not been previously ordered using a purchase order. Both of these purchases will affect inventory and are, thus, recorded in the Items detail section of a bill. The last two bills are services that were rendered and thus do not affect inventory and are therefore recorded in the Category details section of a bill.

To record a bill from a vendor for the receipt of products/services on account, do the following:

1 Continue from where you left off.

2 Click the ⬛ + New ⬛ icon, and click **Bill** in the Vendors column as shown in Figure 5.6.

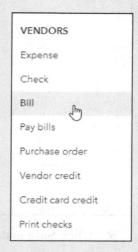

Figure 5.6

+ New window (entering bills)

3 Select **Tige** from the Vendor drop-down list.

4 Accept **Net 30** from the drop-down list of Terms. Type **1/18/27** as the Bill date.

5 Collapse the Category details section of the bill by clicking on the arrow next to Category details.

6 Expand the Item details section of the bill by clicking on the arrow next to Item details.

7 Click **Add** in the Add to Bill section, which identifies an open purchase order #1001 from this vendor located on the right of the bill as shown in Figure 5.7.

Figure 5.7

Bill (adding purchase order information)

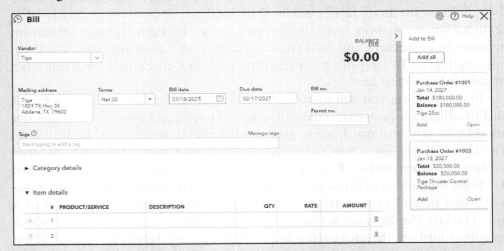

8 The bill now contains information from purchase order #1001 as shown in Figure 5.8. **Trouble?** If information provided in the Product/Service column (or any other column) is cut off or not visible, simply place your cursor between column titles and drag to the left or right to decrease or increase the column width.

Figure 5.8

Bill (after purchase order information is added)

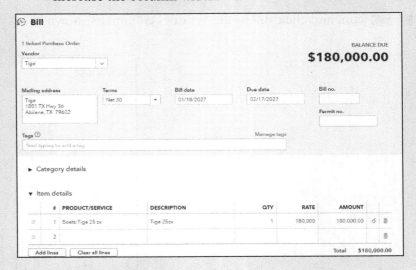

9 Click **Save and new**.

10 Select **Malibu Boats** from the Vendor drop-down list.

11 Select **Net 30** from the drop-down list of Terms. Type **1/18/27** as the Bill date.

12 Select **+ Add new** on line 1 of the bill in the Product/Service column of the Item details section. **Trouble?** If instead of seeing a Product/Service column you see a Category column, you are in the Category details section instead of the Item details section (a common mistake).

13 Add a new product as you have done before—product type: **Inventory**, Name and Description: **Wake Accessory Package**, initial quantity on hand: **0**, As of date: **01/18/2027**, Category: **Parts**, inventory asset account: **Inventory**, Sales price/rate: **500**, cost: **350**, income account: **Sales Parts**, expense account: **Cost of Goods Sold**, Sales tax: Taxable - standard rate. Click **Save and close** in the Product/Service Information window.

14 Type **5** on line 1 of the bill in the QTY column.

15 Click **Save and new**.

16 Type **Best Buy Geek Squad** from the Vendor drop-down list, then click **+ Add new Best Buy Geek Squad**. Type **Best Buy Geek Squad** as the Vendor display name, then click **Save** to save the new vendor.

17 Select **Net 30** from the drop-down list of Terms. Type **1/19/27** as the Bill date.

18 Expand the Category details section of the bill by clicking on the arrow next to Category details.

19 Collapse the Item details section of the bill by clicking on the arrow next to Item details.

20 Select **Rent:Equipment rental** on line 1 of the bill in the Category column.

21 Type **6000** on line 1 of the bill in the Amount column and then press **[Tab]**. Your window should look like Figure 5.9.

Figure 5.9

Bill (for services)

22 Click **Save and new**.

23 Select **Allstate Insurance** from the Choose a vendor drop-down list.

24 Select **Net 30** from the drop-down list of Terms.

25 Type **1/19/27** as the Bill date.

26 Select **Prepaid expenses** on line 1 of the bill in the Category column.

27 Type **2500** on line 1 of the bill in the Amount column and then press **[Tab]**. Your window should look like Figure 5.10.

Figure 5.10

Bill for Prepaid Expenses (recording)

28 Click **Save and close**.

All bills entered increased an asset or an expense account. Inventory purchases were all recorded in the Item details section and increased the quantity of those products (as long as they were originally set up as "tracked" products). Equipment rental was recorded as an expense and the prepaid insurance was recorded as an asset (Prepaid Expenses). All bills increased the accounts payable liability account.

Navigate your browser to the Video Tutorials provided by Intuit (see website address specified in the Preface to this text) and then search on How to Record Bill Payments.

Payment of Bills, Use of a Credit Card, Payments for Items Other Than Bills

In this section, you will focus on recording the payment of a bill for the receipt of services and/or products on account, recording credit card charges, or recording the payment by check for other items.

To pay bills, do the following:

1 Continue from where you left off.

2 Click the `+ New` icon, and click **Pay bills** in the Vendors column as shown in Figure 5.11.

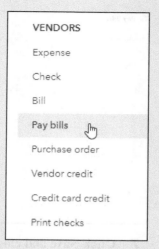

Figure 5.11

+ New window (paying bills)

3 A listing of possible bills that can be paid appears. In the Pay Bills window, select **Checking** as the Payment account and then type **01/18/2027** in the Payment date text box and then type **1001** as the Starting check no. and then press **[Tab]**. Your screen should look like Figure 5.12.

Figure 5.12

Bills to pay

4 Click and hold your mouse between the Payee and Ref No. columns and drag to the right to increase the width of the Payee column.

5 Click and hold your mouse between the Ref No. and Due Date columns and drag to the left to decrease the width of the Ref No. column.

6 Click the **Due Date** column to sort bills by due date and then click in the check box of the **Malibu Boats 12/31/2026** bill to show bills to be paid as shown in Figure 5.13.

Figure 5.13

Bills to pay (selecting)

7   Click **Save and close**.

You have now paid a bill for products/services received for which you received a bill. However, often you will pay for a product/service or another expense for which you have not received a bill. Often, these are vendors who give you no terms and require you to pay immediately. These terms are called *due on receipt*. For example, a credit card charge for fuel or a check for supplies. To record these transactions, you will use either the Expense task or the Check task after clicking the `+ New` icon. For ease of use, you will be directed to use the Expense task for all credit card transactions and the Check task for all checking account payments even though the Expense task can be used for either credit card charges or check payments.

To record a credit card or check payment, do the following:

1   Click the `+ New` icon.

2   Click **Expense** under the Vendors column.

3   Type **Chevron**, in the Payee text box, and then select **+ Add new Chevron**, Type **Chevron** in the Vendor display name text box, then click **Save**.

4   Type **Mastercard** in the Payment account text box, and then click **+ Add new Mastercard**. Select **Credit Card** as the Account Type and Detail Type, then click **Save and close**.

5   Type **1/19/2027** in the Payment date text box, select **Credit Card** in the Payment method text box then select **Vehicle gas & fuel** in row 1 of the Category column, then type **1600** as the amount and then press **[Tab]**. Your window should look like Figure 5.14.

Figure 5.14

Credit card charge

6 Click **Save and close**.

7 Click the ⊕ New icon.

8 Click **Check** under the Vendors column.

9 Type **Verizon** in the Payee text box, then click **+ Add new Verizon,** Type **Verizon** in the Vendor display name text box, then click **Save**.

10 Select **Checking** from the drop-down list in the Bank Account text box.

11 Accept **1002** as the Check no.

12 Select **Phone service** in row 1 of the Category column, and type **1800** as the amount, and then press **[Tab]** as shown in Figure 5.15.

Figure 5.15

Check 1002 payment to Verizon

13 Click **Save and close**.

Trial Balance

The work you completed in this chapter had an effect on the company's trial balance. You decided to create a Trial Balance report and investigate the checking, inventory asset, and accounts payable accounts. In the process, you realized that purchase orders do not affect a company's accounts until products are received or services are rendered.

To create a trial balance and investigate some account activity, do the following:

1 Click **Reports**, then select the **Custom reports** tab, then select **Trial Balance**. Change the to date of the report to **1/19/2027** to view the Trial Balance as shown in Figure 5.16.

Figure 5.16

Trial Balance (upper portion)

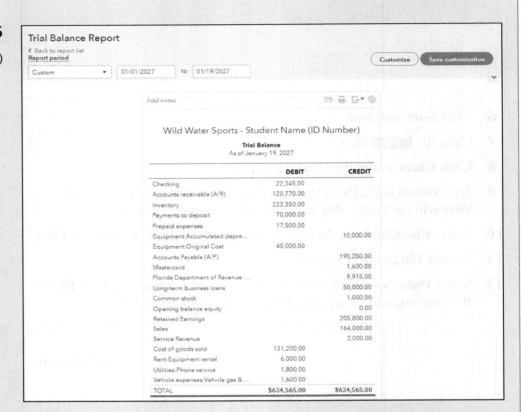

2 Click the Checking account balance of **22,345.00** to produce a Transaction Report for the Checking Account. See Figure 5.17. Note again that your checking account balance may be different.

Figure 5.17

Transaction Report (for the Checking account)

3   Click the **Printer** icon to print this report.

4   Click **Back to report summary**.

5   Click the Inventory account balance of **223,350.00** to produce a Transaction Report for the Inventory account. The two bills for product purchases you recorded earlier in this chapter are shown in Figure 5.18.

Wild Water Sports - Student Name (ID Number)

Transaction Report
January 1-19, 2027

DATE	TRANSACTION TYPE	NUM	NAME	MEMO/DESCRIPTION	ACCOUNT	SPLIT	AMOUNT	BALANCE
▾ Inventory								
Beginning Balance								172,800.00
01/04/2027	Sales Receipt	1001	Southtown Watersports	Malibu Sportster LX	Inventory	Payments to deposit	-41,600.00	131,200.00
01/06/2027	Invoice	1002	Performance Rentals	Malibu Sunset LX	Inventory	Accounts receivable (A/R)	-48,000.00	83,200.00
01/06/2027	Invoice	1002	Performance Rentals	Malibu Sportster LX	Inventory	Accounts receivable (A/R)	-41,600.00	41,600.00
01/15/2027	Inventory Starting Value	START		Tige Thruster Control Packa...	Inventory	Opening balance equity	0.00	41,600.00
01/15/2027	Inventory Starting Value	START		2023 Vi22 - Opening invent...	Inventory	Opening balance equity	0.00	41,600.00
01/18/2027	Inventory Starting Value	START		Wake Accessory Package - ...	Inventory	Opening balance equity	0.00	41,600.00
01/18/2027	Bill		Malibu Boats	Wake Accessory Package	Inventory	Accounts Payable (A/P)	1,750.00	43,350.00
01/18/2027	Bill		Tige	Tige 25zx	Inventory	Accounts Payable (A/P)	180,000.00	223,350.00
Total for Inventory							$50,550.00	
TOTAL							$50,550.00	

Figure 5.18

Transaction Report (for the Inventory account)

6   Click the **Printer** icon to print this report.

7   Click **Back to report summary**.

8   Click the Accounts Payable (A/P) account balance of **190,250.00** to produce a Transaction Report for the Accounts Payable (A/P) account. The bills for product and service purchases and the bill payments you recorded earlier in this chapter are shown in Figure 5.19.

Wild Water Sports - Student Name (ID Number)

Transaction Report
January 1-19, 2027

DATE	TRANSACTION TYPE	NUM	NAME	MEMO/DESCRIPTION	ACCOUNT	SPLIT	AMOUNT	BALANCE
▾ Accounts Payable (A/P)								
Beginning Balance								56,000.00
01/18/2027	Bill		Malibu Boats		Accounts Payable (A/P)	Inventory	1,750.00	57,750.00
01/18/2027	Bill		Tige		Accounts Payable (A/P)	Inventory	180,000.00	237,750.00
01/18/2027	Bill Payment (Check)	1001	Malibu Boats		Accounts Payable (A/P)	Checking	-56,000.00	181,750.00
01/19/2027	Bill		Best Buy Geek Squad		Accounts Payable (A/P)	Rent:Equipment rental	6,000.00	187,750.00
01/19/2027	Bill		Allstate Insurance		Accounts Payable (A/P)	Prepaid expenses	2,500.00	190,250.00
Total for Accounts Payable (A/P)							$134,250.00	
TOTAL							$134,250.00	

Figure 5.19

Transaction Report (for the Accounts Payable account)

9   Click the **Printer** icon to print this report.

10   Click **Back to report summary**.

11   Sign out of QBO.

Be sure to verify that your Trial Balance report matches the one shown above. Create a Detailed Transaction by Account report like you did in Chapter 4 to help locate any discrepancies.

End Note

In this chapter, you added a vendor, a product, purchase orders, bills, payment of bills, a credit card purchase, and a check payment. You also produced a trial balance and drilled down through that trial balance to see the effect the bills and payment of bills affected accounts. In the next chapter, you will work with investing and financing activities.

Chapter 5 Questions

1 Why does a business use purchase orders?

2 Describe the steps to create a new product from within a purchase order.

3 What happens when you create a new purchase order to a vendor from whom you recently placed a different purchase order?

4 What accounts are affected when a bill from a vendor supplying you products is recorded?

5 What appears when you click **Pay bills** after clicking the ⊕ New icon?

6 Describe the process for increasing or decreasing the width of a column in the listing of bills to pay.

7 What are the steps to record a credit card charge?

8 What are the steps to record a check written to pay something other than bills?

9 What are the steps to view a transaction report for the checking account from a trial balance?

10 What are the steps to view a transaction report for the inventory account from a trial balance?

Chapter 5 Matching

a. Purchase order   _____   Purchases that affect inventory are recorded here

b. Due on receipt   _____   An invoice sent by a vendor to a customer

c. Bill   _____   Purchases that don't affect inventory are recorded here

d. Net 30   _____   Task used to record checks in the checking account

e. Item detail section   _____   Suppliers of products and services

f. Category detail section   _____   A formal means to order products from vendors

g. Pay Bills   _____   Pay a bill within 30 days after the bill date

h. Check   _____   Task used to record credit card charges

i. Expense   _____   Terms that provide no credit

j. Vendor   _____   Paying vendors who have billed you

Chapter 5 Cases

The following cases require you to open the company you updated in Chapter 4. Each of the following cases continues throughout the text in a sequential manner. For example, if you are assigned Case 01, you will use the file you modified in this chapter in all of the following chapters. Each of the following cases is similar in concepts assessed but differs in amounts and transactions. See the Preface to this text for a matrix of each student case and its attributes.

To reopen your company, do the following:

1 Open your Internet browser.

2 Type **https://qbo.intuit.com** into your browser's address text box.

3 Type your user ID and password into the text boxes as you have done before.

Case 1

Add some operating activities (purchases, credit card charges, and cash payments) to your company.

Based on what you learned in the text using the Wild Water Sports company, you are to make the following changes to the Case 1 company you modified in Chapter 4:

1 Add a new vendor – Stewart Surfboards, 2102 S El Camino Real, San Clemente, CA 92672, terms: net 30.

2 Add a new vendor – Village Travel, 100 S El Camino Real, San Clemente, CA 92672, terms: due on receipt.

3 Add a new vendor – Office Depot, 101 Main St., San Diego, CA 92600, terms: due on receipt.

4 Add a new account – account type: Credit Card, detail type: Credit Card, name: VISA.

5 Add a new account – account type: Other Current Assets, detail type: Other Current Assets, name: Supplies Asset.

6 Add a new tracked product – Name/description: California Nose Rider, initial quantity on hand: 0, As of date: 01/02/24, inventory asset account: Inventory Asset, price: 3,200.00, cost: 1,700.00, income account: Sales, expense account: Cost of Goods Sold.

7 Add a new tracked product – Name/description: 808, initial quantity on hand: 0, As of date: 01/02/24, inventory asset account: Inventory Asset, price: 2,700.00, cost: 1,500.00, income account: Sales, expense account: Cost of Goods Sold.

8 Record a new purchase order for products on 1/2/24 – Vendor: Channel Islands, product 1: Fred Rubble, QTY: 5, product 2: Rook 15, QTY: 4, product 3: The Water Hog, QTY: 1.

9 Record a new purchase order for products on 1/3/24 – Vendor: Stewart Surfboards, product 1: 808, QTY: 2, product 2: California Nose Rider, QTY: 1.

10 Record a new bill based on a purchase order #1001 on 1/5/24 – Vendor: Channel Islands, terms: Net 15. All items ordered were received.

11 Record a new bill without a purchase order on 1/8/24 – New vendor: San Diego Gas & Electric, terms: Net 15, category: Utilities, amount: 145.00.

12 Record a new bill without a purchase order on 1/9/24 – New vendor: Prime Properties, terms: Net 15, category 1: Rent or Lease, amount: 2,500.00, category 2: Prepaid Expenses, amount: 5,000.00.

13 Pay all bills due to Channel Islands on 1/19/24 using the checking account and starting with check no. 1001.

14 Record a credit card charge on 1/10/24 – vendor: Village Travel, using credit card: VISA, category: Travel, amount: 1,800.00.

15 Record check on 1/11/24 – no.: 1002, vendor: Office Depot, amount: 375.00, account: Supplies Asset.

16 Open your previously customized report named Trial Balance 1/31/24. If a cash or accrual message appears, just close the message. Your report should look like Figure 5.20.

Case 1
TRIAL BALANCE
As of January 31, 2024

	DEBIT	CREDIT
Checking	16,325.00	
Accounts Receivable	1,030.00	
Inventory Asset	11,800.00	
Prepaid Expenses	8,000.00	
Supplies Asset	375.00	
Undeposited Funds	5,000.00	
Furniture & Fixtures:Depreciation		10,000.00
Furniture & Fixtures:Original cost	40,000.00	
Accounts Payable		7,645.00
VISA		1,800.00
Notes Payable		60,000.00
Common Stock		1,000.00
Opening Balance Equity		0.00
Retained Earnings		5,500.00
Sales		2,160.00
Services		170.00
Cost of Goods Sold	1,300.00	
Rent or Lease	2,500.00	
Travel	1,800.00	
Utilities	145.00	
TOTAL	$88,275.00	$88,275.00

Figure 5.20

Trial Balance (as of 1/31/24)

17 Create and print a Transaction Report for the Checking account as you did earlier in the chapter.

18 Create and print a Transaction Report for the Inventory Asset account as you did earlier in the chapter.

19 Create and print a Transaction Report for the Accounts Payable (A/P) account as you did earlier in the chapter.

20 If your trial balance differs from what is shown in Figure 5.20, do the following:

    a.   Make sure all of your changes were dated in January 2024.

    b.   View the Transaction Reports you just created to locate any errors.

    c.   Ask your instructor for assistance.

    d.   Be sure your company matches the above as you will be adding additional business events in Chapter 6.

21 Export your Trial Balance report to Excel, and save it with the file name Student Name (replace with your name) Ch 05 Case 01 Trial Balance.xlsx.

22 Open and print the custom report you created in the last chapter called Transaction Detail by Account.

23 Export your Transactions Detail by Account report to Excel, and save it with the file name Student Name (replace with your name) Ch 05 Case 01 Transaction Detail by Account.xlsx.

24 Sign out of your company.

Case 2

Add some operating activities (purchases, credit card charges, and cash payments) to your company.

Based on what you learned in the text using the Wild Water Sports company, you are to make the following changes to the Case 2 company you modified in Chapter 4:

1 Add a new vendor – E-flite, 700 Annapolis Ln N Suite #175, Plymouth, MN, 55447, terms: net 15.

2 Add a new vendor – Village Steak House, 100 S El Camino Real, San Clemente, CA 92672, terms: due on receipt.

3 Add a new vendor – Staples, 101 Main St., San Diego, CA 92600, terms: due on receipt.

4 Add a new account – account type: Credit Card, detail type: Credit Card, name: AMEX.

5 Add a new account – account type: Other Current Assets, detail type: Other Current Assets, name: Supplies Asset.

6 Add a new product – name/description: Sport Cub S, initial quantity on hand: 0, As of date: 01/02/25, inventory asset account: Inventory Asset, price: 600.00, cost: 479.00, income account: Sales, expense account: Cost of Goods Sold.

7 Add a new product – name/description: Mystique RES, initial quantity on hand: 0, As of date: 01/02/25, inventory asset account: Inventory Asset, price: 450.00, cost: 325.00, income account: Sales, expense account: Cost of Goods Sold.

8 Record a new purchase order for products on 1/2/25 – vendor: E-flite, product 1: Sport Cub S, QTY: 5, product 2: Mystique RES, QTY: 3.

9 Record a new purchase order for products on 1/3/25 – vendor: Kyosho, product 1: Broon F830 Ride, QTY: 4, product 2: GO Aircraft Radio, QTY: 2, product 3: Seawind Carbon Sailboat, QTY: 1.

10 Record a new bill based on a purchase order #1001 on 1/7/25 – vendor: E-flite, terms: Net 15. All items ordered were received.

11 Record a new bill without a purchase order on 1/8/25 – new vendor: San Diego News-Press, terms: Net 15, category: Advertising, amount: 500.00. Note: If your chart of accounts contains Advertising and Marketing, then change the account to read Advertising only.

12 Record a new bill without a purchase order on 1/10/25 – new vendor: Gomez Insurance, terms: Net 15, category 1: Insurance, amount: 400.00, category 2: Prepaid Expenses, amount: 4,400.00.

13 Pay bill due to Kyosho on 1/18/25 using the checking account and starting with check no. 1001.

14 Record a credit card charge on 1/11/25 – vendor: Village Steak House, using credit card: AMEX, category: Meals and Entertainment, amount: 240.00.

15 Record check on 1/14/25 – no.: 1002, vendor: Staples, amount: 450.00, account: Supplies Asset.

16 Open your previously customized report named Trial Balance 1/31/25. Your report should look like Figure 5.21.

Figure 5.21

Trial Balance (as of 1/31/25)

Case 2
TRIAL BALANCE
As of January 31, 2025

	DEBIT	CREDIT
Checking	7,150.00	
Accounts Receivable	1,425.00	
Inventory Asset	5,410.00	
Prepaid Expenses	6,800.00	
Supplies Asset	450.00	
Undeposited Funds	925.00	
Machinery & Equipment:Depreciation		1,000.00
Machinery & Equipment:Original cost	10,000.00	
Accounts Payable		8,670.00
AMEX		240.00
Notes Payable		12,000.00
Common Stock		100.00
Opening Balance Equity		0.00
Retained Earnings		8,385.00
Sales		5,700.00
Services		225.00
Cost of Goods Sold	3,020.00	
Advertising	500.00	
Insurance	400.00	
Meals and Entertainment	240.00	
TOTAL	$36,320.00	$36,320.00

17 Create and print a Transaction Report for the Checking account as you did earlier in the chapter.

18 Create and print a Transaction Report for the Inventory Asset account as you did earlier in the chapter.

19 Create and print a Transaction Report for the Accounts Payable (A/P) account as you did earlier in the chapter.

20 If your trial balance differs from what is shown in Figure 5.21, do the following:

    a. Make sure that all of your changes were dated in January 2025.

    b. View the Transaction Reports you created to locate any errors.

    c. Ask your instructor for assistance.

    d. Be sure your company matches the above as you will be adding additional business events in Chapter 6.

21 Export your Trial Balance report to Excel, and save it with the file name Student Name (replace with your name) Ch 05 Case 02 Trial Balance.xlsx.

22 Open and print the custom report you created in the last chapter called Transaction Detail by Account.

23 Export your Transactions Detail by Account report to Excel, and save it with the file name Student Name (replace with your name) Ch 05 Case 02 Transaction Detail by Account.xlsx.

24 Sign out of your company.

Case 3

Now it's time for you to add some operating activities (purchases, credit card charges, and cash payments) to your company.

Based on what you learned in the text using the Wild Water Sports company, you are to make the following changes to the Case 3 company you modified in Chapter 4:

1 Add a new vendor – Google, Inc., 1600 Amphitheatre Parkway, Mountain View, CA 94043, terms: Net 15.

2 Add a new vendor – Samsung, Inc., 105 Challenger Rd., Ridgefield Park, NJ 07660, terms: Net 15.

3 Add a new vendor – Staples, Inc., 101 Main St., San Diego, CA 92600, terms: Net 30.

4 Modify Apple Inc. (existing Vendor) – Name should be Apple Computer, Inc., address: 1 Infinite Loop Cupertino, CA 95014, terms: Net 15.

5 Add a new account – account type: Credit Card, detail type: Credit Card, name: AMEX.

6 Add a new account – account type: Other Current Assets, detail type: Other Current Assets, name: Supplies Asset.

7 Add a new product – Name/Description & Purchasing information: Samsung Galaxy 8, initial quantity on hand: 0, inventory asset account: Inventory Asset, Sales price: 450.00, cost: 350.00, income account: Sales of Product Income, expense account: Cost of Goods Sold. (Use 01/06/2026 as the "as of date.") Sales tax: Taxable - standard rate.

8 Add a new product – Name/Description & Purchasing information: Samsung Note, initial quantity on hand: 0, inventory asset account: Inventory Asset, Sales price: 850.00, cost: 650.00, income account: Sales of Product Income, expense account: Cost of Goods Sold. (Use 01/06/2026 as the "as of date.") Sales tax: Taxable - standard rate.

9 Record a new purchase order (1001) for products on 1/6/26 – vendor: Google, Inc., Pixel, QTY: 10.

10 Record a new purchase order (1002) for products on 1/7/26 – vendor: Samsung, Inc., product 1: Samsung Galaxy 8, QTY: 5, product 2: Samsung Note, QTY: 8.

11 Record a new bill based on a purchase order #1001 dated 1/6/26 – vendor: Google, Inc., terms: Net 15. All items ordered were received on 1/10/26 (the bill date).

12 Record a new bill without a purchase order on 1/8/26 – new vendor: News-Press, terms: Net 15, category: Advertising & Marketing, amount: 1,300.00.

13 Record a new bill without a purchase order on 1/10/26 – new vendor: Hathaway Insurance, terms: Net 15, category 1: Insurance, amount: 300.00, category 2: Prepaid expenses, amount: 3,300.00.

14 Pay bill due to Apple Computer, Inc. on 1/18/26 using the checking account and starting with check no. 321.

15 Record a credit card charge on 1/11/26 – new vendor: Village Steak House, using credit card: AMEX, category: Meals, amount: 123.00.

16 Record check on 1/14/26 – no.: 322, vendor: Staples, amount: 327.00, category: Supplies Asset.

17 Open and print your previously customized report named Trial Balance 1/31/26. Your report should look like Figure 5.22.

Figure 5.22

Trial Balance as of 1/31/26

Case 03 - Student Name (ID Number)

Trial Balance
As of January 31, 2026

	DEBIT	CREDIT
Checking	15,751.75	
Accounts receivable (A/R)	2,559.38	
Inventory Asset	5,700.00	
Payments to deposit	0.00	
Prepaid expenses	6,050.00	
Supplies Asset	327.00	
Machinery & Equipment:Depreciation		2,000.00
Machinery & Equipment:Original cost	15,000.00	
Accounts Payable (A/P)		8,900.00
AMEX		123.00
California Department of Tax and Fee Administration ...		523.13
Notes Payable		23,000.00
Opening balance equity		0.00
Owner's Equity		10,075.00
Sales of Product Income		6,750.00
Services		240.00
Cost of goods sold	4,500.00	
Advertising & marketing	1,300.00	
Insurance	300.00	
Meals	123.00	
TOTAL	$51,611.13	$51,611.13

18 Create and print a Transaction Report for the Checking account like you did in the chapter.

19 Create and print a Transaction Report for the Accounts Receivable (A/R) account.

20 Create and print a Transaction Report for the Inventory Asset account like you did in the chapter.

21 Create and print a Transaction Report for the Accounts Payable (A/P) account like you did in the chapter.

22 If your trial balance is different than Figure 5.22, do the following:

   a.   Make sure that all of your changes were dated in January 2026.

   b.   View the Transaction Reports you just created to locate any errors.

   c.   Ask your instructor for assistance.

   d.   Be sure your company matches the above as you will be adding additional business events in Chapter 6.

23 Export your Trial Balance report to Excel, and save it with the file name Student Name (replace with your name) Ch 05 Case 03 Trial Balance.xlsx.

24 Open and print the custom report you created in the last chapter called Transaction Detail by Account.

25 Export your Transactions Detail by Account report to Excel, and save it with the file name Student Name (replace with your name) Ch 05 Case 03 Transaction Detail by Account.xlsx.

26 Sign out of your company.

Case 4

Now it's time for you to add some operating activities (purchases and cash payments) to your company.

Based on what you learned in the text using the Wild Water Sports company, you are to make the following changes to the Case 4 company you modified in Chapter 4:

1 Add a new vendor – GEICO Insurance, 335 Park Ave., Los Angeles, CA 90034, terms: Net 15.

2 Add a new account – Account Type: Assets, Save account under: Other Current Assets, Tax form section: Other Current Assets, Account name: Supplies Asset.

3 Add a new account – Account Type: Credit Cards, Save account under: Credit Card, Tax form section: Credit Card, name: VISA.

4 Add a new service – Name/Description information: Towel Service, Sales price/rate: 20.00, income account: Sales, Is taxable: No.

5 Record sales receipt 1004 to a new customer: Enterprise Inc., on 1/4/27 for 5 Monthly Fee – Corporate Membership 50 Employees and 50 Towel Service. Check no. 9847 was received and immediately deposited to the company's checking account in the amount of $31,000.

6 Record a new purchase order (1001) for products on 1/7/27 – vendor: Bowflex, product: Bowflex Dumbbells, QTY: 25.

7 Record a new purchase order (1002) for products on 1/8/27 – vendor: Precor, product: Power Block Elite Dumbbells, QTY: 15.

8 Record a new bill based on a purchase order #1001 dated 1/7/27 – vendor: Bowflex, terms: Net 15. All items ordered were received on 1/15/27 (the bill date).

9 Record a new bill without a purchase order on 1/16/27 – new vendor: Supreme Marketing, terms: Net 15, category: Advertising & marketing, amount: $1,800.00.

10 Record a new bill without a purchase order on 1/18/27 – vendor: Laundry Service, terms: Net 15, category: Supplies Asset, amount: $1,400.00.

11 Pay bills due to Precor and Laundry Service on 1/18/27 using the checking account and starting with check no. 25498.

12 Record credit card charge on 1/20/27 – vendor: GEICO Insurance, using credit card: VISA, category: Insurance, amount: $2,400.00.

13 Record check on 1/21/27 – check no.: 25500, vendor: NordicTrack, amount: $750.00, category: Repairs & Maintenance.

14 Prepare and print the Trial Balance 1/31/27 report you saved previously. Your report should look like Figure 5.23.

Figure 5.23

Trial Balance as of 1/31/27

Trial Balance

As of January 31, 2027

	DEBIT	CREDIT
Checking	45,576.65	
Accounts Receivable (A/R)	22,082.50	
Inventory Asset	8,868.00	
Payments to deposit	0.00	
Prepaid rent	12,000.00	
Supplies Asset	1,400.00	
Furniture:Accumulated Depreciation		10,000.00
Furniture:Original Cost	65,000.00	
Vehicles:Accumulated Depreciation		6,500.00
Vehicles:Original Cost	115,000.00	
Accounts Payable (A/P)		6,800.00
VISA		2,400.00
California Department of Tax and Fee Administration Payable		339.15
Long-term debt		82,000.00
Common Stock		1,000.00
Opening Balance Equity		0.00
Retained Earnings		115,500.00
Sales		48,400.00
Sales of Product Income		3,570.00
Cost of Goods Sold	1,632.00	
Advertising & Marketing	1,800.00	
Insurance	2,400.00	
Repairs & Maintenance	750.00	
TOTAL	**$276,509.15**	**$276,509.15**

15 Create and print a Transaction Report for the Checking account.

16 Create and print a Transaction Report for the Accounts Receivable (A/R) account.

17 Create and print a Transaction Report for the Inventory Asset account.

18 Create and print a Transaction Report for the Accounts Payable (A/P) account.

19 Investigate differences between your trial balance and the trial balance shown above.

20 If necessary, prepare and print the Transaction Detail by Account report you saved previously to investigate identified differences.

    a.   Make sure all your changes were dated in January 2027.

    b.   Click on the line that does not match to view the transaction for that account, and investigate why your answer differs.

    c.   Ask your instructor for assistance.

    d.   Be sure your company matches the above as you will be adding additional business events in Chapter 6.

Case 5

Now it's time for you to add some operating activities (purchases and cash payments) to your company.

Based on using what you learned in the text using the Wild Water Sports company, you are to make the following changes to the Case 5 company you modified in Chapter 4:

1 Add a new vendor – State Farm Insurance, 9542 Argyle Forest Blvd #12, Jacksonville, FL, 32222, terms: Net 30.

2 Add a new account – Account Type: Other Current Assets, Detail Type: Other Current Assets, name: Supplies.

3 Add a new account – Account Type: Credit Card, Detail Type: Credit Card, name: AMEX.

4 Add a new service – Name and description: Training, Sales price/rate: 100.00, income account: Training (a new account type: Income, detail type: Service/Fee income, nontaxable).

5 Record sales receipt 1004 to Blue Origin on 1/13/22 for 35 hours of Training and 10 Training Materials Volume 1. Check no. 105866 was received and immediately deposited to the company's checking account in the amount of $167,000 (including sales tax).

6 Record a new purchase order on 1/14/22 – vendor: HP Computers, product: Computer Workstation 100, QTY: 50.

7 Record a new purchase order on 1/17/22 – vendor: Wild Research, Inc., product 1: Training Materials – Volume 1, QTY: 10, product 2: Training Materials – Volume 2, QTY: 10.

8 Record a new bill based on a purchase order dated 1/14/22 – vendor: HP Computers, terms: Net 30. All items ordered were received on 1/18/22 (the bill date).

9 Record a new bill without a purchase order on 1/19/22 – new vendor: Acme Equipment, terms: Net 15, category: Equipment rental, amount: $7,500.

10 Record a new bill without a purchase order on 1/20/22 – vendor: State Farm Insurance, terms: Net 30, category: Prepaid Expenses, amount: $12,000.

11 Pay bills to Wild Research, Inc., and Acme Equipment on 1/19/22 using the checking account and starting with check no. 3005.

12 Record credit card charge on 1/20/22 – vendor: Indeed, using credit card: AMEX, category: Recruiting, amount: $6,300.

13 Record check on 1/21/22 – check no.: 3007, new vendor: Rocket Marketing, amount: $3,000, category: Advertising & Marketing.

14 Prepare and print the Trial Balance 1/31/22 report you saved previously. Your report should look like Figure 5.24.

Figure 5.24

Trial Balance as of 1/31/22

Case 05 - Student Name (ID Number)

TRIAL BALANCE

As of January 31, 2022

	DEBIT	CREDIT
Checking	254,000.00	
Accounts Receivable (A/R)	158,350.00	
Inventory	722,000.00	
Prepaid Expenses	22,000.00	
Undeposited Funds	0.00	
Fixed Asset Computers:Depreciation		25,000.00
Fixed Asset Computers:Original cost	250,000.00	
Fixed Asset Furniture:Depreciation		8,000.00
Fixed Asset Furniture:Original cost	80,000.00	
Accounts Payable (A/P)		362,000.00
AMEX		6,300.00
Alabama Department of Revenue Payable		6,600.00
Alabama, Huntsville Payable		7,425.00
Alabama, Madison County Payable		825.00
Notes Payable		545,000.00
Opening Balance Equity		0.00
Owner's Equity		382,000.00
Consulting		79,500.00
Sales		165,000.00
Training		3,500.00
Cost of Goods Sold	88,000.00	
Advertising & Marketing	3,000.00	
Equipment Rental	7,500.00	
Recruiting	6,300.00	
TOTAL	$1,591,150.00	$1,591,150.00

15 Create and print a Transaction Report for the Checking account.

16 Create and print a Transaction Report for the Accounts Receivable (A/R) account.

17 Create and print a Transaction Report for the Inventory account.

18 Create and print a Transaction Report for the Accounts Payable (A/P) account.

19 Investigate differences between your trial balance and the trial balance shown above.

20 If necessary, prepare and print the Transaction Detail by Account report you saved previously to investigate identified differences.

a. Make sure all your changes were dated in January 2022.

b. Click on the line that does not match to view the transaction for that account and investigate why your answer differs.

c. Ask your instructor for assistance.

d. Be sure your company matches the above as you will be adding additional business events in Chapter 6.

Case 6

Now it's time for you to add some operating activities (purchases and cash payments) to your company.

Based on using what you learned in the text using the Wild Water Sports company, you are to make the following changes to the Case 6 company you modified in Chapter 4:

1 Add a new vendor – State Farm Insurance, 2764 1st Ave S, Suite 110, Seattle, WA 98134, terms: Net 15.

2 Add a new vendor – National Covers, 2270 Cosmos Court #100, Carlsbad, CA, 92011, terms: Net 15.

3 Add a new account – Account Type: Other Current Assets, Detail Type: Investments - Other, name: Investments.

4 Add a new account – Account Type: Credit Card, Detail Type: Credit Card, name: AMEX.

5 Add a new product.

   a. Name – 2023 Airstream Globetrotter 30RB

   b. Inventory asset account – Inventory Asset

   c. Description – 2023 Airstream Globetrotter 30RB

   d. Sales price/rate – $125,000

   e. Income account – Sales of Product Income

   f. Sales tax category – Taxable - standard rate

   g. Purchasing information – 2023 Globetrotter 30RB

   h. Cost – $100,000

   i. Expense account – Cost of Goods Sold

   j. Preferred Vendor – Airstream, Inc.

   k. Initial quantity on hand – 0

   l. As of date – 12/31/22

6 Add a new product.

   a. Name – RV Cover

   b. Inventory asset account – Inventory Parts

   c. Description – RV Cover

   d. Sales price/rate – $600

   e. Income account – Sales of Product Income

   f. Sales tax category – Taxable - standard rate

   g. Purchasing information – RV Cover

   h. Cost – $480

   i. Expense account – Cost of Goods Sold

   j. Preferred Vendor – National Covers

   k. Initial quantity on hand – 0

   l. As of date – 12/31/22

7   Add a new product.

    a.   Name – Trailer Cover

    b.   Inventory asset account – Inventory Parts

    c.   Description – Trailer Cover

    d.   Sales price/rate – $500

    e.   Income account – Sales of Product Income

    f.   Sales tax category – Taxable - standard rate

    g.   Purchasing information – Trailer Cover

    h.   Cost – $400

    i.   Expense account – Cost of Goods Sold

    j.   Preferred Vendor – National Covers

    k.   Initial quantity on hand – 0

    l.   As of date – 12/31/22

8   Record a new purchase order (1001) for two trailers on 1/7/23 – vendor: Airstream, Inc., product 1: 2023 Airstream Flying Cloud 27FB TWIN, QTY:1, product 2: 2023 Airstream Globetrotter 30RB, QTY: 1.

9   Record a new purchase order (1002) for inventory parts on 1/8/23 – vendor: National Covers, product 1: RV Cover, QTY: 5, product 2: Trailer Cover, QTY: 4.

10   Record a new bill based on a purchase order #1001 dated 1/13/23 – vendor: Airstream, Inc., terms: Net 30. All items ordered were received on 1/13/23 (the bill date).

11   Record a new bill without a purchase order on 1/16/23 – new vendor: Pacific Marketing, terms: Net 15, account: Advertising & Marketing, amount: $8,000.

12   Record a new bill without a purchase order on 1/17/23 – vendor: State Farm Insurance, terms: Net 15, account: Prepaid Expenses, amount: $18,000.

13   Paid $150,000 on bill due to Winnebago, Inc. on 1/18/23 using the checking account and starting Check no. 589.

14   Record expense on 1/19/23 – new vendor: Elite Events, using credit card: AMEX, account: Advertising & Marketing, amount: $6,000.

15   Record check on 1/19/23, Check no.: 590, new vendor: Jay's Detail, amount: $1,800, account: Contractors.

16   Record a new bill based on a purchase order #1002 dated 1/8/23 – vendor: National Covers, terms: Net 30. All items ordered were received on 1/20/23 (the bill date).

17   Prepare and print the Trial Balance 1/31/23 report you saved previously. Your report should look like Figure 5.25.

Figure 5.25

Trial Balance as of 1/31/23

Case 06 - Student Name (ID Number)

TRIAL BALANCE
As of January 31, 2023

	DEBIT	CREDIT
Checking	72,150.00	
Accounts Receivable (A/R)	153,020.00	
Inventory Asset	524,000.00	
Inventory Parts	4,000.00	
Loans To Officers	15,000.00	
Prepaid Expenses	18,000.00	
Undeposited Funds	0.00	
Buildings:Depreciation		15,000.00
Buildings:Original cost	150,000.00	
Machinery & Equipment:Depreciation		10,000.00
Machinery & Equipment:Original cost	100,000.00	
Accounts Payable (A/P)		524,000.00
AMEX		6,000.00
Washington State Department of Revenue Payable		26,970.00
Notes Payable		100,000.00
Common Stock		1,000.00
Opening Balance Equity		0.00
Paid-In Capital		250,000.00
Retained Earnings		61,000.00
Sales of Product Income		290,000.00
Cost of Goods Sold	232,000.00	
Advertising & Marketing	14,000.00	
Contractors	1,800.00	
TOTAL	$1,283,970.00	$1,283,970.00

18 Investigate differences between your trial balance and the trial balance shown above.

19 If necessary, prepare and print the Transaction Detail by Account report for all dates you saved previously to investigate identified differences.

a. Make sure all your changes were dated in January 2023.

b. Click on the line that does not match to view the transaction for that account, and investigate why your answer differs.

c. Ask your instructor for assistance.

d. Be sure your company matches the above as you will be adding additional business events in Chapter 6.

chapter

6

Recording Investing and Financing Activities

Student Learning Outcomes

Upon completion of this chapter, the student will be able to do the following:

- Record the acquisition of a fixed asset
- Record the acquisition of a long-term investment
- Record the sale of common stock
- Record the payment of a dividend
- Record a long-term borrowing (long-term debt)
- Record payment on long-term borrowing (long-term debt)
- Record the acquisition of a fixed asset by taking on new debt

Overview

In Chapter 5 you added new vendors, purchase orders, bills, credit card charges, and checks to your Wild Water Sports company and then paid some bills. In this chapter you will add some investing and financing like the acquisition of a fixed asset and a long-term investment as well as the sale of stock payment of dividends, acquiring and paying long-term debt. At the end of this chapter you will perform similar tasks on the case assigned by your instructor.

To verify the accuracy of your Wild Water Sports company:

1   Sign into your QBO account, then open the Wild Water Sports company you used in Chapter 5.

2   Click **Reports**, then click the **Custom reports** tab, then double-click **Trial Balance** to open the Trial Balance report. Set the from and to dates to **1/1/27** and **1/31/27** respectively. Compare your report to Figure 6.1. If your report doesn't match Figure 6.1, go back to your work in Chapter 5 to fix your errors. Otherwise, close your Trial Balance report.

Figure 6.1

Wild Water Sports trial balance as of 1/31/27

Wild Water Sports - Student Name (ID Number)		
Trial Balance — As of January 31, 2027		
	DEBIT	**CREDIT**
Checking	22,345.00	
Accounts receivable (A/R)	120,770.00	
Inventory	223,350.00	
Payments to deposit	70,000.00	
Prepaid expenses	17,500.00	
Equipment:Accumulated depreciation		10,000.00
Equipment:Original Cost	40,000.00	
Accounts Payable (A/P)		190,250.00
Mastercard		1,600.00
Florida Department of Revenue Payable		9,915.00
Long-term business loans		50,000.00
Common stock		1,000.00
Opening balance equity		0.00
Retained Earnings		205,800.00
Sales		164,000.00
Service Revenue		2,000.00
Cost of goods sold	131,200.00	
Rent:Equipment rental	6,000.00	
Utilities:Phone service	1,800.00	
Vehicle expenses:Vehicle gas & fuel	1,600.00	
TOTAL	$634,565.00	$634,565.00

Fixed Assets

In this section, you will be recording the acquisition of fixed assets. Fixed assets are long-term tangible property that a firm owns and uses in the production of its income and is not expected to be consumed or converted into cash any sooner than at least one year's time. Normally, a fixed asset's cost is depreciated over time as a means of allocating its cost over its useful life. The depreciation is recorded to a depreciation expense account and added to an accumulated depreciation (contra-asset) account. That process will be explained in the chapter on adjusting entries.

To add an asset, you will use the Check task accessed by clicking the [+ New] icon. Alternatively, you could purchase new fixed assets with using a credit card or take on new debt. The Wild Water Sports company has a fixed asset account for equipment, which you'll use to record the purchase of a computer. If you were to purchase some other type of fixed asset, furniture for example, you would need to create two additional subaccounts to the Furniture & Fixtures account: Original Cost and Accumulated Depreciation.

To record the purchase of a new computer and network equipment, do the following:

1 Continue from above.

2 Make sure the navigation bar is open.

3 Click the [+ New] icon and then click **Check**.

4   Select + **Add new** from the drop-down list in the Choose a payee text box.

5   Type **Best Buy** in the Company name text box, select **Vendor** as the Contact type, and click **Save**.

6   Type **1/20/27** as the Payment date and **1003** as the Check no.

7   Select **Original cost** under Equipment in the Category column of line 1.

8   Type **8000** in the Amount column of line 1 and then press **[Tab]**. Your screen should look like Figure 6.2.

Figure 6.2

Purchase of computer

9   Click **Save and new**.

10   Select + **Add new** in the Payee text box and then type **Office Max** as the vendor, then click **Save**, then type **1/20/27** as the Payment date.

11   Select + **Add new** from the drop-down list in the Category column of line 1.

12   Select **Fixed Assets** from the drop-down list in the Account Type text box.

13   Select **Fixed Asset Furniture** from the drop-down list in the Detail type text box.

14   Type **Furniture** in the Name text box, then place a check in the Track depreciation of this asset check box, and then click **Save and close**.

15   Type **Furniture:Original cost** in the Category column of line 1.

16   Type **10000** in the Amount column of line 1 and then press **[Tab]** to see Figure 6.3.

Figure 6.3

Purchase of furniture

17   Click **Save and close**.

You have recorded the purchase of two new fixed assets.

Long-Term Investments

The acquisition of a long-term investment is another type of investing activity. In general, a long-term investment is the purchase of a financial instrument (bond, common stock, and preferred stock) that matures in more than one year.

To record the purchase of a long-term investment, do the following:

1   Continue from where you left off.

2   Click the (+ New) icon, and select **Check**.

3   Select + **Add new** from the drop-down list in the Choose a payee text box.

4   Type **Scottrade** in the Company name text box, select **Vendor** as the Type, and click **Save**.

5   Type **1/21/27** as the payment date and **1005** as the check no.

6   Select + **Add new** from the drop-down list in the Category column of line 1.

7   Select **Other Assets** from the drop-down list in the Account Type text box.

8   Select **Other Long-term Assets** from the drop-down list in the Detail Type text box.

9   Type **Investments** in the Name text box, and click **Save and close**.

10   Type **3000** in the Amount column of line 1 and then press [**Tab**] to see Figure 6.4. Note that your check number may be different than shown below.

Figure 6.4

Purchase of a long-term investment

11   Click **Save and close**.

You have recorded the purchase of a long-term investment.

Equity Transactions (Common Stock, Dividends, Owner Investments, and Owner Withdrawals)

In a corporation, the sale of common stock and the payment of cash dividends to shareholders are two common financing activities. Common stock is a stockholders' equity account. Dividends are a distribution of earnings to shareholders and are accounted for as a reduction in retained earnings. Both of these are cash activities in that the sale of stock results in a cash receipt (you will account for it as a bank deposit), whereas the payment of a cash dividend results in a cash payment. One previous payment from a customer (Refugio) appears when you attempt to record a bank deposit from the issuance of stock. These payments have been received but not recorded. Ignore those for now. To simplify this transaction, we will assume that the common stock is no-par common stock, and thus, no additional paid-in capital exists. Also, we'll assume that the dividend declaration, record, and payment dates are all the same.

In a sole proprietorship, there is no common stock or dividends. Instead, there are owner investments and owner withdrawals. Owner investments are recorded by entering a bank deposit to the Owner's Equity account. Owner withdrawals are recorded by entering a check to the Owner's Equity account. Since the Wild Water Sports company is a corporation, an example of sole proprietorship transactions is not provided.

To record the sale of stock and payment of cash dividends do the following:

1 Continue where you left off.

2 Click the ☐ + New ☐ icon and then select **Bank Deposit**.

3 Select + **Add new** from the drop-down list in the Received From column of line 1 in the Add funds to this deposit section. The Add funds to this deposit section is below the Select the payments included in this deposit section so you may have to scroll down the page to find it. Note that the check box next to the customer Refugio remains unchecked. This will be deposited later.

4 Type **WB Investments** in the Company name text box, select **Vendor** in the Contact type box, and click **Save**.

5 Type **1/21/27** in Date text box.

6 Type **Common stock** in the Account column of line 1.

7 Select **Check** as the Payment Method and then type **56000** as the Ref No.

8 Type **10000** in the Amount column of line 1, and press [**Tab**]. Your screen should look like Figure 6.5.

Figure 6.5

Recording the deposit of funds from the sale of common stock

9 Click **Save and close**.

10 Click the ⟨ + New ⟩ icon, and select **Check**.

11 Type **Shareholders** in the Payee text box and select **+ Add new Shareholders**. In the new Vendor window enter **Shareholders** in the Vendor display name text box, select **Vendor** in the Contact type box, and click **Save**.

12 Type **1/22/2027** in the Payment date text box and then type **1006** in the Check no. text box.

13 Select **Retained Earnings** from the drop-down list in the Category column of line 1.

14 Type **1500** in the Amount column of line 1, and press [**Tab**]. Your screen should look like Figure 6.6.

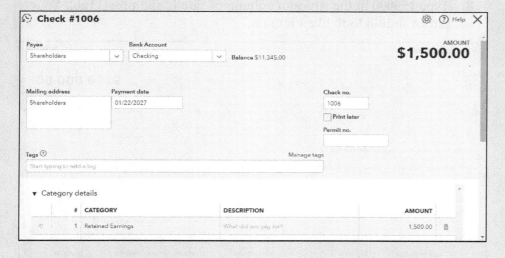

Figure 6.6

Payment of dividends

15 Click **Save and close**.

Long-Term Debt

The borrowing of funds on a long-term basis and the repayment of debt are two additional financing activities. Both of these are cash activities in that the borrowing of funds results in a cash receipt (you will account for it as a bank deposit), whereas the payment of the debt results in a cash payment. There is one previous payment from a customer that appears when you attempt to record a bank deposit from the borrowing of funds. These payments have been received but not recorded. You'll ignore those for now. This company decided to refinance their existing long-term business loan with Chase Bank. Thus, you will have to record the receipt of cash from the new loan and pay off the old long-term debt with interest.

To record the receipt of funds from borrowing and the payment of long-term debt in the Wild Water Sports company do the following:

1 Continue from where you left off.

2 Click the icon and then select **Bank Deposit**.

3 Select **Chase Bank** from the drop-down list in the Received From column of line 1 in the Add funds to this deposit section.

4 Select **Checking** from the Bank Account text box.

5 Type **1/23/27** in the Date text box.

6 Select **Long-term business loans** from the drop-down list in the Account column of line 1.

7 Select **Check** from the drop-down list in the Payment Method column of line 1.

8 Type **150000** in the Amount column of line 1, and press [**Tab**]. Your screen should look like Figure 6.7.

Figure 6.7

Recording the deposit of funds from refinancing

9   Click **Save and close**.

10 Click the [+ New] icon, and select **Check**.

11 Select **Chase Bank** from the drop-down list in the Payee text box.

12 Select **Checking** from the Bank Account text box.

13 Type **1/23/27** in the Payment date text box and **1007** in the Check no. text box.

14 Select **Long-term business loans** from the drop-down list in the Category column of line 1.

15 Type **50000** in the Amount column of line 1 and then press [**Tab**]. Note this is the amount shown on the trial balance before the refinancing.

16 Select **Interest paid** from the drop-down list in the Account column of line 2.

17 Type **2500** in the Amount column of line 2, and press [**Tab**]. Your screen should look like Figure 6.8.

Figure 6.8

Repayment of long-term debt with interest

18 Click **Save and close**.

Acquisition of a Fixed Asset in Exchange for Long-Term Debt

You completed the process for recording an investing activity (purchase of a fixed asset) and a financing activity (borrowing on a long-term basis). Both of these transactions were recorded by affecting the checking account (cash).

Occasionally, a company acquires a fixed asset by issuing long-term debt, for example, purchasing equipment in exchange for a long-term business loan. This cannot be recorded using the checking account since no funds were exchanged. Instead, you will use the journal entry process to record the fixed asset acquisition and the long-term debt borrowing.

To record the purchase of a fixed asset by issuing debt, do the following:

1   Continue from where you left off.

2   Click the [+ New] icon, and select **Journal Entry**.

3   Type **1/25/27** as the Journal date and **5** as the Journal number.

4   Select **Equipment:Original Cost** from the drop-down list in the Account column of line 1.

5   Type **5000** in the Debits column of line 1.

6   Select **Long-term business loans** from the drop-down list in the Account column of line 2.

7   Accept **5000** in the Credits column of line 2, and press **[Tab]** to view the journal entry as shown in Figure 6.9.

Figure 6.9

Journal Entry to record purchase of fixed asset in exchange for long-term debt

Journal Entry #5   ⚙ ⑦ Help ✕

Journal date	Journal no.
01/25/2027	5

#	ACCOUNT	DEBITS	CREDITS	DESCRIPTION	NAME	
1	Equipment:Original Cost	5,000.00				🗑
2	Long-term business loans		5,000.00			🗑

8   Click **Save and close**.

The work you completed in this chapter influenced the company's trial balance. As in previous chapters, you decided to create a Trial Balance report after entering all business events described in this chapter and investigate any differences between your report and that shown in Figure 6.10.

To create a trial balance:

1 Click **Reports**, then select the **Custom reports** tab, then select Trial Balance. Change the to date of the report to 1/31/2027 to view the Trial Balance as shown in Figure 6.10.

Figure 6.10

Trial Balance

Wild Water Sports - Student Name (ID Number)

Trial Balance
As of January 31, 2027

	DEBIT	CREDIT
Checking	107,345.00	
Accounts receivable (A/R)	120,770.00	
Inventory	223,350.00	
Payments to deposit	70,000.00	
Prepaid expenses	17,500.00	
Equipment:Accumulated depreciation		10,000.00
Equipment:Original Cost	53,000.00	
Furniture:Original cost	10,000.00	
Investments	3,000.00	
Accounts Payable (A/P)		190,250.00
Mastercard		1,600.00
Florida Department of Revenue Paya...		9,915.00
Long-term business loans		155,000.00
Common stock		11,000.00
Opening balance equity		0.00
Retained Earnings		204,300.00
Sales		164,000.00
Service Revenue		2,000.00
Cost of goods sold	131,200.00	
Interest paid	2,500.00	
Rent:Equipment rental	6,000.00	
Utilities:Phone service	1,800.00	
Vehicle expenses:Vehicle gas & fuel	1,600.00	
TOTAL	$748,065.00	$748,065.00

2 Compare your trial balance report with Figure 6.10.

3 If you note any differences, click **Reports**, then select the **Custom reports** tab, then select **Transaction Detail by Account All Dates** to identify the source of any differences.

End Note

In this chapter, you recorded investing activities: the acquisition of fixed assets and of long-term investments, the sale of common stocks, the payment of a dividend, the borrowing and payment of long-term debt, and the acquisition of fixed assets by taking on new debt. In the next chapter, you will work with payroll.

Chapter 6 Questions

1 What are the steps to record the acquisition of a fixed asset using a check?

2 What are the steps to record the acquisition of a fixed asset for a note payable?

3 What are the steps to record the sale of common stock?

4 What are the steps to record the payment of dividends?

5 What are the steps to record borrowing on a note payable?

Chapter 6 Matching

a. Operating activity	_____	Long-term tangible property that a firm owns
b. Investing activity	_____	Distribution of earnings to shareholders
c. Financing activity	_____	A stockholders' equity account
d. Fixed assets	_____	Used to record purchase of a fixed asset for a note
e. Long-term investment	_____	A five-year note payable
f. Common stock	_____	Sales receipt
g. Dividends	_____	A financial instrument that matures in more than one year
h. Long-term debt	_____	Used to record amounts received from a note payable
i. Bank deposit	_____	Sale of common stock
j. Journal entry	_____	Purchase of common stock

Chapter 6 Cases

The following cases require you to open the company you updated in Chapter 5. Each of the following cases is continued throughout the text in a sequential manner. For example, if you are assigned Case 01, you will use the file you modified in this chapter in all following chapters. Each of the following cases is similar in concepts assessed but differs in amounts and transactions.

To reopen your company, do the following:

1 Open your Internet browser.

2 Type **https://qbo.intuit.com** into your browser's address text box.

3 Type your user ID and password into the text boxes as you have done before.

Case 1

Now add some investing and financing activities to your company.

Based on what you learned in the text using the Wild Water Sports company, you are to make the following changes to the Case 1 company you modified in Chapter 5:

1 Create a new fixed asset account with an account type: Fixed Asset, detail type: Machinery & Equipment, name: Equipment. Track depreciation of this asset.

2 Create a new asset account with an account type: Other Assets, detail type: Other Long-Term Assets, name: Investments.

3 Record the purchase of a new computer on 1/10/24 from Office Depot, check: 1003, amount: $1,375, category: Equipment:Original Cost.

4 Record a long-term investment on 1/11/24 to Etrade (a new vendor), check: 1004, amount: $4,000, category: Investments.

5 Record the sale of common stock on 1/12/24 to Shareholders (a new vendor), deposit amount: $20,000, account: Common Stock payment method: Check.

6 Record the payment of dividends to Shareholders on 1/15/24, check: 1005, in the amount of $500.

7 Record the deposit of funds from a new note payable signed on 1/16/24 with Bank of CA (a new vendor) in the amount of $65,000 payment method: Check.

8 Record the payment to Rabo Bank (a new vendor) to retire an existing note payable on 1/16/24 of $60,000 with interest of $600 using check 1006.

9 Record the purchase of an additional computer on 1/17/24 from Office Depot in exchange for a note payable of $1,800, account: Equipment:Original Cost.

10 Change the name of account Interest Paid to Interest Expense, then open your previously customized report named Trial Balance 1/31/24. Your report should look like Figure 6.11.

11 Create and print a Transaction Report for the Checking account.

12 Create and print a Transaction Report for the Equipment:Original Cost account.

13 Create and print a Transaction Report for the Notes Payable account.

14 Create and print a Transaction Report for the Common Stock account.

15 If your trial balance differs from Figure 6.11, do the following:

    a.   Make sure that all of your changes were dated in January 2024.

    b.   View the Transaction Reports you just created to locate any errors.

    c.   Ask your instructor for assistance.

    d.   Be sure your company matches the above as you will be adding additional business events in Chapter 7.

Case 1
TRIAL BALANCE
As of January 31, 2024

	DEBIT	CREDIT
Checking	34,850.00	
Accounts Receivable	1,030.00	
Inventory Asset	11,800.00	
Prepaid Expenses	8,000.00	
Supplies Asset	375.00	
Undeposited Funds	5,000.00	
Equipment:Original Cost	3,175.00	
Furniture & Fixtures:Depreciation		10,000.00
Furniture & Fixtures:Original cost	40,000.00	
Investments	4,000.00	
Accounts Payable		7,645.00
VISA		1,800.00
Notes Payable		66,800.00
Common Stock		21,000.00
Opening Balance Equity		0.00
Retained Earnings		5,000.00
Sales		2,160.00
Services		170.00
Cost of Goods Sold	1,300.00	
Interest Expense	600.00	
Rent or Lease	2,500.00	
Travel	1,800.00	
Utilities	145.00	
TOTAL	$114,575.00	$114,575.00

Figure 6.11

Trial Balance as of 1/31/24

16 Export your Trial Balance report to Excel, and save it with the file name Student Name (replace with your name) Ch 06 Case 01 Trial Balance.xlsx.

17 Sign out of your company.

Case 2

Now add some investing and financing activities to your company.

Based on what you learned in the text using the Wild Water Sports company, you are to make the following changes to the Case 2 company you modified in Chapter 5:

1 Create a new fixed asset account with an account type: Fixed Asset, detail type: Furniture & Fixtures, name: Furniture. Track depreciation of this asset.

2 Create a new asset account with an account type: Other Assets, detail type: Other Long-Term Assets, name: Investments.

3 Record the purchase of new furniture on 1/11/25 from Staples, check: 1003, amount: $2,250, category: Furniture:Original Cost.

4 Record a long-term investment on 1/11/25 to Raymond James (a new vendor), check: 1004, amount: $3,200, category: Investments.

5 Record the sale of common stock on 1/14/25 to Shareholders (a new vendor), deposit amount: $25,000, account: Common Stock, payment method: Check.

6 Record the payment of dividends to Shareholders on 1/15/25, check: 1005, amount: $800, category: Retained Earnings.

7 Record the deposit of funds from a new note payable signed on 1/16/25 with Bank of TJ (a new vendor) in the amount of $25,000, payment method: Check.

8 Record the payment to Community Bank (a new vendor) to retire an existing note payable on 1/16/25 of $12,000 with interest of $300 using check 1006.

9 Record the purchase of additional furniture from Staples on 1/17/25 in exchange for a note payable of $2,625, account: Furniture:Original Cost.

10 Change the name of account Interest Paid to Interest Expense, then open your previously customized report named Trial Balance 1/31/25. Your report should look like Figure 6.12.

Figure 6.12

Trial Balance as of 1/31/25

Case 2
TRIAL BALANCE
As of January 31, 2025

	DEBIT	CREDIT
Checking	38,600.00	
Accounts Receivable	1,425.00	
Inventory Asset	5,410.00	
Prepaid Expenses	6,800.00	
Supplies Asset	450.00	
Undeposited Funds	925.00	
Furniture:Original Cost	4,875.00	
Machinery & Equipment:Depreciation		1,000.00
Machinery & Equipment:Original cost	10,000.00	
Investments	3,200.00	
Accounts Payable		8,670.00
AMEX		240.00
Notes Payable		27,625.00
Common Stock		25,100.00
Opening Balance Equity		0.00
Retained Earnings		7,585.00
Sales		5,700.00
Services		225.00
Cost of Goods Sold	3,020.00	
Advertising	500.00	
Insurance	400.00	
Interest Expense	300.00	
Meals and Entertainment	240.00	
TOTAL	$76,145.00	$76,145.00

11 Create and print a Transaction Report for the Checking account.

12 Create and print a Transaction Report for the Furniture:Original Cost account.

13 Create and print a Transaction Report for the Notes Payable account.

14 Create and print a Transaction Report for the Common Stock account.

15 If your trial balance differs from Figure 6.12, do the following:

    a. Make sure that all of your changes were dated in January 2025.

    b. View the Transaction Reports you created to locate any errors.

    c. Ask your instructor for assistance.

    d. Be sure your company matches the above as you will be adding additional business events in Chapter 7.

16 Export your Trial Balance report to Excel, and save it with the file name Student Name (replace with your name) Ch 06 Case 02 Trial Balance.xlsx.

17 Open and print the custom report you created in the last chapter called Transaction Detail by Account.

18 Export your Transactions Detail by Account report to Excel, and save it with the file name Student Name (replace with your name) Ch 06 Case 02 Transaction Detail by Account.xlsx.

19 Sign out of your company.

Case 3

Now it's time for you to add some investing and financing activities to your company.

Based on what you learned in the text using the Wild Water Sports company, you are to make the following changes to the Case 3 company you modified in Chapter 5:

1 Open your chart of accounts. Create a new fixed asset account with an account type: Fixed Asset, detail type: Fixed Asset Computers, name: Computers. Track depreciation of this asset.

2 Create a new asset account with a category type: Other Assets, detail type: Other Long-Term Assets, name: Investments.

3 Open your chart of accounts and confirm that it contains an equity account with an account type: Equity, detail type: Owner's Equity, and name: Owner's Equity.

4 Record the purchase of a new computer on 1/12/26 from Staples, Inc., check: 323, amount: $3,000, category: Computers: Original Cost.

5 Record a long-term investment on 1/13/26 to E-Trade (a new vendor), check: 324, amount: $5,700, category: Investments.

6 Record an owner's contribution on 1/14/26 to Owners (a new vendor) after receiving a check that was immediately deposited in the amount: $40,000 to account: Owner's Equity.

7 Record the deposit of funds from a new note payable signed on 1/16/26 with Chase Bank (a new vendor) in the amount of $32,000.

8 Record the payment to Rabobank (a new vendor) to retire an existing note payable on 1/17/26 of $23,000 with interest of $300 using check 325 for a total of $23,300.

9 Record the purchase of machinery and equipment from Leeds, Inc. (a new vendor) on 1/17/26 in exchange for a note payable of $31,800.

10 Open and print your previously customized report named Trial Balance 1/31/26. Your report should look like Figure 6.13.

Figure 6.13

Trial Balance as of 1/31/26

Case 03 - Student Name (ID Number)

Trial Balance
As of January 31, 2026

	DEBIT	CREDIT
Checking	55,751.75	
Accounts receivable (A/R)	2,559.38	
Inventory Asset	5,700.00	
Payments to deposit	0.00	
Prepaid expenses	6,050.00	
Supplies Asset	327.00	
Computers:Original cost	3,000.00	
Machinery & Equipment:Depreciation		2,000.00
Machinery & Equipment:Original cost	46,800.00	
Investments	5,700.00	
Accounts Payable (A/P)		8,900.00
AMEX		123.00
California Department of Tax and Fee Administratio...		523.13
Notes Payable		63,800.00
Opening balance equity		0.00
Owner's Equity		50,075.00
Sales of Product Income		6,750.00
Services		240.00
Cost of goods sold	4,500.00	
Advertising & marketing	1,300.00	
Insurance	300.00	
Interest paid	300.00	
Meals	123.00	
TOTAL	$132,411.13	$132,411.13

11 Create and print a Transaction Report for the Checking account.

12 Create and print a Transaction Report for the Computers:Original Cost account.

13 Create and print a Transaction Report for the Notes Payable account.

14 Create and print a Transaction Report for the Owner's Equity account.

15 If your trial balance is different than Figure 6.13, do the following:

    a. Make sure that all of your changes were dated in January 2026.

    b. View the Transaction Reports you just created to locate any errors.

    c. Ask your instructor for assistance.

    d. Be sure your company matches the above as you will be adding additional business events in Chapter 7.

16 Export your Trial Balance report to Excel, and save it with the file name Student Name (replace with your name) Ch 06 Case 03 Trial Balance.xlsx.

17 Open and print the custom report you created in the last chapter called Transaction Detail by Account.

18 Export your Transactions Detail by Account report to Excel, and save it with the file name Student Name (replace with your name) Ch 06 Case 03 Transaction Detail by Account.xlsx.

19 Sign out of your company.

Case 4

Now it's time for you to add some investing and financing activities to your company.

Based on what you learned in the text using the Wild Water Sports company, you are to make the following changes to the Case 4 company you modified in Chapter 5:

1 Record the signing of a new long-term business loan (a new Long-Term Liabilities type account) on 1/01/27 with Coast Bank (a new vendor) in the amount of $18,000. A check was received from Coast Bank and immediately deposited.

2 Record the purchase of Furniture on 1/23/27 from ABC Holdings (a new vendor), check: 25501, amount: $35,000.

3 Record the purchase of a long-term investment on 1/25/27 from Barber Investments, Inc. (a new vendor), check: 25502, amount: $8,000. Record to a new Other Assets account type, Other Long-term Assets detail type account named Long-term investments.

4 Record the sale of common stock on 1/26/27 to Shareholders (a new vendor) receiving a $10,000 check that was immediately deposited.

5 Record the purchase of furniture from Pacific Furniture (a new vendor) on 1/27/27 in exchange for a Long-term business loan of $6,000 using journal no. 3.

6 Record the payment of principle ($694) and interest ($120) to Coast Bank on the $18,000 long-term business loan on 1/31/27 with check 25503. Note: principle payment reduces the long-term business loans account.

7 Record the payment of $1,000 in dividends to Shareholders on 1/31/27, check: 25504.

8 Use journal entry 4 to reclassify $82,000 in Long-term debt (Debit) to Long-term business loans (Credit) on 1/31/27.

9 Prepare and print the Trial Balance 1/31/27 report you saved previously. Your report should look like Figure 6.14.

Figure 6.14

Trial Balance as of 1/31/27

Trial Balance As of January 31, 2027	DEBIT	CREDIT
Checking	28,762.65	
Accounts Receivable (A/R)	22,082.50	
Inventory Asset	8,868.00	
Payments to deposit	0.00	
Prepaid rent	12,000.00	
Supplies Asset	1,400.00	
Furniture:Accumulated Depreciation		10,000.00
Furniture:Original Cost	106,000.00	
Vehicles:Accumulated Depreciation		6,500.00
Vehicles:Original Cost	115,000.00	
Long-term investments	8,000.00	
Accounts Payable (A/P)		6,800.00
VISA		2,400.00
California Department of Tax and Fee Administration Payable		339.15
Long-term business loans		105,306.00
Long-term debt		0.00
Common Stock		11,000.00
Opening Balance Equity		0.00
Retained Earnings		114,500.00
Sales		48,400.00
Sales of Product Income		3,570.00
Cost of Goods Sold	1,632.00	
Advertising & Marketing	1,800.00	
Insurance	2,400.00	
Interest Paid	120.00	
Repairs & Maintenance	750.00	
TOTAL	$308,815.15	$308,815.15

10 Investigate differences between your trial balance and the trial balance shown above.

11 If necessary, prepare and print the Transaction Detail by Account report you saved previously to investigate identified differences.

    a. Make sure all your changes were dated in January 2027.

    b. Click on the line that does not match to view the transaction for that account, and investigate why your answer differs.

    c. Ask your instructor for assistance.

    d. Be sure your company matches the above as you will be adding additional business events in Chapter 7.

Case 5

Now it's time for you to add some investing and financing activities to your company.

Based on what you learned in the text using the Wild Water Sports company, you are to make the following changes to the Case 5 company you modified in Chapter 5:

1 Create a new fixed asset account with an account type: Fixed Assets, detail type: Fixed Asset Copiers, name: Fixed Asset Copiers. Track depreciation of this asset.

2 Create a new asset account with an account type: Other Assets, detail type: Other Long-Term Assets, name: Investments.

3 Create an expense account with an account type: Expenses, detail type: Interest Paid, name: Interest Expense.

4 Record the signing of a new 6%, 36-month note payable on 1/01/22 with Gold Coast Bank (a new vendor) in the amount of $25,000. A check was received from Gold Coast Bank and immediately deposited.

5 Record the purchase of a new copier on 1/03/22 from Coastal Copy (a new vendor), check: 3008, amount: $25,000.

6 Record the purchase of a long-term investment on 1/25/22 from Fleet Investments, Inc. (a new vendor), check: 3009, amount: $50,000.

7 Record the additional investment as a deposit on 1/26/22 from Owners (a new vendor) receiving an $80,000 check that was immediately deposited as an increase in Owner's Equity.

8 Record the purchase of computers (fixed asset) from Acme Equipment on 1/3/22 in exchange for a note payable to Acme Equipment of $30,000.

9 Record the payment of $20,907 (principal $18,182 and interest $2,725) to Chase Bank on a note payable on 1/31/22 with check 3010.

10 Record the payment of $761 (principal $636 and interest $125) to Gold Coast Bank on a note payable on 1/31/22 with check 3011.

11 Record the payment of $913 (principal $763 and interest $150) to Acme Equipment on a note payable on 1/31/22 with check 3012.

12 Record the payment of $5,000 in withdrawals (use Owner's Equity category) to Owners on 1/31/22, check: 3013.

13 Record a new invoice 1005 on 1/31/22 to a new customer Northrup (Net 15 terms) for 30 Computer Workstation 100 items for a total invoice of $490,500 including sales tax. (Be sure to click **See the math**.)

14 Prepare and print the Trial Balance 1/31/22 report you saved previously. Your report should look like Figure 6.15.

Figure 6.15

Trial Balance as of 1/31/22

TRIAL BALANCE As of January 31, 2022	DEBIT	CREDIT
Checking	256,419.00	
Accounts Receivable (A/R)	648,850.00	
Inventory	512,000.00	
Prepaid Expenses	22,000.00	
Undeposited Funds	0.00	
Fixed Asset Computers:Depreciation		25,000.00
Fixed Asset Computers:Original cost	280,000.00	
Fixed Asset Copiers:Original cost	25,000.00	
Fixed Asset Furniture:Depreciation		8,000.00
Fixed Asset Furniture:Original cost	80,000.00	
Investments	50,000.00	
Accounts Payable (A/P)		362,000.00
AMEX		6,300.00
Alabama Department of Revenue Payable		24,600.00
Alabama, Huntsville Payable		27,675.00
Alabama, Madison County Payable		3,075.00
Notes Payable		580,419.00
Opening Balance Equity		0.00
Owner's Equity		457,000.00
Consulting		79,500.00
Sales		615,000.00
Training		3,500.00
Cost of Goods Sold	298,000.00	
Advertising & Marketing	3,000.00	
Equipment Rental	7,500.00	
Interest Expense	3,000.00	
Recruiting	6,300.00	
TOTAL	$2,192,069.00	$2,192,069.00

15 Investigate differences between your trial balance and the trial balance shown above.

16 If necessary, prepare and print the Transaction Detail by Account report you saved previously to investigate identified differences.

a. Make sure all your changes were dated in January 2022.

b. Click on the line that does not match to view the transaction for that account, and investigate why your answer differs.

c. Ask your instructor for assistance.

d. Be sure your company matches the above as you will be adding additional business events in Chapter 7.

Case 6

Now it's time for you to add some investing and financing activities to your company.

Based on what you learned in the text using the Wild Water Sports company, you are to make the following changes to the Case 6 company you modified in Chapter 5:

1. Create a new fixed asset account with an account type: Fixed Asset, detail type: Fixed Asset Computers, name: Computers. Track depreciation of this asset.

2. Change the name of the Interest Paid category to Interest Expense using the Chart of Accounts edit feature.

3. Record the signing of a new 4%, 36-month note payable on 1/01/23 with Seattle Bank (a new vendor) in the amount of $20,000. This was an addition to the existing $100,000 note payable that existed on 12/31/22. A check was received from Seattle Bank and immediately deposited.

4. Record the purchase of a new computer on 1/23/23 from Best Buy (a new vendor), check: 591, amount: $8,000.

5. Record the purchase of a long-term investment on 1/25/23 from McConnel Investments, Inc. (a new vendor), check: 592, amount: $12,000.

6. Record the sale of common stock on 1/26/23 to Shareholders (a new vendor) receiving a $10,000 check that was immediately deposited ($100 common stock $9,900 Paid-In Capital).

7. Record the purchase of machinery & equipment from GM (a new vendor) on 1/27/23 in exchange for a note payable of $12,000.

8. Record the payment of $3,542.88 (principle $3,142.88 and interest $400.00) to Seattle Bank on the $120,000 note payable on 1/31/23 with check 593.

9. Record the payment of $500 in dividends to Shareholders on 1/31/23, check: 594 (remember to use Retained Earnings to record dividends).

10. Prepare and print the Trial Balance 1/31/23 report you saved previously. Your report should look like Figure 6.16.

Figure 6.16

Trial Balance as of 1/31/23

Case 06 - Student Name (ID Number)		
TRIAL BALANCE		
As of January 31, 2023		
	DEBIT	**CREDIT**
Checking	78,107.12	
Accounts Receivable (A/R)	153,020.00	
Inventory Asset	524,000.00	
Inventory Parts	4,000.00	
Investments	12,000.00	
Loans To Officers	15,000.00	
Prepaid Expenses	18,000.00	
Undeposited Funds	0.00	
Buildings:Depreciation		15,000.00
Buildings:Original cost	150,000.00	
Computers	8,000.00	
Machinery & Equipment	12,000.00	
Machinery & Equipment:Depreciation		10,000.00
Machinery & Equipment:Original cost	100,000.00	
Accounts Payable (A/P)		524,000.00
AMEX		6,000.00
Washington State Department of Revenue Payable		26,970.00
Notes Payable		128,857.12
Common Stock		1,100.00
Opening Balance Equity		0.00
Paid-In Capital		259,900.00
Retained Earnings		60,500.00
Sales of Product Income		290,000.00
Cost of Goods Sold	232,000.00	
Advertising & Marketing	14,000.00	
Contractors	1,800.00	
Interest Expense	400.00	
TOTAL	$1,322,327.12	$1,322,327.12

11 Investigate differences between your trial balance and the trial balance shown above.

12 Prepare and print the Transaction Detail by Account report for all dates you saved previously to investigate identified differences.

   a. Make sure all your changes were dated in January 2023.

   b. Click on the line that does not match to view the transaction for that account, and investigate why your answer differs.

   c. Ask your instructor for assistance.

   d. Be sure your company matches the above as you will be adding additional business events in Chapter 7.

7

Recording Payroll

Student Learning Outcomes

Upon completion of this chapter, the student will be able to do the following:

- Add a new employee
- Add payroll-related general ledger accounts
- Pay employees and record payroll expenses and liabilities

Overview

In Chapter 6, you added some investing and financing activities like the acquisition of a fixed asset and a long-term investment as well as the sale of stock, payment of dividends, and acquiring and paying long-term debt to your Wild Water Sports company. In this chapter, you will add payroll activities like adding employees, adding payroll-related accounts, and recording payroll expenses and liabilities to your Wild Water Sports company. At the end of this chapter, you will perform similar tasks on the case assigned by your instructor.

To verify the accuracy of your Wild Water Sports company:

1 Sign into your QBO account, then open the Wild Water Sports company you used in Chapter 6.

2 Click **Reports**, then click the **Custom reports** tab, then double-click **Trial Balance** to open the Trial Balance report. Set the from and to dates to **1/1/27** and **1/31/27**, respectively. Compare your report to Figure 7.1. If your report doesn't match Figure 7.1, go back to your work in Chapter 6 to fix your errors. Otherwise, close your Trial Balance report.

Figure 7.1

Wild Water Sports trial balance as of 1/31/27

Wild Water Sports - Student Name (ID Number)

Trial Balance
As of January 31, 2027

	DEBIT	CREDIT
Checking	107,345.00	
Accounts receivable (A/R)	120,770.00	
Inventory	223,350.00	
Payments to deposit	70,000.00	
Prepaid expenses	17,500.00	
Equipment:Accumulated depreciation		10,000.00
Equipment:Original Cost	53,000.00	
Furniture:Original cost	10,000.00	
Investments	3,000.00	
Accounts Payable (A/P)		190,250.00
Mastercard		1,600.00
Florida Department of Revenue Paya…		9,915.00
Long-term business loans		155,000.00
Common stock		11,000.00
Opening balance equity		0.00
Retained Earnings		204,300.00
Sales		164,000.00
Service Revenue		2,000.00
Cost of goods sold	131,200.00	
Interest paid	2,500.00	
Rent:Equipment rental	6,000.00	
Utilities:Phone service	1,800.00	
Vehicle expenses:Vehicle gas & fuel	1,600.00	
TOTAL	$748,065.00	$748,065.00

Employees

In this section, you will be adding a new employee to QBO.

To add a new employee to the Wild Water Sports company, do the following:

1 Continue from above.

2 Make sure the navigation bar is open.

3 Click **Payroll** and then click **Employees** from the navigation bar.

4 Do not click the **Get Started** button. Instead click **Add an employee** text.

5 Click the **Not right now** button when asked to Turn payroll on.

6 Type **Donna Chandler** as the employee's name and provide the following address information: **12 Ridgeway Lane, Orlando, FL, 32807**. Your screen should look like Figure 7.2.

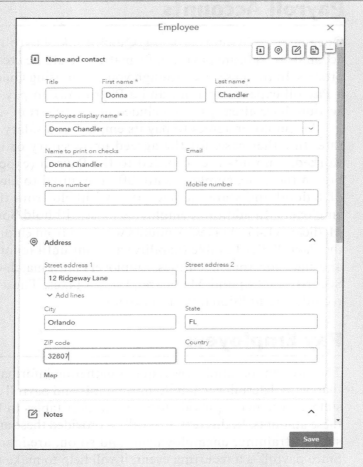

Figure 7.2

Employee Information (adding a new employee)

7 Click **Save**.

8 Click **Add an employee**, then add **Karen Vordale, 1554 Rose Ave. #4, Orlando, FL, 32804** as a second employee. Then click **Save**.

9 Click **Add an employee**, then add **Ryder Zacovic, 12 Spaceport Court, Orlando, FL, 32804** as a second employee. Then click **Save**.

10 Your Employees window should now reflect three employees as shown in Figure 7.3.

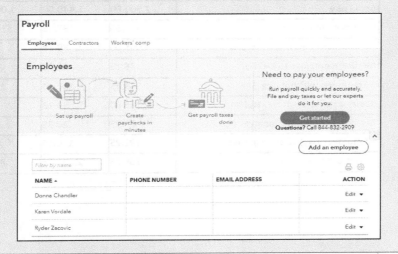

Figure 7.3

Employees

Payroll Accounts

Once again, if you were using QuickBooks Payroll Online, general ledger accounts to capture payroll information would be created for you in the setup process. In this case, even though you're not using QuickBooks Payroll Online, a Payroll expense account and a Payroll tax to pay other current liabilities account have already been included in your chart of accounts.

An employer agrees to pay its employees a salary per month or an hourly rate. In either case, for the agreed upon salary or hourly rate times hours worked, amounts are recorded to the Payroll (expense) account. Depending on the state, employees are often required to have an estimated amount of federal and state income taxes withheld from their paychecks by their employers. In addition, employers must withhold Social Security (6.2%) and Medicare (1.45%) taxes. Amounts withheld from employees will be recorded in the Payroll Tax Payable (liability) account until remitted to the U.S. Treasury and state government entities. Employers must match those amounts for Social Security (6.2%) and Medicare (1.45%) taxes. These matching costs will be recorded as additional Payroll expense.

Pay Employees

The payment of employees requires gathering information from each employee that helps determine withholding amounts and payroll expenses. The federal and state governments provide formulas and/or tables to help employers calculate these amounts. In this text, you will be provided these amounts. Additional taxes, such as training, unemployment, and so on, are ignored for this illustration. Since payroll is a recurring event, it will help to make these checks recur, which can be edited for each payroll for changes in hours worked where applicable. In this example, payroll is paid semimonthly.

See Figure 7.4 for a payroll for your Wild Water Sports company.

Figure 7.4

Semimonthly payroll information

Pay/Tax/Withholding	Donna	Karen	Ryder	Total
Hours if applicable	n/a	80	60	
Annual salary or hourly rate	$ 60,000	$ 18.00	$ 18.00	
Gross pay	2,500.00	1,440.00	1,080.00	5,020.00
Federal withholding	342.50	197.28	147.96	687.74
Social security employee (6.2%)	155.00	89.28	66.96	311.24
Medicare employee (1.45%)	36.25	20.88	15.66	72.79
Employee withholding	533.75	307.44	230.58	1,071.77
Social security employer (6.2%)	155.00	89.28	66.96	311.24
Medicare company employer (1.45%)	36.25	20.88	15.66	72.79
Employer payroll tax expense	191.25	110.16	82.62	384.03
Net Check amount	1,966.25	1,132.56	849.42	3,948.23

To record the payment of employees in the Wild Water Sports company, do the following:

1 Continue from where you left off.

2 Click the (+ New) icon, and select **Check**.

3 Select **Donna Chandler** from the drop-down list in the **Payee** text box. (Note: Employees are located at the bottom of the list.)

4 Type **1/15/2027** as the payment date and **1008** as the Check no.

5 Select **Payroll expenses** from the drop-down list in the Category column of line 1.

6 Type **2500** in the Amount column of line 1, and press **[Tab]** once.

7 Select **Payroll wages and tax to pay** from the drop-down list in the Category column of line 2.

8 Type **−533.75** in the Amount column of line 1, and press **[Tab]** once. (Be sure to enter this amount as a negative number.)

9 Select **Payroll expenses** from the drop-down list in the Category column of line 3.

10 Type **191.25** in the Amount column of line 3, and press **[Tab]** once.

11 Select **Payroll wages and tax to pay** from the drop-down list in the Category column of line 4.

12 Type **−191.25** in the Amount column of line 4, and press **[Tab]** once. (Be sure to enter this amount as a negative number.) Your screen should look like Figure 7.5.

Figure 7.5

Check #1008 (paycheck for Donna Chandler)

13 Click **Make recurring** located at the bottom of the screen.

14 Select **Unscheduled** from the drop-down list in the Type text box.

15 Click **Save template**.

16 Click the **Gear** icon.

17 Select **Recurring Transactions** located in the List column.

18 Click **Use** located in the Action column of the Donna Chandler row. The check window will appear again completed like that shown in Figure 7.5.

19 Make sure the date is correct and then click **Save and new**.

20 Enter payroll information found in Figure 7.4 for Karen and Ryder in the same way as you entered payroll information for Donna above. Be sure to make each of these unscheduled recurring events.

21 After entering the last check to record payroll above, click **Save and close**.

22 Click **Reports** from the navigation bar.

23 Click the **Custom reports** tab, then click **Trial Balance** to open the Trial Balance report. Set the from and to dates to **1/1/27** and **1/31/27**, respectively, then click **Run Report** to view the report, which is shown in Figure 7.6.

Figure 7.6

Trial Balance

Wild Water Sports - Student Name (ID Number)

Trial Balance
As of January 31, 2027

	DEBIT	CREDIT
Checking	103,396.77	
Accounts receivable (A/R)	120,770.00	
Inventory	223,350.00	
Payments to deposit	70,000.00	
Prepaid expenses	17,500.00	
Equipment:Accumulated de...		10,000.00
Equipment:Original Cost	53,000.00	
Furniture:Original cost	10,000.00	
Investments	3,000.00	
Accounts Payable (A/P)		190,250.00
Mastercard		1,600.00
Florida Department of Reve...		9,915.00
Payroll wages and tax to pay		1,455.80
Long-term business loans		155,000.00
Common stock		11,000.00
Opening balance equity		0.00
Retained Earnings		204,300.00
Sales		164,000.00
Service Revenue		2,000.00
Cost of goods sold	131,200.00	
Interest paid	2,500.00	
Payroll expenses	5,404.03	
Rent:Equipment rental	6,000.00	
Utilities:Phone service	1,800.00	
Vehicle expenses:Vehicle ga...	1,600.00	
TOTAL	$749,520.80	$749,520.80

24 Click the **103,396.77** amount on the Checking line to view a transaction report for the checking account as shown in Figure 7.7.

Figure 7.7

Transaction Report (checking account)

25 Match your screen with Figure 7.7.

26 Click **Ryder Zacovic** to view the payroll check as shown in Figure 7.8.

Figure 7.8

Check #1010 (Ryder Zacovic payroll check)

27 Match your screen to Figure 7.8, and close the check window.

28 Click **Back to report summary** to return to the Trial Balance report.

You have recorded payroll for one semimonthly period. You can practice with another payroll using the recurring transactions you have set up.

29 Click the **Gear** icon, and click **Recurring Transactions** located in the Lists column to view a list of recurring transactions as shown in Figure 7.9. (If your list does not contain the three employees you recorded, you will need to return to these transactions, and click the **Make recurring** button.)

Figure 7.9

Recurring Transactions

30 Click **Use** on the **Ryder Zacovic** template to view a new payroll check for Ryder.

31 Type **1/31/2027** in the Payment date text box and then type **1011** in the Check no. text box.

32 Payroll information for this next semimonthly period is shown in Figure 7.10. Note that the hours worked are different, and Karen received an increase in her hourly rate.

Figure 7.10

Semimonthly payroll information

Pay/Tax/Withholding	Donna	Karen	Ryder	Total
Hours if applicable	n/a	75	63	
Annual salary or hourly rate	$ 60,000	$ 20.00	$ 18.00	
Gross pay	2,500.00	1,500.00	1,134.00	5,134.00
Federal withholding	342.50	205.50	155.36	703.36
Social security employee (6.2%)	155.00	93.00	70.31	318.31
Medicare employee (1.45%)	36.25	21.75	16.44	74.44
Employee withholding	533.75	320.25	242.11	1,096.11
Social security employer (6.2%)	155.00	93.00	70.31	318.31
Medicare company employer (1.45%)	36.25	21.75	16.44	74.44
Employer payroll tax expense	191.25	114.75	86.75	392.75
Net Check amount	1,966.25	1,179.75	891.89	4,037.89

33 Type **1134** in the Amount column on line 1.

34 Type **−242.11** in the Amount column on line 2.

35 Type **86.75** in the Amount column on line 3.

36 Type **−86.75** in the Amount column on line 4. Your screen should now look like Figure 7.11.

Figure 7.11

Check #1011 (Ryder Zacovic payroll check)

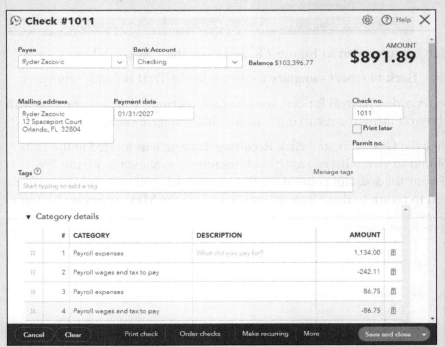

37 Click **Save and close**.

38 Use the same process (clicking **Use** from the Recurring Transactions list) for Karen and Donna to record their paychecks based on the new information shown in Figure 7.10. (Since Donna is salaried, her information remains the same each pay period, so nothing needs to be changed from the recurring transaction information provided.)

39 Click **Reports**, then click the **Custom reports** tab, then double-click **Trial Balance** to open the Trial Balance report. Confirm that the from and to dates are **1/1/27** and **1/31/27** respectively, then click **Run Report** to view the report shown in Figure 7.12.

Figure 7.12

Trial Balance

Wild Water Sports - Student Name (ID Number)

Trial Balance
As of January 31, 2027

	DEBIT	CREDIT
Checking	99,358.88	
Accounts receivable (A/R)	120,770.00	
Inventory	223,350.00	
Payments to deposit	70,000.00	
Prepaid expenses	17,500.00	
Equipment:Accumulated depreciation		10,000.00
Equipment:Original Cost	53,000.00	
Furniture:Original cost	10,000.00	
Investments	3,000.00	
Accounts Payable (A/P)		190,250.00
Mastercard		1,600.00
Florida Department of Revenue Payable		9,915.00
Payroll wages and tax to pay		2,944.66
Long-term business loans		155,000.00
Common stock		11,000.00
Opening balance equity		0.00
Retained Earnings		204,300.00
Sales		164,000.00
Service Revenue		2,000.00
Cost of goods sold	131,200.00	
Interest paid	2,500.00	
Payroll expenses	10,930.78	
Rent:Equipment rental	6,000.00	
Utilities:Phone service	1,800.00	
Vehicle expenses:Vehicle gas & fuel	1,600.00	
TOTAL	$751,009.66	$751,009.66

40 Click the **99,358.88** amount on the Checking line to view a transaction report for the checking account as shown in Figure 7.13.

Figure 7.13

Transaction Report (checking account)

Wild Water Sports - Student Name (ID Number)

Transaction Report
January 2027

DATE	TRANSACTION TYPE	NUM	NAME	MEMO/DESCRIPTION	ACCOUNT	SPLIT	AMOUNT	BALANCE
▼ Checking								
Beginning Balance								25,000.00
01/13/2027	Deposit		Southtown Watersports		Checking	Payments to deposit	55,145.00	80,145.00
01/15/2027	Check	1008	Donna Chandler		Checking	-Split-	-1,966.25	78,178.75
01/15/2027	Check	1009	Karen Vordale		Checking	-Split-	-1,132.56	77,046.19
01/15/2027	Check	1010	Ryder Zacovic		Checking	-Split-	-849.42	76,196.77
01/18/2027	Bill Payment (Check)	1001	Malibu Boats		Checking	Accounts Payable (A/P)	-56,000.00	20,196.77
01/19/2027	Check	1002	Verizon		Checking	Utilities:Phone service	-1,800.00	18,396.77
01/20/2027	Check	1004	Office Max		Checking	Furniture:Original cost	-10,000.00	8,396.77
01/20/2027	Check	1003	Best Buy		Checking	Equipment:Original Cost	-8,000.00	396.77
01/21/2027	Check	1005	Scotttrede		Checking	Investments	-3,000.00	-2,603.23
01/21/2027	Deposit		WB Investments		Checking	Common stock	10,000.00	7,396.77
01/22/2027	Check	1006	Shareholders		Checking	Retained Earnings	-1,500.00	5,896.77
01/23/2027	Check	1007	Chase Bank		Checking	-Split-	-52,500.00	-46,603.23
01/23/2027	Deposit		Chase Bank		Checking	Long-term business loans	150,000.00	103,396.77
01/31/2027	Check	1011	Ryder Zacovic		Checking	-Split-	-891.89	102,504.88
01/31/2027	Check	1012	Karen Vordale		Checking	-Split-	-1,179.75	101,325.13
01/31/2027	Check	1013	Donna Chandler		Checking	-Split-	-1,966.25	99,358.88
Total for Checking							$74,358.88	
TOTAL							$74,358.88	

41   Compare your screen with Figure 7.13, then compare your trial balance with Figure 7.12. Take note of any differences.

42   Click any payroll-related transaction if you want to drill down to the payroll check you recorded to see if you can fix any differences noted.

43   Fix any errors you discover.

You have recorded two semimonthly payroll checks for the Wild Water Sports company.

End Note

In this chapter, you added new employees, and paid employees. In the next chapter, you will work with budgets and bank reconciliations.

Chapter 7 Questions

1 What are the steps to create a new employee?

2 What are the steps to create a new account?

3 What are the two minimum accounts needed to account for payroll?

4 What types of costs are included in the Payroll (expense) account?

5 What types of costs are included in the Payroll Tax Payable (liability) account?

Chapter 7 Matching

a. 6.2%   _____   Account used to record the liability for Federal income tax withheld

b. 1.45%   _____   An add-on feature to QBO

c. Payroll   _____   Rate used to calculate an employee's Medicare tax

d. Payroll tax payable _____   Hours worked times hourly rate

e. QBO Payroll   _____   Use to more efficiently record periodic payroll

f. Gross pay   _____   Payroll tax payable

g. Recurring transactions _____   Accessed by clicking an amount on the trial balance

h. Transaction report _____   One type of recurring event

i. Unscheduled   _____   Account used to record all payroll expenses

j. Record as negative amounts _____   Rate used to calculate an employee's Social Security tax

Chapter 7 Cases

The following cases require you to open the company you updated in Chapter 6. Each of the following cases continues throughout the text in a sequential manner. For example, if you are assigned Case 01, you will use the file you modified in this chapter in all following chapters. Each of the following cases is similar in concepts assessed but differs in amounts and transactions.

To reopen your company, do the following:

1 Open your Internet browser.

2 Type **https://qbo.intuit.com** into your browser's address text box.

3 Type your user ID and password into the text boxes as you have done before.

Case 1

Now add some payroll activities to your company. Do not install QBO Payroll. Based on what you learned in the text using the Wild Water Sports company, you are to make the following changes to the Case 1 company you modified in Chapter 6:

1   Add two new accounts like you did in the chapter: Payroll (expense) and Payroll Tax Payable (liability) if they are not already present.

2   Add a new employee: Ben Franklin, 32 Ocean View Lane, La Jolla, CA, 92037, employee ID number: 556-12-3467.

3   Add a second employee: Betsy Ross, 2323 1st Street, La Jolla, CA, 92037, employee ID number: 458-87-1974.

4   Payroll is paid twice a month on the 17th and the last day of each month.

5   Record payroll (as you did in the chapter) for 1/17/24 based on the information shown in Figure 7.14. After recording each employee's check, be sure to designate it as a recurring transaction.

Figure 7.14

Payroll information (for 1/17/24)

Pay/Tax/Withholding	Ben	Betsy	Total
Hours if applicable	n/a	73	
Annual salary or hourly rate	$ 95,000	$ 21.50	
Gross pay	**3,958.33**	**1,569.50**	**5,527.83**
Federal withholding	542.29	215.02	**757.31**
Social security employee (6.2%)	245.42	97.31	**342.73**
Medicare employee (1.45%)	57.40	22.76	**80.16**
Employee withholding	**845.11**	**335.09**	**1,180.20**
Social security employer (6.2%)	245.42	97.31	**342.73**
Medicare company employer (1.45%)	57.40	22.76	**80.16**
Employer payroll tax expense	**302.82**	**120.07**	**422.89**
Net Check amount	3,113.22	1,234.41	**4,347.63**

6   Use the recurring transactions template you created above to help you record payroll (as you did in the chapter) for 1/31/24 based on the information shown in Figure 7.15.

Figure 7.15

Payroll information (for 1/31/24)

Pay/Tax/Withholding	Ben	Betsy	Total
Hours if applicable	n/a	68	
Annual salary or hourly rate	$ 95,000	$ 21.50	
Gross pay	3,958.33	1,462.00	5,420.33
Federal withholding	542.29	200.29	742.58
Social security employee (6.2%)	245.42	90.64	336.06
Medicare employee (1.45%)	57.40	21.20	78.60
Employee withholding	845.11	312.13	1,157.24
Social security employer (6.2%)	245.42	90.64	336.06
Medicare company employer (1.45%)	57.40	21.20	78.60
Employer payroll tax expense	302.82	111.84	414.66
Net Check amount	3,113.22	1,149.87	4,263.09

7 Open your previously customized report named Trial Balance 1/31/24. Your report should look like Figure 7.16.

Figure 7.16

Trial Balance (as of 1/31/24)

	DEBIT	CREDIT
Checking	26,239.28	
Accounts Receivable	1,030.00	
Inventory Asset	11,800.00	
Prepaid Expenses	8,000.00	
Supplies Asset	375.00	
Undeposited Funds	5,000.00	
Equipment:Original Cost	3,175.00	
Furniture & Fixtures:Depreciation		10,000.00
Furniture & Fixtures:Original cost	40,000.00	
Investments	4,000.00	
Accounts Payable		7,645.00
Visa		1,800.00
Payroll Tax Payable		3,174.99
Notes Payable		66,800.00
Common Stock		21,000.00
Opening Balance Equity		0.00
Retained Earnings		5,000.00
Sales		2,160.00
Services		170.00
Cost of Goods Sold	1,300.00	
Interest Expense	600.00	
Payroll	11,785.71	
Rent or Lease	2,500.00	
Travel	1,800.00	
Utilities	145.00	
TOTAL	$117,749.99	$117,749.99

8 Create and print a Transaction Report for the Checking account.

9 Create and print a Transaction Report for the Payroll Tax Payable account.

10 If your trial balance differs from the one in Figure 7.16, do the following:

    a. Make sure all of your changes were dated in January 2024.

    b. View the Transaction Reports you created to locate any errors.

    c. Ask your instructor for assistance.

    d. Be sure your company matches the above as you will be adding additional business events in Chapter 8.

11 Export your Trial Balance report to Excel, and save it with the file name Student Name (replace with your name) Ch 07 Case 01 Trial Balance.xlsx.

12 Open and print the custom report you created in the last chapter called Transaction Detail by Account.

13 Export your Transactions Detail by Account report to Excel, and save it with the file name Student Name (replace with your name) Ch 07 Case 01 Transaction Detail by Account.xlsx.

14 Sign out of your company.

Case 2

Now add some payroll activities to your company. Do not install QBO Payroll. Based on what you learned in the text using the Wild Water Sports company, you are to make the following changes to the Case 2 company you modified in Chapter 6:

1 Add two new accounts like you did in the chapter: Payroll (expense) and Payroll Tax Payable (liability) if they are not already present.

2 Add a new employee: Frank Benjamin, 32 Ocean View Lane, La Jolla, CA, 92037, employee ID number: 556-12-3467.

3 Add a second employee: Sara Juarez, 2323 1st Street, La Jolla, CA, 92037, employee ID number: 458-87-1974.

4 Payroll is paid twice a month on the 16th and the last day of each month.

5 Record payroll (like you did in the chapter) for 1/16/25 based on the information shown in Figure 7.17. After recording each employee's check, be sure to designate it as a recurring transaction.

Pay/Tax/Withholding	Frank	Sara	Total
Hours if applicable	n/a	71	
Annual salary or hourly rate	$ 72,000	$ 18.75	
Gross pay	3,000.00	1,331.25	4,331.25
Federal withholding	411.00	182.38	593.38
Social security employee (6.2%)	186.00	82.54	268.54
Medicare employee (1.45%)	43.50	19.30	62.80
Employee withholding	640.50	284.22	924.72
Social security employer (6.2%)	186.00	82.54	268.54
Medicare company employer (1.45%)	43.50	19.30	62.80
Employer payroll tax expense	229.50	101.84	331.34
Net Check amount	2,359.50	1,047.03	3,406.53

Figure 7.17

Payroll information (for 1/16/25)

6 Use the recurring transactions template you created above to help you record payroll (as you did in the chapter) for 1/31/25 based on the information shown in Figure 7.18.

Pay/Tax/Withholding	Frank	Sara	Total
Hours if applicable	n/a	66	
Annual salary or hourly rate	$ 72,000	$ 18.75	
Gross pay	3,000.00	1,237.50	4,237.50
Federal withholding	411.00	169.54	580.54
Social security employee (6.2%)	186.00	76.73	262.73
Medicare employee (1.45%)	43.50	17.94	61.44
Employee withholding	640.50	264.21	904.71
Social security employer (6.2%)	186.00	76.73	262.73
Medicare company employer (1.45%)	43.50	17.94	61.44
Employer payroll tax expense	229.50	94.67	324.17
Net Check amount	2,359.50	973.29	3,332.79

Figure 7.18

Payroll information (for 1/31/25)

7 Open your previously customized report named Trial Balance 1/31/25. Your report should look like Figure 7.19.

Figure 7.19

Trial Balance (as of 1/31/25)

Case 2
TRIAL BALANCE
As of January 31, 2025

	DEBIT	CREDIT
Checking	31,860.68	
Accounts Receivable	1,425.00	
Inventory Asset	5,410.00	
Prepaid Expenses	6,800.00	
Supplies Asset	450.00	
Undeposited Funds	925.00	
Furniture:Original Cost	4,875.00	
Machinery & Equipment:Depreciation		1,000.00
Machinery & Equipment:Original cost	10,000.00	
Investments	3,200.00	
Accounts Payable		8,670.00
AMEX		240.00
Payroll Tax Payable		2,484.94
Notes Payable		27,625.00
Common Stock		25,100.00
Opening Balance Equity		0.00
Retained Earnings		7,585.00
Sales		5,700.00
Services		225.00
Cost of Goods Sold	3,020.00	
Advertising	500.00	
Insurance	400.00	
Interest Expense	300.00	
Meals and Entertainment	240.00	
Payroll	9,224.26	
TOTAL	$78,629.94	$78,629.94

8 Create and print a Transaction Report for the Checking account.

9 Create and print a Transaction Report for the Payroll Tax Payable account.

10 If your trial balance differs from the one in Figure 7.19, do the following:

a. Make sure all of your changes were dated in January 2025.

b. View the Transaction Reports you created to locate any errors.

c. Ask your instructor for assistance.

d. Be sure your company matches the above as you will be adding additional business events in Chapter 8.

11 Export your Trial Balance report to Excel, and save it with the file name Student Name (replace with your name) Ch 07 Case 02 Trial Balance.xlsx.

12 Open and print the custom report you created in the last chapter called Transaction Detail by Account.

13 Export your Transactions Detail by Account report to Excel, and save it with the file name Student Name (replace with your name) Ch 07 Case 02 Transaction Detail by Account.xlsx.

14 Sign out of your company.

Case 3

Now add some payroll activities to your company. Do not install QBO Payroll. Based on what you learned in the text using the Wild Water Sports company, you are to make the following changes to the Case 3 company you modified in Chapter 6:

1 If necessary, add two new accounts like you did in the chapter: Payroll (expense) and Payroll Tax Payable (liability).

2 Add a new employee: Kira Jennings, 32 Ocean View Lane, La Jolla, CA, 92037, employee ID number: 556-33-3467.

3 Add a second employee: Jedi Vu, 2323 1st Street, La Jolla, CA, 92037, employee ID number: 458-22-1974.

4 Payroll is paid twice a month on the 16th and the last day of each month.

5 Record payroll (like you did in the chapter) for 1/16/26 based on the information shown in Figure 7.20 using checks 326 and 327. Be sure to designate both as a recurring transaction.

Pay/Tax/Withholding	Kira	Jedi	Total
Hours if applicable	n/a	70	
Annual salary or hourly rate	$ 48,000	$ 17.00	
Gross pay	2,000.00	1,190.00	3,190.00
Federal withholding	274.00	163.03	437.03
Social security employee (6.2%)	124.00	73.78	197.78
Medicare employee (1.45%)	29.00	17.26	46.26
Employee withholding	427.00	254.07	681.07
Social security employer (6.2%)	124.00	73.78	197.78
Medicare company employer (1.45%)	29.00	17.26	46.26
Employer payroll tax expense	153.00	91.04	244.04
Net Check amount	1,573.00	935.93	2,508.93

Figure 7.20

Payroll information for 1/16/26

6 Use the recurring transactions template you created above to help you record payroll (like you did in the chapter) for 1/31/26 based on the information shown in Figure 7.21 using checks 328 and 329.

Figure 7.21

Payroll information for 1/31/26

Pay/Tax/Withholding	Kira	Jedi	Total
Hours if applicable	n/a	75	
Annual salary or hourly rate	$ 48,000	$ 17.00	
Gross pay	**2,000.00**	**1,275.00**	**3,275.00**
Federal withholding	274.00	174.68	**448.68**
Social security employee (6.2%)	124.00	79.05	**203.05**
Medicare employee (1.45%)	29.00	18.49	**47.49**
Employee withholding	**427.00**	**272.22**	**699.22**
Social security employer (6.2%)	124.00	79.05	**203.05**
Medicare company employer (1.45%)	29.00	18.49	**47.49**
Employer payroll tax expense	**153.00**	**97.54**	**250.54**
Net Check amount	1,573.00	1,002.78	**2,575.78**

7 Open your previously customized report named Trial Balance 1/31/26. Your report should look like Figure 7.22.

Figure 7.22

Trial Balance as of 1/31/26

Case 03 - Student Name (ID Number)

Trial Balance
As of January 31, 2026

	DEBIT	CREDIT
Checking	50,667.04	
Accounts receivable (A/R)	2,559.38	
Inventory Asset	5,700.00	
Payments to deposit	0.00	
Prepaid expenses	6,050.00	
Supplies Asset	327.00	
Computers:Original cost	3,000.00	
Machinery & Equipment:Depreciation		2,000.00
Machinery & Equipment:Original cost	46,800.00	
Investments	5,700.00	
Accounts Payable (A/P)		8,900.00
AMEX		123.00
California Department of Tax and Fe...		523.13
Payroll Tax Payable		1,874.87
Notes Payable		63,800.00
Opening balance equity		0.00
Owner's Equity		50,075.00
Sales of Product Income		6,750.00
Services		240.00
Cost of goods sold	4,500.00	
Advertising & marketing	1,300.00	
Insurance	300.00	
Interest paid	300.00	
Meals	123.00	
Payroll	6,959.58	
TOTAL	$134,286.00	$134,286.00

8   Create and print a Transaction Report for the Checking account.

9   Create and print a Transaction Report for the Payroll Tax Payable account.

10   If your trial balance is different than Figure 7.22, do the following:

    a.   Make sure that all of your changes were dated in January 2026.

    b.   View the Transaction Reports you just created to locate any errors.

    c.   Ask your instructor for assistance.

    d.   Be sure your company matches the above as you will be adding additional business events in Chapter 8.

11   Export your Trial Balance report to Excel, and save it with the file name Student Name (replace with your name) Ch 07 Case 03 Trial Balance.xlsx.

12   Open and print the customized report you created in the last chapter called Transaction Detail by Account.

13   Export your Transactions Detail by Account report to Excel, and save it with the file name Student Name (replace with your name) Ch 07 Case 03 Transaction Detail by Account.xlsx.

14   Sign out of your company.

Case 4

Now add some payroll activities to your company. Do not install QBO Payroll. Based on what you learned in the text using the Wild Water Sports company, you are to make the following changes to the Case 4 company you modified in Chapter 6:

1   Add two new accounts: Payroll expense and Payroll tax to pay (liability) if they are not already present.

2   Add a new employee: Graham O'Leary.

3   Add additional employees: Allegra Munoz and Beckett Yamamomo.

4   Payroll is paid twice a month on the 15th and the last day of each month.

5   Record payroll (like you did in the chapter) for 1/15/27 based on the information shown in Figure 7.23. After recording each employee's check, be sure to designate it as an unscheduled recurring transaction.

Figure 7.23

Payroll information for 1/15/27

Pay/Tax/Withholding	Graham	Allegra	Beckett	Total
Hours if applicable	n/a	75	83	
Annual salary or hourly rate	$ 75,000	$ 25.00	$ 22.00	
Gross pay	**3,125.00**	**1,875.00**	**1,826.00**	**6,826.00**
Federal withholding	428.13	256.88	250.16	**935.16**
Social security employee (6.2%)	193.75	116.25	113.21	**423.21**
Medicare employee (1.45%)	45.31	27.19	26.48	**98.98**
Employee withholding	**667.19**	**400.32**	**389.85**	**1,457.35**
Social security employer (6.2%)	193.75	116.25	113.21	**423.21**
Medicare company employer (1.45%)	45.34	27.19	26.48	**99.01**
Employer payroll tax expense	**239.09**	**143.44**	**139.69**	**522.22**
Net Check amount	2,457.81	1,474.68	1,436.15	**5,368.64**

6 Use the recurring transactions template you created above to help you record payroll (as you did in the chapter) for 1/31/27 based on the information shown in Figure 7.24.

Figure 7.24

Payroll information for 1/31/27

Pay/Tax/Withholding	Graham	Allegra	Beckett	Total
Hours if applicable	n/a	70	88	
Annual salary or hourly rate	$ 75,000	$ 25.00	$ 22.00	
Gross pay	**3,125.00**	**1,750.00**	**1,936.00**	**6,811.00**
Federal withholding	428.13	239.75	265.23	**933.11**
Social security employee (6.2%)	193.75	108.50	120.03	**422.28**
Medicare employee (1.45%)	45.31	25.38	28.07	**98.76**
Employee withholding	**667.19**	**373.63**	**413.33**	**1,454.15**
Social security employer (6.2%)	193.75	108.50	120.03	**422.28**
Medicare company employer (1.45%)	45.34	25.38	28.07	**98.79**
Employer payroll tax expense	**239.09**	**133.88**	**148.10**	**521.07**
Net Check amount	2,457.81	1,376.37	1,522.67	**5,356.85**

7 Prepare and print the Trial Balance 1/31/27 report you saved previously. Your report should look like Figure 7.25.

Figure 7.25

Trial Balance as of 1/31/27

Trial Balance As of January 31, 2027	DEBIT	CREDIT
Checking	18,037.16	
Accounts Receivable (A/R)	22,082.50	
Inventory Asset	8,868.00	
Payments to deposit	0.00	
Prepaid rent	12,000.00	
Supplies Asset	1,400.00	
Furniture:Accumulated Depreciation		10,000.00
Furniture:Original Cost	106,000.00	
Vehicles:Accumulated Depreciation		6,500.00
Vehicles:Original Cost	115,000.00	
Long-term investments	8,000.00	
Accounts Payable (A/P)		6,800.00
VISA		2,400.00
California Department of Tax and Fee Administration Payable		339.15
Payroll wages and tax to pay		3,954.80
Long-term business loans		105,306.00
Long-term debt		0.00
Common Stock		11,000.00
Opening Balance Equity		0.00
Retained Earnings		114,500.00
Sales		48,400.00
Sales of Product Income		3,570.00
Cost of Goods Sold	1,632.00	
Advertising & Marketing	1,800.00	
Insurance	2,400.00	
Interest Paid	120.00	
Payroll expenses	14,680.29	
Repairs & Maintenance	750.00	
TOTAL	$312,769.95	$312,769.95

8 Investigate differences between your trial balance and the trial balance shown above.

9 If necessary, prepare and print the Transaction Detail by Account report you saved previously to investigate identified differences.

a. Make sure all your changes were dated in January 2027.

b. Click on the line that does not match to view the transaction for that account, and investigate why your answer differs.

c. Ask your instructor for assistance.

d. Be sure your company matches the above as you will be adding additional business events in Chapter 8.

Case 5

Now add some payroll activities to your company. Do not install QBO Payroll. Based on what you learned in the text using the Wild Water Sports company, you are to make the following changes to the Case 5 company you modified in Chapter 6:

1 Add two new accounts like you did in the chapter: Payroll (expense) and Payroll Tax Payable (liability) if they are not already present.

2 Add a new employee: Jamal Hope.

3 Add a second employee: Rebecca Fairly.

4 Add a third employee: Sarah Lockwood.

5 Payroll is paid twice a month on the 15th and the last day of each month.

6 Record payroll (like you did in the chapter) for 1/15/22 based on the information shown in Figure 7.26. After recording each employee's check, be sure to designate it as a recurring transaction.

Figure 7.26

Payroll information for 1/15/22

Pay/Tax/Withholding	Jamal	Rebecca	Sarah	Total
Hours if applicable	n/a	n/a	80	
Annual salary or hourly rate	$ 125,000	$ 100,000	$ 40.00	
Gross pay	**5,208.33**	**4,166.67**	**3,200.00**	**12,575.00**
Federal withholding	713.54	570.83	438.40	1,722.78
Social security employee (6.2%)	322.92	258.33	198.40	779.65
Medicare employee (1.45%)	75.52	60.42	46.40	182.34
Employee withholding	**1,111.98**	**889.58**	**683.20**	**2,684.76**
Social security employer (6.2%)	322.92	258.33	198.40	779.65
Medicare company employer (1.45%)	75.55	60.45	46.40	182.40
Employer payroll tax expense	**398.47**	**318.78**	**244.80**	**962.05**
Net Check amount	4,096.35	3,277.09	2,516.80	**9,890.24**

7 Use the recurring transactions template you created above to help you record payroll (as you did in the chapter) for 1/31/22 based on the information shown in Figure 7.27. You may enter payroll for employees in any order; just keep in mind that your check numbers may not match the Transactions Detail by Account report.

Figure 7.27

Payroll information for 1/31/22

Pay/Tax/Withholding	Jamal	Rebecca	Sarah	Total
Hours if applicable	n/a	n/a	75	
Annual salary or hourly rate	$ 125,000	$ 100,000	$ 40.00	
Gross pay	**5,208.33**	**4,166.67**	**3,000.00**	**12,375.00**
Federal withholding	713.54	570.83	411.00	1,695.38
Social security employee (6.2%)	322.92	258.33	186.00	767.25
Medicare employee (1.45%)	75.52	60.42	43.50	179.44
Employee withholding	**1,111.98**	**889.58**	**640.50**	**2,642.06**
Social security employer (6.2%)	322.92	258.33	186.00	767.25
Medicare company employer (1.45%)	75.55	60.45	43.50	179.50
Employer payroll tax expense	**398.47**	**318.78**	**229.50**	**946.75**
Net Check amount	4,096.35	3,277.09	2,359.50	**9,732.94**

8 Prepare and print the Trial Balance 1/31/22 report you saved previously. Your report should look like Figure 7.28.

TRIAL BALANCE
As of January 31, 2022

	DEBIT	CREDIT
Checking	236,795.82	
Accounts Receivable (A/R)	648,850.00	
Inventory	512,000.00	
Prepaid Expenses	22,000.00	
Undeposited Funds	0.00	
Fixed Asset Computers:Depreciation		25,000.00
Fixed Asset Computers:Original cost	280,000.00	
Fixed Asset Copiers:Original cost	25,000.00	
Fixed Asset Furniture:Depreciation		8,000.00
Fixed Asset Furniture:Original cost	80,000.00	
Investments	50,000.00	
Accounts Payable (A/P)		362,000.00
AMEX		6,300.00
Alabama Department of Revenue Payable		24,600.00
Alabama, Huntsville Payable		27,675.00
Alabama, Madison County Payable		3,075.00
Payroll Tax Payable		7,235.62
Notes Payable		580,419.00
Opening Balance Equity		0.00
Owner's Equity		457,000.00
Consulting		79,500.00
Sales		615,000.00
Training		3,500.00
Cost of Goods Sold	298,000.00	
Advertising & Marketing	3,000.00	
Equipment Rental	7,500.00	
Interest Expense	3,000.00	
Payroll	26,858.80	
Recruiting	6,300.00	
TOTAL	$2,199,304.62	$2,199,304.62

Figure 7.28

Trial Balance as of 1/31/22

9 Investigate differences between your trial balance and the trial balance shown above.

10 If necessary, prepare and print the Transaction Detail by Account report you saved previously to investigate identified differences.

    a. Make sure all your changes were dated in January 2022.

    b. Click on the line that does not match to view the transaction for that account, and investigate why your answer differs.

    c. Ask your instructor for assistance.

    d. Be sure your company matches the above as you will be adding additional business events in Chapter 8.

Case 6

Now add some payroll activities to your company. Do not install QBO Payroll. Based on what you learned in the text using the Wild Water Sports company, you are to make the following changes to the Case 6 company you modified in Chapter 6:

1 Add two new accounts like you did in the chapter: Payroll (expense) and Payroll Tax Payable (liability) if they are not already present.

2 Add new employees:

    a. Oliver Peters, 4737 Forest Ave SE, Mercer Island, WA, 98040, employee ID number: 1347.

    b. Rhett Brady, 1706 9th Ave SE, Puyallup, WA, 98372, employee ID number: 1348.

    c. Emelia Carlstrom, 518 Guptil Ave, Sumer, WA, 98390, employee ID number: 1349.

3 Payroll is paid twice a month on the 15th and the last day of each month.

4 Record payroll (like you did in the chapter) for 1/15/23 based on the information shown in Figure 7.29 using checks 595, 596, and 597. After recording each employee's check, be sure to designate it as a recurring transaction.

Figure 7.29

Payroll information for 1/15/23

Pay/Tax/Withholding	Oliver	Rhett	Emelia
Hours if applicable	n/a	n/a	80
Annual salary or hourly rate	$ 85,000	$ 60,000	$ 35.00
Gross pay	3,541.67	2,500.00	2,800.00
Federal withholding	485.22	342.50	383.60
Social security employee (6.2%)	219.58	155.00	173.60
Medicare employee (1.45%)	51.35	36.25	40.60
Employee withholding	756.15	533.75	597.80
Social security employer (6.2%)	219.59	155.00	173.60
Medicare company employer (1.45%)	51.38	36.28	40.60
Employer payroll tax expense	270.97	191.28	214.20
Net Check amount	2,785.52	1,966.25	2,202.20

5 Use the recurring transactions templates you created above to help you record payroll (as you did in the chapter) for 1/31/23 based on the information shown in Figure 7.30 using checks 598, 599, and 600.

Figure 7.30

Payroll information for 1/31/23

Pay/Tax/Withholding	Oliver	Rhett	Emelia
Hours if applicable	n/a	n/a	75
Annual salary or hourly rate	$ 85,000	$ 60,000	$ 35.00
Gross pay	3,541.67	2,500.00	2,625.00
Federal withholding	485.22	342.50	359.63
Social security employee (6.2%)	219.58	155.00	162.75
Medicare employee (1.45%)	51.35	36.25	38.06
Employee withholding	756.15	533.75	560.44
Social security employer (6.2%)	219.59	155.00	162.75
Medicare company employer (1.45%)	51.38	36.28	38.06
Employer payroll tax expense	270.97	191.28	200.81
Net Check amount	2,785.52	1,966.25	2,064.56

6 Prepare and print the Trial Balance 1/31/23 report you saved previously. Your report should look like Figure 7.31.

Case 06 - Student Name (ID Number)		
TRIAL BALANCE		
As of January 31, 2023		
	DEBIT	CREDIT
Checking	64,336.82	
Accounts Receivable (A/R)	153,020.00	
Inventory Asset	524,000.00	
Inventory Parts	4,000.00	
Investments	12,000.00	
Loans To Officers	15,000.00	
Prepaid Expenses	18,000.00	
Undeposited Funds	0.00	
Buildings:Depreciation		15,000.00
Buildings:Original cost	150,000.00	
Computers	8,000.00	
Machinery & Equipment	12,000.00	
Machinery & Equipment:Depreciation		10,000.00
Machinery & Equipment:Original cost	100,000.00	
Accounts Payable (A/P)		524,000.00
AMEX		6,000.00
Payroll Tax Payable		5,077.55
Washington State Department of Revenue Payable		26,970.00
Notes Payable		128,857.12
Common Stock		1,100.00
Opening Balance Equity		0.00
Paid-In Capital		259,900.00
Retained Earnings		60,500.00
Sales of Product Income		290,000.00
Cost of Goods Sold	232,000.00	
Advertising & Marketing	14,000.00	
Contractors	1,800.00	
Interest Expense	400.00	
Payroll	18,847.85	
TOTAL	**$1,327,404.67**	**$1,327,404.67**

Figure 7.31

Trial Balance as of 1/31/23

7 Investigate differences between your trial balance and the trial balance shown above.

8 If necessary, prepare and print the Transaction Detail by Account report you saved previously to investigate identified differences.

a. Make sure all your changes were dated in January 2023.

b. Click on the line that does not match to view the transaction for that account and investigate why your answer differs.

c. Ask your instructor for assistance.

d. Be sure your company matches the above as you will be adding additional business events in Chapter 8.

Establishing Budgets and Preparing Bank Reconciliations

Student Learning Outcomes

Upon completion of this chapter, the student will be able to do the following:

- Add budget amounts to create a budget
- Create Profit and Loss budget reports
- Reconcile a checking account and print a reconciliation report

Overview

In Chapter 7, you added payroll activities like adding employees, adding payroll-related accounts, and recording payroll expenses and liabilities to your Wild Water Sports company. In this chapter, you will add a budget, add a Profit and Loss budget report, and add a bank reconciliation to your Wild Water Sports company. At the end of this chapter, you will perform the similar tasks on the case assigned by your instructor.

To verify the accuracy of your Wild Water Sports company:

1   Sign into your QBO account then open the Wild Water Sports company you used in Chapter 7.

2   Click **Reports**, then click the **Custom reports** tab, then double-click **Trial Balance** to open the Trial Balance report. Set the from and to dates to **1/1/27** and **1/31/27** respectively. Compare your report to Figure 8.1. If your report doesn't match Figure 8.1, go back to your work in Chapter 7 to fix your errors. Otherwise, close your Trial Balance report.

Wild Water Sports - Student Name (ID Number)		
Trial Balance		
As of January 31, 2027		
	DEBIT	**CREDIT**
Checking	99,358.88	
Accounts receivable (A/R)	120,770.00	
Inventory	223,350.00	
Payments to deposit	70,000.00	
Prepaid expenses	17,500.00	
Equipment:Accumulated depreciation		10,000.00
Equipment:Original Cost	53,000.00	
Furniture:Original cost	10,000.00	
Investments	3,000.00	
Accounts Payable (A/P)		190,250.00
Mastercard		1,600.00
Florida Department of Revenue Payable		9,915.00
Payroll wages and tax to pay		2,944.66
Long-term business loans		155,000.00
Common stock		11,000.00
Opening balance equity		0.00
Retained Earnings		204,300.00
Sales		164,000.00
Service Revenue		2,000.00
Cost of goods sold	131,200.00	
Interest paid	2,500.00	
Payroll expenses	10,930.78	
Rent:Equipment rental	6,000.00	
Utilities:Phone service	1,800.00	
Vehicle expenses:Vehicle gas & fuel	1,600.00	
TOTAL	$751,009.66	$751,009.66

Figure 8.1

Wild Water Sports trial balance as of 1/31/27

Budget Creation

In this section, you will be establishing a Profit and Loss budget in QBO, which tracks amounts in income and expense accounts. QBO will interview you to determine budget amounts. You will be creating your budget from scratch since you have no historical amounts in QBO.

To create a Profit and Loss budget for the Wild Water Sports company, do the following:

1 Continue from above.

2 Make sure the navigation bar is open.

3 Click the **Gear** icon, and select **Budgeting** as shown in Figure 8.2.

Figure 8.2

Budgeting window (accessing the budgeting process)

4   Click **Add budget**.

5   Select **FY2027 (Jan 2027–Dec 2027)** from the Fiscal Year drop-down list, and type **Budget 1** as the Budget name.

6   Click **Next**.

7   Click in the JAN **Sales** account.

8   Type **180000** in the Jan text box, and then place your cursor over the Copy Across button as shown in Figure 8.3.

Figure 8.3

Budget worksheet

Budget 1				
Name *				
Budget 1				
ACCOUNTS	**JAN**	**FEB**	**MAR**	**APR**
▾ INCOME				
Billable Expense Income				
Discounts given				
Sales	180000 ❯			
Sales of Product Income				
Sales Parts				
Service Revenue				

Click to copy the value across on the row

9   Click the **Copy Across** button to view Figure 8.4.

ACCOUNTS	JAN	FEB	MAR	APR	MAY	JUN	JUL	AUG	SEP	OCT	NOV	DEC	TOTAL
▾ INCOME													
Billable Expense Income													
Discounts given													
Sales	180,000.00	180,000.00	180,000.00	180,000.00	180,000.00	180,000.00	180,000.00	180,000.00	180,000.00	180,000.00	180,000.00	180,000.00	2,160,000.

Figure 8.4

Budget worksheet for Sales

10   Type **5000** in the Jan Service Revenue text box. Copy across the Service Revenue amount for the entire year and then click **Save**.

11   Click the **Gear** icon in the budget window then select **Year** to view by year. Place a check in the **Hide blank rows** check box and then place a check in the **Compact** check box under Display density. Your newly entered amounts are shown in Figure 8.5.

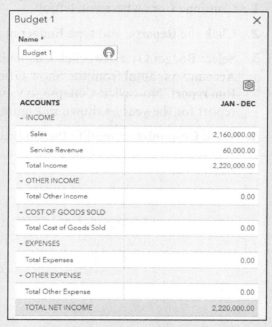

ACCOUNTS	JAN - DEC
▾ INCOME	
Sales	2,160,000.00
Service Revenue	60,000.00
Total Income	2,220,000.00
▾ OTHER INCOME	
Total Other Income	0.00
▾ COST OF GOODS SOLD	
Total Cost of Goods Sold	0.00
▾ EXPENSES	
Total Expenses	0.00
▾ OTHER EXPENSE	
Total Other Expense	0.00
TOTAL NET INCOME	2,220,000.00

Budget 1

Name *
Budget 1

Figure 8.5

Budget worksheet for annual Income

12   Click the **Gear** icon again and then click **Month** to change the view by to Month and uncheck the **Hide blank rows** check box.

13   Scroll down the budget worksheet, and type additional January amounts for cost of goods sold: **135000**, advertising & marketing **10000**, interest paid **2500**, payroll expenses **11000**, equipment rental **5000**, Supplies **3000**, Internet & TV services **4000**, phone service **2000**, and vehicle gas & fuel **1000**. Copy across each amount entered for the entire year. Click the **Gear** icon in the budget window then select **Year** to view by year. Place a check in the **Hide blank rows** check box.

14   Click **Save and close**.

You have entered budgeted amounts and stored them in QBO. Now, view budget reports.

Budget Reports

QBO has two basic budget-related reports: Budget Overview and Budget vs. Actual. The overview report only lists budget data. The Budget vs. Actual lists budget data compared to actual transactions inputted into QBO.

To view budget reports in the Wild Water Sports company, do the following:

1 Continue from where you left off.

2 Click the **Reports**, and type **Budget** in the Find report by name text box.

3 Select **Budget Overview**, click **Customize**, click **Rows/Columns**, select **Accounts vs. Total** from the Show Grid drop-down list, and then click **Run report**. Now click **Collapse** to view the collapsed Budget Overview report for the year as shown in Figure 8.6.

4 Click **Customize** to modify the Budget Overview report.

Figure 8.6

Budget Overview (collapsed report)

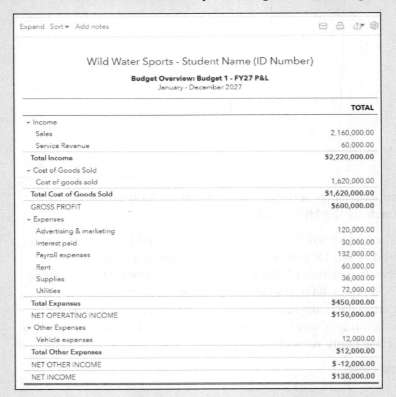

Expand Sort ▼ Add notes

Wild Water Sports - Student Name (ID Number)

Budget Overview: Budget 1 - FY27 P&L
January - December 2027

	TOTAL
▾ Income	
Sales	2,160,000.00
Service Revenue	60,000.00
Total Income	$2,220,000.00
▾ Cost of Goods Sold	
Cost of goods sold	1,620,000.00
Total Cost of Goods Sold	$1,620,000.00
GROSS PROFIT	$600,000.00
▾ Expenses	
Advertising & marketing	120,000.00
Interest paid	30,000.00
Payroll expenses	132,000.00
Rent	60,000.00
Supplies	36,000.00
Utilities	72,000.00
Total Expenses	$450,000.00
NET OPERATING INCOME	$150,000.00
▾ Other Expenses	
Vehicle expenses	12,000.00
Total Other Expenses	$12,000.00
NET OTHER INCOME	$ -12,000.00
NET INCOME	$138,000.00

5   Check the **Without cents** check box as shown in Figure 8.7.

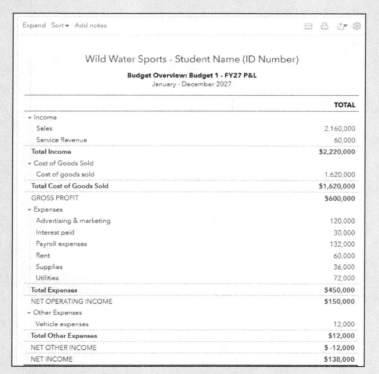

Figure 8.7

Customizing Budget Overview

6   Click **Run report** to view the customized Budget Overview report as shown in Figure 8.8.

Figure 8.8

Budget Overview
(customized report)

Wild Water Sports - Student Name (ID Number)

Budget Overview: Budget 1 - FY27 P&L
January - December 2027

	TOTAL
▾ Income	
Sales	2,160,000
Service Revenue	60,000
Total Income	**$2,220,000**
▾ Cost of Goods Sold	
Cost of goods sold	1,620,000
Total Cost of Goods Sold	**$1,620,000**
GROSS PROFIT	$600,000
▾ Expenses	
Advertising & marketing	120,000
Interest paid	30,000
Payroll expenses	132,000
Rent	60,000
Supplies	36,000
Utilities	72,000
Total Expenses	**$450,000**
NET OPERATING INCOME	$150,000
▾ Other Expenses	
Vehicle expenses	12,000
Total Other Expenses	**$12,000**
NET OTHER INCOME	$ -12,000
NET INCOME	$138,000

7   Click **Save customization**, type **Budget Overview** in the Custom report name text box, and then click **Save**.

8   Click **Reports**, once again type **Budget** into the Find report by name text box, and then select **Budget vs. Actuals** from the list of recommended reports.

9   Click **Collapse**.

10 Click **Customize** to modify the Budget vs. Actuals report.

11 Change the From: and To: dates to **1/1/27** and **1/31/27**, respectively.

12 Click **Rows/Columns**, select **Accounts vs. Total** in the drop-down list in the Show Grid text box, and then check the **Without cents** check box as shown in Figure 8.9.

Figure 8.9

Customizing Budget vs. Actuals

13 Click **Run report**. A partial view of the customized Budget vs. Actuals report is shown in Figure 8.10. Note: Your actual and budget amounts should match this figure.

Figure 8.10

Budget vs. Actual report

Wild Water Sports - Student Name (ID Number)

Budget vs. Actuals: Budget 1 - FY27 P&L

January 2027

			TOTAL		
	ACTUAL	BUDGET	OVER BUDGET	% OF BUDGET
▼ Income				
Sales	164,000	180,000	-16,000	91.00 %
Service Revenue	2,000	5,000	-3,000	40.00 %
Total Income	**$166,000**	**$185,000**	**$ -19,000**	**90.00 %**
▼ Cost of Goods Sold				
Cost of goods sold	131,200	135,000	-3,800	97.00 %
Total Cost of Goods Sold	**$131,200**	**$135,000**	**$ -3,800**	**97.00 %**
GROSS PROFIT	$34,800	$50,000	$ -15,200	70.00 %
▼ Expenses				
Advertising & marketing		10,000	-10,000	
Interest paid	2,500	2,500	0	100.00 %
Payroll expenses	10,931	11,000	-69	99.00 %
Rent	6,000	5,000	1,000	120.00 %
Supplies		3,000	-3,000	
Utilities	1,800	6,000	-4,200	30.00 %
Total Expenses	**$21,231**	**$37,500**	**$ -16,269**	**57.00 %**
NET OPERATING INCOME	$13,569	$12,500	$1,069	109.00 %
▼ Other Expenses				
Vehicle expenses	1,600	1,000	600	160.00 %
Total Other Expenses	**$1,600**	**$1,000**	**$600**	**160.00 %**
NET OTHER INCOME	$ -1,600	$ -1,000	$ -600	160.00 %
NET INCOME	$11,969	$11,500	$469	104.00 %

14 Click **Save customization**, type **Budget vs. Actuals** in the Custom report name text box, and then click **Save**.

Bank Reconciliation

Good internal control requires frequent reconciliations between bank records and a company's records of cash receipts and payments completed by someone other than the accountant or bookkeeper who is responsible for maintaining accounting records. The process involves comparing items that appear in the checking account with those items appearing on the bank statement. Deposits that appear in the checking account but do not appear on the bank statement are referred to as deposits in transit. Checks that appear in the checking account but do not appear on the bank statement are referred to as outstanding checks. They usually appear as checks on the next bank statement.

In QBO, if you discover a deposit recorded by the bank but not recorded in the checking account (determined to be an error in the checking account), you should correct the checking account by recording the deposit. Likewise, if you discover a check recorded by the bank but not recorded in the checking account (determined to be an error in the checking account), you should correct the checking account by recording the check. In the following example, neither was identified.

To create reconciliation for the Wild Water Sports company, do the following:

1 Continue from above.

2 Make sure the navigation bar is open.

3 Click the **Gear** icon, and select **Reconcile** as shown in Figure 8.11.

Figure 8.11

Reconciliation process (access)

TOOLS

Order checks

Import data

Import desktop data

Export data

Reconcile

Budgeting

Audit log

SmartLook

Case center

4 Click **Get Started**, click **Let's get reconciled**, and then make sure the **Checking** account is selected in the Reconcile window as shown in Figure 8.12.

Figure 8.12

Reconcile window

Reconcile

Which account do you want to reconcile?

Account

Checking

Add the following information

Beginning balance	Ending balance *	Ending date *
25,000.00		

Enter the service charge or interest earned, if necessary

Date	Service charge	Expense account
	0.00	Account

Date	Interest earned	Income account
	0.00	Account

Start reconciling

5 Type **1/31/2027** as the Ending date and type **103396.77** as the Ending balance.

6 Click **Start reconciling**.

7 The Reconcile—Checking form shown in Figure 8.13 should appear. Note: The column widths in this figure have been adjusted.

Figure 8.13

Partial view of the Reconcile—Checking form

8 After a review of the company's most recent bank statement and a comparison with the company's checking account, you discover some checks and payments recorded in the checking account that did not appear on the bank statement. Click the **Payments** tab. Place a check next to all checks and payments *except* for checks 1011, 1012, and 1013, none of which had cleared the bank.

9 After a review of the company's most recent bank statement and a comparison with the company's checking account, you discover some deposits and other credits recorded in the checking account that did not appear on the bank statement. Click the **Deposits** tab. Place a check next to all deposits and other credits.

10 Click the **All** tab. Your account is reconciled as shown by the 0 difference between the Statement Ending Balance and the Cleared Balance as shown in Figure 8.14.

Figure 8.14

Reconcile—Checking form (reconciled account)

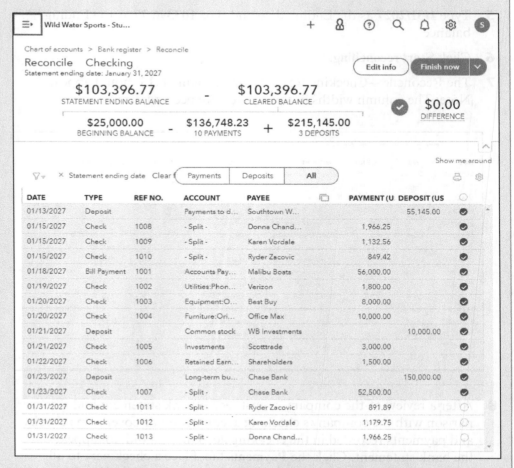

11 Once you have reconciled the checking account and the $0 difference is displayed, click **Finish now** and then click **Done**.

12 Click the text **History by account**. A summary of all reconciliation reports completed should appear as shown in Figure 8.15.

Figure 8.15

Reconcile (reconciliation summary)

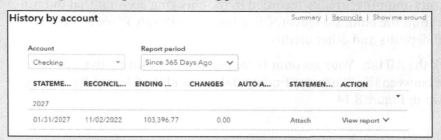

13 Click **View report** to view the reconciliation report. Place a check in the **Hide additional information** check box. The upper summary portion of that report is shown in Figure 8.16.

Figure 8.16

Summary Reconciliation Report

Wild Water Sports - Student Name (ID Number)
Checking, Period Ending 01/31/2027

RECONCILIATION REPORT

Reconciled on: 11/02/2022

Reconciled by: Sample Student

Any changes made to transactions after this date aren't included in this report.

Summary	USD
Statement beginning balance	25,000.00
Checks and payments cleared (10)	-136,748.23
Deposits and other credits cleared (3)	215,145.00
Statement ending balance	103,396.77
Uncleared transactions as of 01/31/2027	-4,037.89
Register balance as of 01/31/2027	99,358.88

Details

Checks and payments cleared (10)

DATE	TYPE	REF NO.	PAYEE	AMOUNT (USD)
01/15/2027	Check	1008	Donna Chandler	-1,966.25
01/15/2027	Check	1009	Karen Vordale	-1,132.56
01/15/2027	Check	1010	Ryder Zacovic	-849.42
01/18/2027	Bill Payment	1001	Malibu Boats	-56,000.00
01/19/2027	Check	1002	Verizon	-1,800.00
01/20/2027	Check	1004	Office Max	-10,000.00
01/20/2027	Check	1003	Best Buy	-8,000.00
01/21/2027	Check	1005	Scotttrade	-3,000.00
01/22/2027	Check	1006	Shareholders	-1,500.00

14 Click the **Printer** icon, click **Print**, and click **Close** to print the report
and close its window.

End Note

In this chapter, you created a Profit and Loss budget for 12 months, prepared a
Budget Overview report and Budget vs. Actual report, and reconciled your checking account. In the next chapter, you will work with adjusting journal entries.

Chapter 8 Questions

1 What are the steps to create a Profit and Loss budget?

2 What value do budgets provide a business?

3 Why should a business reconcile a checking account?

4 Who should prepare a bank reconciliation?

5 Explain the difference between the Budget Overview report and the Budget vs. Actual report.

6 What button is used to replicate amounts across several months in the budget worksheet?

7 How do you know if you have correctly reconciled an account?

8 What are the steps to change a Budget Overview report from covering a year to covering just one month?

9 What should you do if you discover a deposit was recorded by the bank but not recorded in the checking account (determined to be an error in the checking account)?

10 What are the initial steps to begin a bank reconciliation?

Chapter 8 Matching

a. Budget Overview report

b. Budget vs. Actual report

c. Deposits in transit

d. Outstanding checks

e. Collapse

f. Customize

_____ Condenses a report

_____ Do not appear on the bank statement

_____ Used to change report dates

_____ Includes only budget amounts

_____ Usually appear as checks on the next bank statement

_____ Includes both budget and actual amounts

Chapter 8 Cases

The following cases require you to open the company you updated in Chapter 7. Each of the following cases continues throughout the text in a sequential manner. For example, if you are assigned Case 01, you will use the file you modified in this chapter in all following chapters. Each of the following cases is similar in concepts assessed but differs in amounts and transactions.

To reopen your company, do the following:

1 Open your Internet browser.

2 Type **https://qbo.intuit.com** into your browser's address text box.

3 Type your user ID and password into the text boxes as you have done before.

Case 1

Now it is time to create a budget and reconcile a bank account. Based on what you learned in the text using the Wild Water Sports company, you are to make the following changes to the Case 1 company you modified in Chapter 7:

1   Add an invoice on 1/30/24 to customer: Blondie's Boards, terms: Net 30, for 4 Fred Rubbles, 7 Water Hogs, and 8 Rook 15 surfboards.

2   Add an invoice on 1/31/24 to a new customer: Surf Rider Foundation, terms: Net 30, for 100 hours of consulting.

3   Create a new budget titled "Budget 1." Be sure to select FY 2024 (Jan 2024–Dec 2024) from the Fiscal Year drop-down list in the new budget window. Enter the following budgeted amounts: sales: 40000, services: 3000, cost of goods sold: 23500, interest expense: 600, payroll: 12000, rent or lease: 2500, travel: 500, and utilities: 200. Amounts provided should be input for each month of 2024.

4   Create and customize, save customization as Budget Overview Budget 1, print, and export to Excel a Budget Overview report for the month of January 2024. Your report should look like Figure 8.17.

Figure 8.17

Budget Overview (January 2024)

Case 1
BUDGET OVERVIEW: BUDGET 1 - FY24 P&L
January 2024

	TOTAL
Income	
Sales	40,000.00
Services	3,000.00
Total Income	**$43,000.00**
Cost of Goods Sold	
Cost of Goods Sold	23,500.00
Total Cost of Goods Sold	**$23,500.00**
Gross Profit	**$19,500.00**
Expenses	
Interest Expense	600.00
Payroll	12,000.00
Rent or Lease	2,500.00
Travel	500.00
Utilities	200.00
Total Expenses	**$15,800.00**
Net Operating Income	**$3,700.00**
Net Income	**$3,700.00**

5   Create and customize, save customization as Budget vs. Actual Budget 1, print, and export to Excel a Budget vs. Actuals report for the month of January 2024. Your report should look like Figure 8.18.

Figure 8.18

Budget vs. Actuals (January 2024)

Case 1
BUDGET VS. ACTUALS: BUDGET 1 - FY24 P&L
January 2024

	TOTAL			
	ACTUAL	BUDGET	OVER BUDGET	% OF BUDGET
Income				
Sales	17,180.00	40,000.00	-22,820.00	42.95 %
Services	2,670.00	3,000.00	-330.00	89.00 %
Total Income	$19,850.00	$43,000.00	$ -23,150.00	46.16 %
Cost of Goods Sold				
Cost of Goods Sold	10,400.00	23,500.00	-13,100.00	44.26 %
Total Cost of Goods Sold	$10,400.00	$23,500.00	$ -13,100.00	44.26 %
Gross Profit	$9,450.00	$19,500.00	$ -10,050.00	48.46 %
Expenses				
Interest Expense	600.00	600.00	0.00	100.00 %
Payroll	11,785.71	12,000.00	-214.29	98.21 %
Rent or Lease	2,500.00	2,500.00	0.00	100.00 %
Travel	1,800.00	500.00	1,300.00	360.00 %
Utilities	145.00	200.00	-55.00	72.50 %
Total Expenses	$16,830.71	$15,800.00	$1,030.71	106.52 %
Net Operating Income	$ -7,380.71	$3,700.00	$ -11,080.71	-199.48 %
Net Income	$ -7,380.71	$3,700.00	$ -11,080.71	-199.48 %

6   Open and print the custom report you created in the last chapter called Transaction Detail by Account.

7   Export your Transactions Detail by Account report to Excel, and save it with the file name Student Name (replace with your name) Ch 08 Case 01 Transaction Detail by Account.xlsx.

8   Reconcile your company's checking account. No service charges were incurred or interest earned. The ending bank statement balance on 1/31/24 was $29,202.37.

9   After a review of the company's most recent bank statement and a comparison with the company's checking account, you discover some checks and payments recorded in the checking account that did not appear on the bank statement. Place a check next to all checks and payments *except* for check 1009 to Ben Franklin for 3,113.22 and check 1010 to Betsy Ross for 1,149.87, neither of which had cleared the bank.

10   After a review of the company's most recent bank statement and a comparison with the company's checking account, you discover some deposits and other credits recorded in the checking account that did not appear on the bank statement. Place a check next to all deposits and other credits *except* for a deposit on 1/8/24 from Blondie's Boards for 1,300, which had not cleared the bank.

11   Print the resulting Reconciliation Report. Select **All dates** from the Report Period drop-down text box, then click **2024**, and then click **View Report** on the statement ending date 01/31/24 line.

12   Sign out of your company.

Case 2

Now it is time to create a budget and reconcile a bank account. Based on what you learned in the text using the Wild Water Sports company, you are to make the following changes to the Case 2 company you modified in Chapter 7:

1   Add an invoice on 1/30/25 to customer: Hagen's Toys, terms: Net 30, for 100 hours of custom painting.

2   Add an invoice on 1/31/25 to a new customer: Zack's RC, terms: Net 30, for 2 Sea Wind Carbon Sailboats and 2 Mystique RES.

3   Create a new budget titled "Budget 1." Be sure to select FY 2025 (Jan 2025–Dec 2025) from the Fiscal Year drop-down list in the new budget window. Enter the following budgeted amounts: sales: 10,000, services: 4,000, cost of goods sold: 5,000, advertising: 500, insurance: 425, interest expense: 300, meals and entertainment: 250, and payroll: 9,000. Amounts provided should be input for each month of 2025.

4   Create and customize, save customization as Budget Overview Budget 1, print, and export to Excel a Budget Overview report for the month of January 2025. Your report should look like Figure 8.19.

Figure 8.19

Budget Overview (January 2025)

Case 2
BUDGET OVERVIEW: BUDGET 1 - FY25 P&L
January 2025

	TOTAL
Income	
Sales	10,000.00
Services	4,000.00
Total Income	**$14,000.00**
Cost of Goods Sold	
Cost of Goods Sold	5,000.00
Total Cost of Goods Sold	**$5,000.00**
Gross Profit	**$9,000.00**
Expenses	
Advertising	500.00
Insurance	425.00
Interest Expense	300.00
Meals and Entertainment	250.00
Payroll	9,000.00
Total Expenses	**$10,475.00**
Net Operating Income	**$ -1,475.00**
Net Income	**$ -1,475.00**

5   Create and customize, save customization as Budget vs. Actuals Budget 1, print, and export to Excel a Budget vs. Actuals report for the month of January 2025. Your report should look like Figure 8.20.

Figure 8.20

Budget vs. Actuals (January 2025)

Case 2
BUDGET VS. ACTUALS: BUDGET 1 - FY25 P&L
January 2025

	ACTUAL	BUDGET	OVER BUDGET	% OF BUDGET
Income				
Sales	9,000.00	10,000.00	-1,000.00	90.00 %
Services	4,725.00	4,000.00	725.00	118.13 %
Total Income	**$13,725.00**	**$14,000.00**	**$ -275.00**	**98.04 %**
Cost of Goods Sold				
Cost of Goods Sold	4,910.00	5,000.00	-90.00	98.20 %
Total Cost of Goods Sold	**$4,910.00**	**$5,000.00**	**$ -90.00**	**98.20 %**
Gross Profit	**$8,815.00**	**$9,000.00**	**$ -185.00**	**97.94 %**
Expenses				
Advertising	500.00	500.00	0.00	100.00 %
Insurance	400.00	425.00	-25.00	94.12 %
Interest Expense	300.00	300.00	0.00	100.00 %
Meals and Entertainment	240.00	250.00	-10.00	96.00 %
Payroll	9,224.26	9,000.00	224.26	102.49 %
Total Expenses	**$10,664.26**	**$10,475.00**	**$189.26**	**101.81 %**
Net Operating Income	**$ -1,849.26**	**$ -1,475.00**	**$ -374.26**	**125.37 %**
Net Income	**$ -1,849.26**	**$ -1,475.00**	**$ -374.26**	**125.37 %**

6   Open and print the custom report you created in the last chapter called Transaction Detail by Account.

7   Export your Transactions Detail by Account report to Excel, and save it with the file name Student Name (replace with your name) Ch 08 Case 02 Transaction Detail by Account.xlsx.

8   Reconcile your company's checking account. No service charges were incurred or interest earned. The ending bank statement balance on 1/31/25 was $30,693.47.

9   After a review of the company's most recent bank statement and a comparison with the company's checking account, you discover some checks and payments recorded in the checking account that did not appear on the bank statement. Place a check next to all checks and payments *except* for check 1009 to Frank Benjamin for 2,359.50 and check 1010 to Sara Juarez for 973.29, neither of which had cleared the bank.

10   After a review of the company's most recent bank statement and a comparison with the company's checking account, you discover a deposit and other credit recorded in the checking account that did not appear on the bank statement. Place a check next to all deposits and other credits *except* for a deposit on 1/7/25 from Benson's RC for 4,500, which had not cleared the bank.

11   Print the resulting Reconciliation Report. Select **All dates** from the Report Period drop-down text box, then click **2025**, and then click **View Report** on the statement ending date 01/31/25 line.

12   Sign out of your company.

Case 3

Now it is time to create a budget and reconcile a bank account. Based on what you learned in the text using the Wild Water Sports company, you are to make the following changes to the Case 3 company you modified in Chapter 7:

1   Add the following bill and product received from Samsung, Inc. on 1/30/26, terms: Net 15, received 5 Samsung Galaxy 8 and 8 Samsung Note phones.

2   Add an invoice on 1/30/26 to a new taxable customer: Diamond Girl, Inc., terms: Net 30, for 4 Samsung Galaxy 8 and 5 Samsung Note phones and 6 hours of Phone Consulting. Click **See the math** to update sales tax amounts.

3   Add a payment received from GHO Marketing on 1/31/26 for $2,559.38, which was deposited the same day into the checking account.

4   Create a new budget titled "Budget 1." Be sure to select FY 2026 (Jan 2026–Dec 2026) from the Fiscal Year drop-down list in the new budget window. Enter the following budgeted amounts: sales of product income: 20,000, services: 1,000, cost of goods sold: 10,000, advertising & marketing: 1,000, insurance: 500, interest paid: 350, meals: 250, and payroll: 7,000. Amounts provided should be input for each month of 2026.

5   Create a Budget Overview report for January 2026. Customize your report to show accounts vs. totals. Save customization as Budget Overview. Your report should look like Figure 8.21.

Case 03 - Student Name (ID Number)	
Budget Overview: Budget 1 - FY26 P&L January 2026	
	TOTAL
▾ Income	
Sales of Product Income	20,000.00
Services	1,000.00
Total Income	**$21,000.00**
▾ Cost of Goods Sold	
Cost of goods sold	10,000.00
Total Cost of Goods Sold	**$10,000.00**
GROSS PROFIT	**$11,000.00**
▾ Expenses	
Advertising & marketing	1,000.00
Insurance	500.00
Interest paid	350.00
Meals	250.00
Payroll	7,000.00
Total Expenses	**$9,100.00**
NET OPERATING INCOME	**$1,900.00**
NET INCOME	**$1,900.00**

Figure 8.21

Budget Overview (January 2026)

6   Create a Budget vs. Actuals report for the month of January 2026. Customize and save your report to show accounts vs. totals without cents. Your report should look like Figure 8.22.

Figure 8.22

Budget vs. Actuals for January 2026

Case 03 - Student Name (ID Number)

Budget vs. Actuals: Budget 1 - FY26 P&L

January 2026

	ACTUAL	BUDGET	OVER BUDGET	% OF BUDGET
			TOTAL	
▾ Income				
Sales of Product Income	12,800	20,000	-7,200	64.00 %
Services	450	1,000	-550	45.00 %
Total Income	**$13,250**	**$21,000**	**$ -7,750**	**63.00 %**
▾ Cost of Goods Sold				
Cost of goods sold	9,150	10,000	-850	92.00 %
Total Cost of Goods Sold	**$9,150**	**$10,000**	**$ -850**	**92.00 %**
GROSS PROFIT	**$4,100**	**$11,000**	**$ -6,900**	**37.00 %**
▾ Expenses				
Advertising & marketing	1,300	1,000	300	130.00 %
Insurance	300	500	-200	60.00 %
Interest paid	300	350	-50	86.00 %
Meals	123	250	-127	49.00 %
Payroll	6,960	7,000	-40	99.00 %
Total Expenses	**$8,983**	**$9,100**	**$ -117**	**99.00 %**
NET OPERATING INCOME	$ -4,883	$1,900	$ -6,783	-257.00 %
NET INCOME	$ -4,883	$1,900	$ -6,783	-257.00 %

7   Reconcile your company's checking account. No service charges were incurred or interest earned. The ending bank statement balance on 1/31/26 was $51,669.82.

8   After a review of the company's most recent statement and a comparison with the company's checking account, you note that one check and one deposit that were recorded in the checking account did not appear on the bank statement. Place a check next to all checks and payments *except* for check 329 to Jedi Vu for 1,002.78 and the deposit from GHO Marketing for 2,559.38, which had not cleared the bank.

9   Print the resulting Reconciliation Report after hiding additional information.

10 Sign out of your company.

Case 4

Now it is time to create a budget and reconcile a bank account. Based on what you learned in the text using the Wild Water Sports company, you are to make the following changes to the Case 4 company you modified in Chapter 7:

1. Create a new budget titled "Budget 1." Be sure to select FY 2027 (Jan 2027–Dec 2027) from the Fiscal Year drop-down list in the new budget window. Enter the following budgeted amounts for 2027: sales: 50,000, sales of product income: 4,000, cost of goods sold: 1,500, advertising & marketing: 2,400, insurance: 2,000, interest paid: 300, payroll expense: 15,000, and repairs & maintenance: $500. Amounts provided should be input for each month of 2027.

2. Create, customize (save customization as Budget Overview), and print a Budget Overview report for the month of January 2027 without cents showing accounts vs. totals. Your report should look like Figure 8.23.

Figure 8.23

Budget Overview for January 2027

Case 04 - Student Name (ID Number)

Budget Overview: Budget 1 - FY27 P&L

January 2027

	TOTAL
▾ Income	
Sales	50,000
Sales of Product Income	4,000
Total Income	**$54,000**
▾ Cost of Goods Sold	
Cost of goods sold	1,500
Total Cost of Goods Sold	**$1,500**
GROSS PROFIT	$52,500
▾ Expenses	
Advertising & marketing	2,400
Insurance	2,000
Interest paid	300
Payroll expenses	15,000
Repairs & maintenance	500
Total Expenses	**$20,200**
NET OPERATING INCOME	$32,300
NET INCOME	$32,300

3. Create, customize (save customization as Budget vs. Actuals), and print a Budget vs. Actuals report for the month of January 2027 without cents showing accounts vs. totals. Your report should look like Figure 8.24.

Figure 8.24

Budget vs. Actuals for
January 2027

Case 04 - Student Name (ID Number)

Budget vs. Actuals: Budget 1 - FY27 P&L
January 2027

	ACTUAL	BUDGET	OVER BUDGET	% OF BUDGET
			TOTAL	
▾ Income				
Sales	48,400	50,000	-1,600	97.00 %
Sales of Product Income	3,570	4,000	-430	89.00 %
Total Income	$51,970	$54,000	$ -2,030	96.00 %
▾ Cost of Goods Sold				
Cost of goods sold	1,632	1,500	132	109.00 %
Total Cost of Goods Sold	$1,632	$1,500	$132	109.00 %
GROSS PROFIT	$50,338	$52,500	$ -2,162	96.00 %
▾ Expenses				
Advertising & marketing	1,800	2,400	-600	75.00 %
Insurance	2,400	2,000	400	120.00 %
Interest paid	120	300	-180	40.00 %
Payroll expenses	14,680	15,000	-320	98.00 %
Repairs & maintenance	750	500	250	150.00 %
Total Expenses	$19,750	$20,200	$ -450	98.00 %
NET OPERATING INCOME	$30,588	$32,300	$ -1,712	95.00 %
NET INCOME	$30,588	$32,300	$ -1,712	95.00 %

4   Reconcile your company's checking account. No service charges were incurred or interest earned. The ending bank statement balance on 1/31/27 was $10,936.20.

5   After a review of the company's most recent statement and a comparison with the company's checking account, you note that a $10,000 deposit on 1/26/27 and checks 25509 and 25510 (for $1,376.37 and $1,522.67 respectfully) had not cleared the bank.

6   Print the resulting Reconciliation Report (hide additional information).

7   Sign out of your company.

Case 5

Now it is time to create a budget and reconcile a bank account. Based on what you learned in the text using the Wild Water Sports company, you are to make the following changes to the Case 5 company you modified in Chapter 7:

1   Create a new budget titled "Budget 1." Be sure to select FY 2022 (Jan 2022–Dec 2022) from the Fiscal Year drop-down list in the new budget window. Enter the following budgeted amounts for January 2022: consulting: 75,000, sales: 500,000, training: 4,000, cost of goods sold: 250,000, advertising & marketing: 3,500, equipment rental: 8,000, insurance: 6,000, interest expense: 4,000, payroll: 30,000, recruiting: 4,000, and repairs & maintenance: $2,500. Amounts provided should be copied for each month of 2022.

2 Create, customize (save customization as Budget Overview), and print a Budget Overview report for the month of January 2022 without cents showing accounts vs. totals. Your report should look like Figure 8.25.

Case 05 - Student Name (ID Number)

BUDGET OVERVIEW: BUDGET 1 - FY22 P&L
January 2022

	TOTAL
▼ Income	
Consulting	75,000
Sales	500,000
Training	4,000
Total Income	**$579,000**
▼ Cost of Goods Sold	
Cost of Goods Sold	250,000
Total Cost of Goods Sold	**$250,000**
GROSS PROFIT	$329,000
▼ Expenses	
Advertising & Marketing	3,500
Equipment Rental	8,000
Insurance	6,000
Interest Expense	4,000
Payroll	30,000
Recruiting	4,000
Repairs & Maintenance	2,500
Total Expenses	**$58,000**
NET OPERATING INCOME	$271,000
NET INCOME	$271,000

Figure 8.25

Budget Overview for January 2022

---

3 Create, customize (save customization as Budget vs. Actuals), and print a Budget vs. Actuals report for the month of January 2022 without cents showing accounts vs. totals. Your report should look like Figure 8.26.

4 Reconcile your company's checking account. No service charges were incurred or interest earned. The ending bank statement balance on 1/31/22 was $194,109.76.

5 After a review of the company's most recent statement and a comparison with the company's checking account, you note that a $80,000 deposit on 1/26/22 and all checks written on 1/31/22 had not cleared the bank.

Figure 8.26

Budget vs. Actuals for
January 2022

Case 05 - Student Name (ID Number)

BUDGET VS. ACTUALS: BUDGET 1 - FY22 P&L

January 2022

	TOTAL			
	ACTUAL	BUDGET	OVER BUDGET	% OF BUDGET
Income				
Consulting	79,500	75,000	4,500	106.00 %
Sales	615,000	500,000	115,000	123.00 %
Training	3,500	4,000	-500	88.00 %
Total Income	**$698,000**	**$579,000**	**$119,000**	**121.00 %**
Cost of Goods Sold				
Cost of Goods Sold	298,000	250,000	48,000	119.00 %
Total Cost of Goods Sold	**$298,000**	**$250,000**	**$48,000**	**119.00 %**
GROSS PROFIT	**$400,000**	**$329,000**	**$71,000**	**122.00 %**
Expenses				
Advertising & Marketing	3,000	3,500	-500	86.00 %
Equipment Rental	7,500	8,000	-500	94.00 %
Insurance		6,000	-6,000	
Interest Expense	3,000	4,000	-1,000	75.00 %
Payroll	26,859	30,000	-3,141	90.00 %
Recruiting	6,300	4,000	2,300	158.00 %
Repairs & Maintenance		2,500	-2,500	
Total Expenses	**$46,659**	**$58,000**	**$ -11,341**	**80.00 %**
NET OPERATING INCOME	**$353,341**	**$271,000**	**$82,341**	**130.00 %**
NET INCOME	**$353,341**	**$271,000**	**$82,341**	**130.00 %**

6 Print the resulting Reconciliation Report. Select **All dates** from the Report Period drop-down text box, then click **2022**, and then click **View Report** on the statement ending date 01/31/22 line. A partial view of that report should look like Figure 8.27.

Figure 8.27

Bank Reconciliation as of
1/31/22 (partial view)

Case 05 - Student Name (ID Number)

Checking, Period Ending 01/31/2022

RECONCILIATION REPORT

Any changes made to transactions after this date aren't included in this report.

Summary	USD
Statement beginning balance	30,000.00
Checks and payments cleared (8)	-115,390.24
Deposits and other credits cleared (3)	279,500.00
Statement ending balance	194,109.76
Uncleared transactions as of 01/31/2022	42,686.06
Register balance as of 01/31/2022	236,795.82

7 Sign out of your company.

Case 6

Now it is time to create a budget and reconcile a bank account. Based on what you learned in the text using the Wild Water Sports company, you are to make the following changes to the Case 6 company you modified in Chapter 7:

1   Create a new budget titled "Budget 1." Be sure to select FY 2023 (Jan 2023–Dec 2023) from the Fiscal Year drop-down list in the new budget window. Enter the following budgeted amounts for 2023: sales: 10,000, sales of product income: 300,000, cost of goods sold: 230,000, advertising & marketing: 15,000, contractors: 2,000, insurance: 3,000, interest expense: 500, payroll: 20,000, repairs: 500, and depreciation: 1,000. Amounts provided should be input for each month of 2023.

2   Create, customize (save customization as Budget Overview), and print a Budget Overview report for the month of January 2023 without cents showing accounts vs. totals. Your report should look like Figure 8.28

Case 06 - Student Name (ID Number)

BUDGET OVERVIEW: BUDGET 1 - FY23 P&L

January 2023

	TOTAL
▾ Income	
Sales	10,000
Sales of Product Income	300,000
Total Income	**$310,000**
▾ Cost of Goods Sold	
Cost of Goods Sold	230,000
Total Cost of Goods Sold	**$230,000**
GROSS PROFIT	$80,000
▾ Expenses	
Advertising & Marketing	15,000
Contractors	2,000
Insurance	3,000
Interest Expense	500
Payroll	20,000
Repairs	500
Total Expenses	**$41,000**
NET OPERATING INCOME	$39,000
▾ Other Expenses	
Depreciation	1,000
Total Other Expenses	**$1,000**
NET OTHER INCOME	$ -1,000
NET INCOME	$38,000

Figure 8.28

Budget Overview for January 2023

3 Create, customize (save customization as Budget vs. Actuals), and print a Budget vs. Actuals report for the month of January 2023 without cents showing accounts vs. totals. Your report should look like Figure 8.29.

Figure 8.29

Budget vs. Actuals for January 2023

Case 06 - Student Name (ID Number)

BUDGET VS. ACTUALS: BUDGET 1 - FY23 P&L

January 2023

		TOTAL		
	ACTUAL	BUDGET	OVER BUDGET	% OF BUDGET
▾ Income				
Sales		10,000	-10,000	
Sales of Product Income	290,000	300,000	-10,000	97.00 %
Total Income	**$290,000**	**$310,000**	**$ -20,000**	**94.00 %**
▾ Cost of Goods Sold				
Cost of Goods Sold	232,000	230,000	2,000	101.00 %
Total Cost of Goods Sold	**$232,000**	**$230,000**	**$2,000**	**101.00 %**
GROSS PROFIT	**$58,000**	**$80,000**	**$ -22,000**	**73.00 %**
▾ Expenses				
Advertising & Marketing	14,000	15,000	-1,000	93.00 %
Contractors	1,800	2,000	-200	90.00 %
Insurance		3,000	-3,000	
Interest Expense	400	500	-100	80.00 %
Payroll	18,848	20,000	-1,152	94.00 %
Repairs		500	-500	
Total Expenses	**$35,048**	**$41,000**	**$ -5,952**	**85.00 %**
NET OPERATING INCOME	**$22,952**	**$39,000**	**$ -16,048**	**59.00 %**
▾ Other Expenses				
Depreciation		1,000	-1,000	
Total Other Expenses	**$0**	**$1,000**	**$ -1,000**	**0%**
NET OTHER INCOME	**$0**	**$ -1,000**	**$1,000**	**0.00 %**
NET INCOME	**$22,952**	**$38,000**	**$ -15,048**	**60.00 %**

4 Reconcile your company's checking account. No service charges were incurred or interest earned. The ending bank statement balance on 1/31/23 was $65,196.03.

5 After a review of the company's most recent statement and a comparison with the company's checking account, you note that a $10,000 deposit on 1/26/23 and checks 593, 594, 598, 599, and 600 had not cleared the bank.

6 Print the resulting Reconciliation Report.

7 Sign out of your company.

Analysis and Recording of Adjusting Entries

Student Learning Outcomes

Upon completion of this chapter, the student will be able to do the following:

- Prepare an unadjusted trial balance
- Make adjusting entries for the following:
  - o Prepaid expenses
  - o Accrued expenses
  - o Unearned revenue
  - o Accrued revenue
  - o Depreciation

Overview

In Chapter 8 you added a budget, a Profit and Loss budget report, and a bank reconciliation to your Wild Water Sports company. In this chapter you will add adjusting journal entries. At the end of this chapter you will perform the similar tasks on the case assigned by your instructor.

Prior to the creation of periodic financial statements, generally accepted accounting principles (GAAP) require that accounting records be adjusted to reflect accrual accounting. This process ensures revenues are recorded in the period in which they are earned and that expenses are recorded in the period in which they were consumed. In the process, expenses will be matched in the same period to the revenues generated from incurring those expenses.

There are five types of adjusting entries. Expenses paid, prior to being consumed, should be deferred (supplies, rent, insurance, etc.) and recorded as assets (supplies asset, prepaid rent, prepaid insurance, etc.) until they are consumed. To defer is to postpone. Expenses incurred prior to being paid (payroll, rent, utilities, etc.) must be recorded and accrued as a liability. To accrue is to increase. Revenue collected prior to being earned must be deferred (sales, services, etc.) and recorded as liabilities (unearned revenue, etc.) until they are earned. Revenues earned prior to being collected (sales and services, etc.) must be recorded and accrued as a receivable. Lastly, fixed assets (buildings, furniture, equipment, vehicles, etc.) must be depreciated over their useful life to match costs with revenues.

Trial Balance

In this section, you will create a trial balance (before adjusting entries), which must be analyzed in light of end of the period business events to determine the required adjusting entries.

To create a trial balance for the Wild Water Sports company, do the following:

1   Open your Internet browser.

2   Open your QBO account and the Wild Water Sports company like you've done in previous chapters.

3   Click **Reports** from the navigation bar.

4   Click the **Custom reports** tab and then click **Trial Balance** shown in Figure 9.1.

Figure 9.1

Trial Balance report (partial view)

Wild Water Sports - Student Name (ID Number)

Trial Balance
As of January 31, 2027

	DEBIT	CREDIT
Checking	99,358.88	
Accounts receivable (A/R)	120,770.00	
Inventory	223,350.00	
Payments to deposit	70,000.00	
Prepaid expenses	17,500.00	
Equipment:Accumulated depreciation		10,000.00
Equipment:Original Cost	53,000.00	
Furniture:Original cost	10,000.00	
Investments	3,000.00	
Accounts Payable (A/P)		190,250.00
Mastercard		1,600.00
Florida Department of Revenue Payable		9,915.00
Payroll wages and tax to pay		2,944.66
Long-term business loans		155,000.00
Common stock		11,000.00
Opening balance equity		0.00
Retained Earnings		204,300.00
Sales		164,000.00
Service Revenue		2,000.00
Cost of goods sold	131,200.00	
Interest paid	2,500.00	
Payroll expenses	10,930.78	
Rent:Equipment rental	6,000.00	
Utilities:Phone service	1,800.00	
Vehicle expenses:Vehicle gas & fuel	1,600.00	
TOTAL	$751,009.66	$751,009.66

Adjusting Journal Entries: Prepaid Expenses

Further investigation of this trial balance and period end business activities indicates that $500 of Vehicle gas & fuel were recorded as an expense but should have been deferred as a supplies asset until consumed in some future period. Thus, an adjusting entry is necessary.

To record an adjusting entry for supplies in the Wild Water Sports company, do the following:

1 Continue from where you left off.

2 Click the ⬛ + New icon and then click **Journal Entry**.

3 Type **1/31/27** as the Journal date, then accept as the Journal no.

4 Type **Supplies asset** on line 1 of the Account column, and click **+ Add Supplies asset** as shown in Figure 9.2. (This is another way to add a new account in QBO.)

Figure 9.2

Journal Entry (adding a new account)

5 Select **Other Current Assets** from the drop-down list in the Account Type text box.

6 Select **Other Current Assets** from the drop-down list in the Detail Type text box.

7 Click **Save and close**.

8 Type **500** into the Debits column of line 1.

9 Select **Vehicle gas & fuel** from the drop-down list in line 2 of the Accounts column.

10 Accept **500** into the Credits column of line 2 and then press **[Tab]** to view the journal entry as shown in Figure 9.3.

Figure 9.3

Journal Entry #6 (to defer supplies)

> ◷ **Journal Entry #6**
>
> Journal date   Journal no.
>
> 01/31/2027   6
>
> | | # | ACCOUNT | DEBITS | CREDITS |
> |---|---|---|---|---|
> | ⠿ | 1 | Supplies asset | 500.00 | |
> | ⠿ | 2 | Vehicle expenses:Vehicle gas & fuel | | 500.00 |

11 Click **Save and close**.

The same process could be used to defer a cost that had been recorded as an expense but should be deferred as an asset at period end. Examples might include insurance to be deferred as either prepaid insurance or prepaid expenses or rent to be deferred as either prepaid rent or prepaid expenses.

Another example of this occurs when an expense is deferred in a prior period but is consumed or expired in the current period. We will use the Prepaid expenses created as an example assuming $1000 of prepaid expenses (in this case insurance cost paid to Allstate for future coverage) were consumed in the month leaving $16,500 of prepaid expenses as an asset.

To record an adjusting journal entry to record the expiration of prepaid expenses (insurance), do the following:

1 Continue from where you left off.

2 Click the ⬡ + New icon and then click **Journal Entry**.

3 Accept **1/31/27** as the Journal date and **7** as the Journal no.

4 Select **Insurance** from the drop-down list in line 1 of the Account column. (This is an expense account already in the Company's chart of accounts.)

5 Type **1000** into the Debits column of line 1.

6 Select **Prepaid expenses** from the drop-down list in line 2 of the Accounts column.

7 Accept **1000** into the Credits column of line 2 to view the journal entry as shown in Figure 9.4.

Figure 9.4

Journal Entry (recording the expiration of insurance)

8 Click **Save and close**.

9 Closing the journal entry should reveal the trial balance created before. The trial balance has now been updated to reflect the supplies asset account as shown in Figure 9.5.

Figure 9.5

Trial Balance after adjustments

Wild Water Sports - Student Name (ID Number)

Trial Balance
As of January 31, 2027

	DEBIT	CREDIT
Checking	99,358.88	
Accounts receivable (A/R)	120,770.00	
Inventory	223,350.00	
Payments to deposit	70,000.00	
Prepaid expenses	16,500.00	
Supplies asset	500.00	
Equipment:Accumulated depreciation		10,000.00
Equipment:Original Cost	53,000.00	
Furniture:Original cost	10,000.00	
Investments	3,000.00	
Accounts Payable (A/P)		190,250.00
Mastercard		1,600.00
Florida Department of Revenue Payable		9,915.00
Payroll wages and tax to pay		2,944.66
Long-term business loans		155,000.00
Common stock		11,000.00
Opening balance equity		0.00
Retained Earnings		204,300.00
Sales		164,000.00
Service Revenue		2,000.00
Cost of goods sold	131,200.00	
Insurance	1,000.00	
Interest paid	2,500.00	
Payroll expenses	10,930.78	
Rent:Equipment rental	6,000.00	
Utilities:Phone service	1,800.00	
Vehicle expenses:Vehicle gas & fuel	1,100.00	
TOTAL	$751,009.66	$751,009.66

10 Click the Supplies asset **500** amount to reveal a Transaction Report for the Supplies asset account as shown in Figure 9.6.

11 Click **Back to report summary** to return to the Trial Balance report. Click the Prepaid expenses **16,500** amount to reveal a Transaction Report for the Prepaid expense account.

Figure 9.6

Transaction Report (for Supplies asset)

Wild Water Sports - Student Name (ID Number)

Transaction Report
January 2027

DATE	TRANSACTION TYPE	NUM	NAME	MEMO/DESCRIPTION	ACCOUNT	SPLIT	AMOUNT	BALANCE
▾ Supplies asset								
01/31/2027	Journal Entry	6			Supplies asset	-Split-	500.00	500.00
Total for Supplies asset							$500.00	
TOTAL							$500.00	

The first entry deferred $500 from Vehicle expense; the second entry recorded the expiration of insurance reducing the Prepaid expenses account.

Adjusting Journal Entries: Accrued Expenses

Further investigation of this trial balance and period end business activities indicates that a bill for $2,500 was received and recorded in the next month for advertising consumed in the current month. Thus, an adjusting journal entry needs to be made to accrue this expense. For our purposes, we will create a new accrued liabilities account to keep track of these accruals and keep them separate from accounts payable.

To record an adjusting journal entry to record the accrual of advertising expense, do the following:

1 Continue from where you left off.

2 Click the `+ New` icon and then click **Journal Entry**.

3 Accept **1/31/27** as the Journal date and **8** as the Journal no.

4 Select **Advertising & Marketing** from the drop-down list in line 1 of the Account column.

5 Type **2500** into the Debits column of line 1.

6 Type **Accrued liabilities** on line 2 of the Account column and then click + **Add Accrued liabilities**.

7 Select **Other Current Liabilities** from the drop-down list in the Account Type text box.

8 Select **Other Current Liabilities** from the drop-down list in the Detail Type text box.

9 Click **Save and close**.

10 Accept **2500** into the Credits column of line 2 to view the journal entry as shown in Figure 9.7.

Figure 9.7

Journal Entry (accruing advertising & marketing expense)

🕐 **Journal Entry #8**

Journal date	Journal no.
01/31/2027	8

	#	ACCOUNT	DEBITS	CREDITS
⠿	1	Advertising & marketing	2,500.00	
⠿	2	Accrued liabilities		2,500.00

11 Click **Save and close**.

12 Closing the journal entry should reveal the trial balance created before but now updated to reflect the accrual of advertising & marketing expense to the accrued liabilities account.

13 Click the Accrued liabilities **2500** amount to reveal a Transaction Report showing Journal entry 8.

14 Click **Back to report summary** to return to the Trial Balance report.

Adjusting Journal Entries: Unearned Revenue

Further investigation of this trial balance and period end business activities indicates that the sale of a boat recorded on sales receipt #1001 for $55,145 to Southtown Watersports had not been delivered even though cash had been received. Thus, the revenue had not been earned. Delivery is expected to occur next month; thus, this amount of revenue and related sales tax must be deferred and set up as an unearned revenue liability.

To record an adjusting journal entry to reflect unearned revenue, do the following:

1 Continue from where you left off. From the Trial Balance as of 1/31/27 click the Sales amount **164,000** then click sales receipt **1001**. Note this receipt recorded cash received of $55,145, sales of $52,000, and sales tax payable of $3,145. Now close this sales receipt.

2 Click the ⬛ + New icon and then click **Journal Entry**.

3 Accept **1/31/27** as the Journal date and **9** as the Journal no.

4 Select **Sales** from the drop-down list in line 1 of the Account column.

5 Type **52000** into the Debits column of line 1.

6 Select **Southtown Watersports** from the drop-down list of customers in the Name column of line 1.

7 Type **Unearned revenue** on line 2 of the Account column and then click + **Add Unearned revenue**.

8 Select **Other Current Liabilities** from the drop-down list in the Account Type text box.

9 Select **Deferred Revenue** from the drop-down list in the Detail Type text box.

10 Click **Save and close**.

11 Accept **52000** into the Credits column of line 2 and then select **Southtown Watersports** from the drop-down list of customers in the Name column of line 2 to view the journal entry as shown in Figure 9.8.

Figure 9.8

Journal Entry (recording unearned revenue)

12 Click **Save and close**.

13 Closing the journal entry should reveal the trial balance created before but updated to reflect the deferral of revenue to the unearned revenue liability account.

14 Click the Unearned revenue **52,000.00** amount to reveal a Transaction Report.

15 Click **Back to report summary** to return to the Trial Balance report.

Adjusting Journal Entries: Accruing Revenue

Further investigation of this trial balance and period end business activities indicates that a Tige 25 zx boat was sold and delivered to a new customer High Flyer Sports on 1/31/27 on net 30 terms but not invoiced until the next month. Sales tax on that sale amounted to $13,525 and the boat was sold for $225,000. Thus, you will need to record an adjusting journal entry to accrue revenue and an accrued receivable.

To record an adjusting journal entry to reflect earned revenue, do the following:

1 Continue from where you left off.

2 Click the ⬭＋New icon and then click **Journal Entry**.

3 Accept **1/31/27** as the Journal date and **10** as the Journal no.

4 Type **Accrued receivable** on line 1 of the Account column and then click + **Add Accrued receivable**.

5 Select **Other Current Assets** from the drop-down list in the Account Type text box.

6   Select **Other Current Assets** from the drop-down list in the Detail Type text box.

7   Click **Save and close**.

8   Type **238525** into the Debits column of line 1.

9   Type **High Flyer Sports** in the Name column of line 1. Add this as a new customer.

10   Select **Sales** from the drop-down list in line 2 of the Account column.

11   Type **225000** in the Credits column of line 2.

12   Select **High Flyer Sports** from the drop-down list of customers in the Name column of line 2.

13   Select **Sales tax to pay** from the drop-down list in line 3 of the Account column.

14   Type **13525** in the Credits column of line 3.

15   Select **High Flyer Sports** from the drop-down list in line 3 of the Name column. Your journal should look like Figure 9.9.

Figure 9.9

Journal Entry (recording accrued revenue)

16   Click **Save and close**.

17   Closing the journal entry should reveal the trial balance created before but updated to reflect the accrual of revenue to the accrued receivable account.

18   Click the Accrued Receivable **238,525** amount to reveal a Transaction Report.

19   Click **Back to report summary** to return to the Trial Balance report.

Adjusting Journal Entries: Depreciation

Further investigation of this trial balance and period end business activities indicates the company's fixed assets need to be depreciated for the month. Monthly depreciation for equipment and furniture is $1,000 and $250, respectively. Normally, the adjusting entry would debit depreciation expense and credit accumulated depreciation. However, the accounts set up in the chart of accounts need to be edited. Thus, you decide to change the account names first and then record the depreciation adjusting journal entry.

To edit account names and then record an adjusting journal entry to record depreciation, do the following:

1   Continue from where you left off.

2   Click the **Gear** and then click **Chart of Accounts**.

3   Click **Edit** from the drop-down arrow next to the words View Register on the Depreciation line listed under the Furniture account.

4   Type **Accumulated** *in front* of Depreciation in the Account name text box and then click **Save**.

5   Scroll down to the bottom of the chart of accounts and select **Edit** from the drop-down arrow next to the words Run report on the Depreciation line.

6   Type **expense** *after* Depreciation in the Account name text box and then click **Save**.

7   Click the 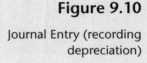 icon and then click **Journal Entry**.

8   Type **1/31/2027** in the journal date text box and accept 11 as the journal no.

9   Select **Depreciation expense** from the drop-down list in line 1 of the Account column.

10   Type **1250** into the Debits column of line 1.

11   Select **Accumulated depreciation** under the Equipment account from the drop-down list in line 2 of the Account column.

12   Type **1000** as the Credits column amount.

13   Select **Furniture: Accumulated Depreciation** from the drop-down list in line 3 of the Account column.

14   Accept **250** as the Credits column amount. Your screen should look like Figure 9.10.

Figure 9.10

Journal Entry (recording depreciation)

⊙ Journal Entry #11					⚙ ⑦ Help ✕

Journal date   Journal no.
01/31/2027   11

#	ACCOUNT	DEBITS	CREDITS	DESCRIPTION	NAME
1	Depreciation expense	1,250.00			
2	Equipment:Accumulated depreciation		1,000.00		
3	Furniture:Accumulated Depreciation		250.00		

15 Click **Save and close**.

16 Click **Reports** from the navigation bar, then click the **Custom reports** tab, and then select **Trial Balance** to view the trial balance shown in Figure 9.11.

<table>
<tr><th colspan="3">Wild Water Sports - Student Name (ID Number)</th></tr>
<tr><th colspan="3">Trial Balance
As of January 31, 2027</th></tr>
<tr><th></th><th>DEBIT</th><th>CREDIT</th></tr>
<tr><td>Checking</td><td>99,358.88</td><td></td></tr>
<tr><td>Accounts receivable (A/R)</td><td>120,770.00</td><td></td></tr>
<tr><td>Accrued receivable</td><td>238,525.00</td><td></td></tr>
<tr><td>Inventory</td><td>223,350.00</td><td></td></tr>
<tr><td>Payments to deposit</td><td>70,000.00</td><td></td></tr>
<tr><td>Prepaid expenses</td><td>16,500.00</td><td></td></tr>
<tr><td>Supplies asset</td><td>500.00</td><td></td></tr>
<tr><td>Equipment:Accumulated depreciation</td><td></td><td>11,000.00</td></tr>
<tr><td>Equipment:Original Cost</td><td>53,000.00</td><td></td></tr>
<tr><td>Furniture:Accumulated Depreciation</td><td></td><td>250.00</td></tr>
<tr><td>Furniture:Original cost</td><td>10,000.00</td><td></td></tr>
<tr><td>Investments</td><td>3,000.00</td><td></td></tr>
<tr><td>Accounts Payable (A/P)</td><td></td><td>190,250.00</td></tr>
</table>

Figure 9.11

Revised Trial Balance report (partial view)

End Note

In this chapter, you recorded adjusting entries to create accrual accounting-based records. In the next chapter, you will create financial statements and useful reports.

Chapter 9 Questions

1 What is an unadjusted trial balance?

2 What is an adjusted trial balance?

3 Why accrue an expense?

4 Why defer an expense?

5 Why accrue revenues?

6 Why defer revenues?

7 What QBO task is used to record accruals and deferrals?

8 Why depreciate a fixed asset?

9 Describe the new method you learned in this chapter to add a new account from within a journal entry.

10 Describe the method you learned in this chapter to add a customer to a transaction within a journal entry.

Chapter 9 Matching

a. Prepaid Expenses _____ Debit this account when recording depreciation

b. Accrue _____ Credit this account when accruing an expense

c. Unearned Revenue _____ Debit this account when accruing revenue

d. Defer _____ Supplies consumed

e. Depreciation Expense _____ Credit this account when recording depreciation

f. Supplies Asset _____ Expenses not yet consumed

g. Supplies Expense _____ Revenue not yet earned

h. Accrued Receivables _____ To increase

i. Accrued Liabilities _____ Supplies not yet consumed

j. Accumulate Depreciation _____ To postpone

Chapter 9 Cases

The following cases require you to open the company you updated in Chapter 8. Each of the following cases continues throughout the text in a sequential manner. For example, if you are assigned Case 01, you will use the file you modified in this chapter in all following chapters. Each of the following cases is similar in concepts assessed but differs in amounts and transactions.

To reopen your company, do the following:

1 Open your Internet browser.

2 Type **https://qbo.intuit.com** into your browser's address text box.

3 Type your user ID and password into the text boxes as you've done before.

Case 1

Now it is time to make some adjusting journal entries. Based on what you learned in the text using the Wild Water Sports company, you are to make the following changes to the Case 1 company you modified in Chapter 8:

1 Open and review your previously customized report named Trial Balance 1/31/24.

2 Record the appropriate adjusting journal entries on 1/31/24 based on the following:

   a. An inventory of supplies reveals that only $75 of supplies remain as of 1/31/24. (You'll need to add a new Supplies account—Account Type: Expenses, Detail Type: Supplies & Materials, Name: Supplies.)

   b. Prepaid expenses of $800 expired (representing prepaid rent) in the month of January.

   c. A bill for $150 was received and recorded in the next month for repairs and maintenance consumed in the current month. Create a new liability account as you did earlier in the chapter.

   d. Consulting services recorded on sales receipt #1004 for $2,500 to Surf Rider Foundation were never performed even though cash had been received. Thus, the revenue had not been earned. Create a new liability account as you did earlier in the chapter.

   e. Consulting services of $8,500 were performed on the last day of the month for a new customer Blazing Boards but not invoiced to the customer or recorded into the accounting records until a few days into the next month. Create a new asset account as you did earlier in the chapter.

   f. Depreciation Expense of $575 ($75 and $500 for Equipment and Furniture & Fixtures, respectively) needed to be recorded for the month. Before recording this journal entry, edit the "Depreciation" expense account so that the new name is "Depreciation Expense." Also, change the account title for Furniture & Fixtures accumulated depreciation from "Depreciation" to "Accumulated Depreciation" as you did earlier in the chapter. This also needs to be done for the Equipment accumulated depreciation account.

3 Open, print, and export to Excel your previously customized report named Trial Balance 1/31/24, which should now reflect your adjusting journal entries.

4 Open, print, and export to Excel your previously customized report named Transaction Detail by Account, which should now reflect your adjusting journal entries.

Case 2

Now it is time to make some adjusting journal entries. Based on what you learned in the text using the Wild Water Sports company, you are to make the following changes to the Case 2 company you modified in Chapter 8:

1 Open and review your previously customized report named Trial Balance 1/31/25.

2 Record the appropriate adjusting journal entries on 1/31/25 based on the following:

  a. An inventory of supplies reveals that only $200 of supplies remain as of 1/31/25. (You'll need to add a new Supplies account—Account Type: Expenses, Detail Type: Supplies & Materials, Name: Supplies.)

  b. Prepaid expenses of $1,800 expired (representing prepaid insurance) in the month of January.

  c. A bill for $750 was received and recorded in the next month for legal fees performed in the current month. Create a new liability account as you did earlier in the chapter.

  d. Custom painting services recorded on invoice #1003 for $4,500 to Hagen's toys were never performed even though invoiced. Thus, the revenue had not been earned. Create a new liability account as you did earlier in the chapter.

  e. Repair services of $6,298 were performed on the last day of the month for a new customer Kelly's Awesome Copters but not invoiced to the customer or recorded into the accounting records until a few days into the next month. Create a new asset account as you did earlier in the chapter.

  f. Depreciation Expense of $1,000 ($375 and $625 for Furniture and Machinery & Equipment, respectively) needed to be recorded for the month. Before recording this journal entry, edit the "Depreciation" expense account so the new name is "Depreciation Expense." Also, change the account title for Machinery & Equipment accumulated depreciation from "Depreciation" to "Accumulated Depreciation" like you did earlier in the chapter. This also needs to be done for the Furniture accumulated depreciation account.

3 Open, print, and export to Excel your previously customized report named Trial Balance 1/31/25, which should reflect your adjusting journal entries.

4 Open, print, and export to Excel your previously customized report named Transaction Detail by Account, which should reflect your adjusting journal entries.

Case 3

Now it is time to make some adjusting journal entries. Based on what you learned in the text using the Wild Water Sports company, you are to make the following changes to the Case 3 company you modified in Chapter 8:

1 Open and review your previously customized report named Trial Balance 1/31/26.

2 Record the appropriate adjusting journal entries on 1/31/26 based on the following:

  a. An inventory of supplies reveals that only $200 of supplies remain as of 1/31/26. (You'll need to add a new Supplies expense account—Account Type: Expenses, Detail Type: Supplies & Materials, Name: Supplies.)

  b. Prepaid expenses of $1,500 expired (representing prepaid insurance) in the month of January.

c. A bill for $350 was received and recorded in the next month from Supreme Marketing (new vendor) for repairs & maintenance performed in the current month. Create a new liability account like you did earlier in the chapter.

d. Phone Consulting services recorded on invoice #1003 for $210 to Diamond Girl, Inc. and recorded as Service income were never performed even though invoiced. Thus, the revenue had not been earned. Create a new liability account like you did earlier in the chapter.

e. Phone Consulting services of $1,800 were performed on the last day of the month for a new customer Graham Engineering, Inc. but not invoiced to the customer or recorded into the accounting records until a few days into the next month. Create a new asset account like you did earlier in the chapter.

f. Depreciation Expense of $1,200 ($850 and $350 for Computers and Machinery & Equipment respectively) needed to be recorded for the month. Before recording this journal entry, edit the "Depreciation" expense account so that the new name is "Depreciation Expense." Also change the account title for the Machinery & Equipment accumulated depreciation from "Depreciation" to "Accumulated Depreciation" like you did earlier in the chapter. This also needs to be done for the Computers accumulation depreciation account.

3 Open, print, and export to Excel your previously customized report named Trial Balance 1/31/26, which should now reflect your adjusting journal entries.

4 Open, print, and export to Excel your previously customized report named Transaction Detail by Account, which should now reflect your adjusting journal entries.

Case 4

Now it is time to make some adjusting journal entries. Based on what you learned in the text using the Wild Water Sports company, you are to make the following changes to the Case 4 company you modified in Chapter 8:

1 Open and review your previously customized report named Trial Balance 1/31/27.

2 Record the appropriate adjusting journal entries on 1/31/27 based on the following:

a. An inventory of supplies reveals that only $200 of supplies remain as of 1/31/27. (You'll need to create a new Supplies Expense account— Account Type: Expenses, Detail Type: Supplies & Materials, Name: Supplies Expense.)

b. Prepaid rent of $1,500 expired (a new expense account called Rent and Lease) in the month of January.

c. A bill for $675 was received and recorded in the next month from FixIt, Inc. (a new vendor) for advertising placed in the current month. Create a new liability account like you did earlier in the chapter.

d. Training services recorded on invoice #1003 for $3,750 to Flyer Corporation were only partially performed even though invoiced. Thus, the $2,000 of sales had not been earned. Create a new liability account like you did earlier in the chapter.

e.   Training services of $750 were performed on the last day of the month for a new customer Jules, Inc. but not invoiced to the customer or recorded into the accounting records until a few days into the next month. Create a new asset account like you did earlier in the chapter and record additional sales.

f.   If necessary, create a new account titled Depreciation Expense. Depreciation Expense of $1,500 ($500, $1,000 for Vehicles, and Furniture, respectively) needed to be recorded for the month.

3 Print your Trial Balance 1/31/27 report that should now reflect your adjusting journal entries.

Case 5

Now it is time to make some adjusting journal entries. Based on what you learned in the text using the Wild Water Sports company, you are to make the following changes to the Case 5 company you modified in Chapter 8:

1 Open and review your previously customized report named Trial Balance 01/31/22.

2 Record the appropriate adjusting journal entries on 01/31/22 based on the following:

a.   Prepaid expenses of $8,000 expired (representing prepaid insurance) in the month of January.

b.   A bill for $2,800 was received and recorded in the next month from Indeed for recruiting services consumed in the current month. Create a new liability account like you did in the chapter.

c.   Consulting services recorded on invoice #1003 for $32,000 to Boeing were only 50% complete as of 01/31/22 even though invoiced in the current month. Thus, $16,000 of consulting services had not been earned. Create an unearned revenue liability account like you did in the chapter.

d.   Training services of $6,700 were performed on the last day of the month for a new customer Raonic but not invoiced to the customer or recorded into the accounting records until a few days into the next month. Create a new asset account like you did in the chapter.

e.   Depreciation Expense of $11,000 ($6,000, $2,000, and $3,000 for Computers, Copiers, and Furniture, respectively) needed to be recorded for the month. Before recording this journal entry, edit the "Depreciation" expense account so that the new name is "Depreciation Expense." Also change the account title for the Computers, Copiers, and Furniture accumulated depreciation from "Depreciation" to "Accumulated Depreciation" like you did in the chapter.

3 Print your Trial Balance 01/31/22 report that should now reflect your adjusting journal entries.

Case 6

Now it is time to make some adjusting journal entries. Based on what you learned in the text using the Wild Water Sports company, you are to make the following changes to the Case 6 company you modified in Chapter 8:

1 Open and review your previously customized report named Trial Balance 1/31/23.

2 Record the appropriate adjusting journal entries on 1/31/23 based on the following:

a. An inventory of supplies reveals that only $400 of supplies remain as of 1/31/23 and $1,000 of supplies were mistakenly recorded as Contractors (an expense). You'll need to create a new Supplies Asset account and journalize $1,000 of Contractors (expense) to the newly created Supplies Asset account. (Note: This a correction of an error journal entry.) Then you'll need to create a new Supplies Expense account (Account Type: Expenses, Detail Type: Supplies & Materials) and journalize $600 of Supplies Asset to the newly created Supplies Expense account. (Note: This requires an adjusting journal entry.)

b. Prepaid expenses of $2,400 expired (representing prepaid insurance) in the month of January. (Note: This requires an adjusting journal entry.)

c. A bill for $1,800 was received and recorded in the next month from Pacific Marketing for advertising placed in the current month. Create a new liability account like you did in the chapter. (Note: This requires an adjusting journal entry.)

d. A Transmission Service of $350 and a Sewer System Repair of $600 were performed on the last day of the month for an existing customer (Deja Smith) but not invoiced to the customer or recorded into the accounting records until a few days into the next month. Create a new asset account like you did in the chapter and then record this as Sales. (Note: This requires an adjusting journal entry.)

e. Depreciation Expense of $2,100 ($1,000, $300, and $800 for Buildings, Computers, and Machinery & Equipment, respectively) needed to be recorded for the month. Before recording this journal entry, edit the "Depreciation" expense account so that the new name is "Depreciation Expense." Also change the account title for the Buildings, Computers, and Machinery & Equipment accumulated depreciation from "Depreciation" to "Accumulated Depreciation" like you did in the chapter. (Note: This requires an adjusting journal entry.)

3 Print your Trial Balance 1/31/23 report that should now reflect your adjusting journal entries.

Preparing Financial Statements and Reports

Overview

In Chapter 9, you added adjusting journal entries to your Wild Water Sports company. In this chapter, you will add several new reports. At the end of this chapter you will perform similar tasks on the case assigned by your instructor.

Four standard reports exist in financial accounting: the income statement, the statement of stockholders' equity, the balance sheet, and the statement of cash flows. QBO does not have a report for stockholders' equity. It does have the others along with a host of other reports so you can understand the underlying business events that have occurred during a particular accounting period. You will be exploring the A/R Aging Summary, A/P Aging Summary, and Inventory Valuation Summary reports. You will also be customizing them by adding columns and removing cents.

Income Statement

In this section, you will create an income statement. Intuit decided years ago to call this report Profit and Loss rather than an Income Statement. Even though this may confuse the accounting professional and accounting student, it resonates with the small business user that uses QBO. This report is designed to communicate the revenues earned and expenses incurred for a business over a month, quarter, or year.

Intuit defines this report as follows: "Shows money you earned (income) and money you spent (expenses), so you can see how profitable you are." That is not exactly how an accounting professional or accounting student was taught but close enough. Accountants define the income statement as a report reflecting revenues less expenses to derive net income. Intuit is not about to change its wording to accommodate us, so we will accept it at face value. Thus, revenues are the same as income in the Profit and Loss report. For simplicity, we will refer to this as the Profit and Loss report.

To create a Profit and Loss report for the Wild Water Sports company, do the following:

1 Open your Internet browser.

2 Open your QBO account and the Wild Water Sports company like you've done in previous chapters.

3 Click **Reports** from the navigation bar.

4 Type **Profit and Loss** in the Find report by name search box and then select the **Profit and Loss** text, which appears below the search text box.

5 Scroll to the top of the report to reveal the report period information. Type **1/1/2027** and **1/31/2027** as the new from and to dates then click **Run Report** as seen in the Report period text boxes at the top of Figure 10.1.

Wild Water Sports - Student Name (ID Number)	
Profit and Loss	
January 2027	
	TOTAL
Income	
Sales	337,000.00
Service Revenue	2,000.00
Total Income	**$339,000.00**
Cost of Goods Sold	
Cost of goods sold	131,200.00
Total Cost of Goods Sold	**$131,200.00**
GROSS PROFIT	**$207,800.00**
Expenses	
Advertising & marketing	2,500.00
Insurance	1,000.00
Interest paid	2,500.00
Payroll expenses	10,930.78
Rent	
Equipment rental	6,000.00
Total Rent	6,000.00
Utilities	
Phone service	1,800.00
Total Utilities	1,800.00
Total Expenses	**$24,730.78**
NET OPERATING INCOME	**$183,069.22**
Other Expenses	
Depreciation expense	1,250.00
Vehicle expenses	
Vehicle gas & fuel	1,100.00
Total Vehicle expenses	1,100.00
Total Other Expenses	**$2,350.00**
NET OTHER INCOME	**$ -2,350.00**
NET INCOME	**$180,719.22**

Figure 10.1

Profit and Loss Report

6   Click **Collapse** to view the report shown in Figure 10.2.

Figure 10.2

Profit and Loss Report
(collapsed)

Wild Water Sports - Student Name (ID Number)

Profit and Loss

January 2027

	TOTAL
Income	
Sales	337,000.00
Service Revenue	2,000.00
Total Income	**$339,000.00**
Cost of Goods Sold	
Cost of goods sold	131,200.00
Total Cost of Goods Sold	**$131,200.00**
GROSS PROFIT	**$207,800.00**
Expenses	
Advertising & marketing	2,500.00
Insurance	1,000.00
Interest paid	2,500.00
Payroll expenses	10,930.78
Rent	6,000.00
Utilities	1,800.00
Total Expenses	**$24,730.78**
NET OPERATING INCOME	**$183,069.22**
Other Expenses	
Depreciation expense	1,250.00
Vehicle expenses	1,100.00
Total Other Expenses	**$2,350.00**
NET OTHER INCOME	**$ -2,350.00**
NET INCOME	**$180,719.22**

By defining the accounting period as the month of January 2027, the only events reported are those recorded during that period. All reports in QBO allow you to drill down to specific transactions recorded in that period. You drill down by clicking an account on a report. That reveals a transactions report for that account for that period. Double-clicking a specific transaction in the transactions report reveals a specific source document, such as an invoice, sales receipt, cash receipt, and bill.

7   Click the **337,000.00** amount next to the Sales account as shown in Figure 10.2 to view the Transaction report for the Sales account for the month of January shown in Figure 10.3, remembering that this figure illustrates the details behind the number you just clicked.

Figure 10.3

Transaction Report
(for the sales account)

Wild Water Sports - Student Name (ID Number)

Transaction Report

January 2027

DATE	TRANSACTION TYPE	NUM	NAME	MEMO/DESCRIPTION	ACCOUNT	SPLIT	AMOUNT	BALANCE
▼ Sales								
01/04/2027	Sales Receipt	1001	Southtown Watersports	Malibu Sportster LX	Sales	Payments to deposit	52,000.00	52,000.00
01/06/2027	Invoice	1002	Performance Rentals	Malibu Sportster LX	Sales	Accounts receivable (A/R)	52,000.00	104,000.00
01/06/2027	Invoice	1002	Performance Rentals	Malibu Sunset LX	Sales	Accounts receivable (A/R)	60,000.00	164,000.00
01/31/2027	Journal Entry	9			Sales	-Split-	-52,000.00	112,000.00
01/31/2027	Journal Entry	10			Sales	-Split-	225,000.00	337,000.00
Total for Sales							**$337,000.00**	
TOTAL							**$337,000.00**	

8 Click on the **Performance Rentals** text to view invoice #1002 shown in Figure 10.4.

Figure 10.4

Invoice #1002 (partial view)

9 Click **X** to return to the transaction report, and click **Back to report summary** to return to the Profit and Loss report.

10 Click the drop-down arrow in the Compare another period text box and then select **% of income**.

11 Click **Customize**.

12 Check the **Without cents** check box.

13 Click **Run report** to view the report shown in Figure 10.5.

Wild Water Sports - Student Name (ID Number)		
Profit and Loss		
January 2027		
	TOTAL	
	JAN 2027	**% OF INCOME**
Income		
Sales	337,000	99.00 %
Service Revenue	2,000	1.00 %
Total Income	**$339,000**	100.00 %
Cost of Goods Sold		
Cost of goods sold	131,200	39.00 %
Total Cost of Goods Sold	**$131,200**	39.00 %
GROSS PROFIT	**$207,800**	61.00 %
Expenses		
Advertising & marketing	2,500	1.00 %
Insurance	1,000	0.00 %
Interest paid	2,500	1.00 %
Payroll expenses	10,931	3.00 %
Rent	6,000	2.00 %
Utilities	1,800	1.00 %
Total Expenses	**$24,731**	7.00 %
NET OPERATING INCOME	**$183,069**	54.00 %
Other Expenses		
Depreciation expense	1,250	0.00 %
Vehicle expenses	1,100	0.00 %
Total Other Expenses	**$2,350**	1.00 %
NET OTHER INCOME	$ -2,350	-1.00 %
NET INCOME	**$180,719**	53.00 %

Figure 10.5

Customized profit and loss report

14   Click **Save customization**.

15   Type **Profit and Loss Custom** as the report name.

16   Click **Save**.

17   Click the **Export** button and then select **Export to Excel** as shown in Figure 10.6.

Figure 10.6

Exporting a report to Excel

18   Click **Save** after you've specified where you'd like to save the Excel worksheet.

19   Open the Excel file you just saved and click **Enable Editing** to view the Excel file shown in Figure 10.7.

Figure 10.7

Exported Excel File

	A	B	C
1	**Wild Water Sports - Student Name (ID Number)**		
2	**Profit and Loss**		
3	January 2027		
4			
5		Total	
6		Jan 2027	% of Income
7	Income		
8	Sales	337,000	99.41%
9	Service Revenue	2,000	0.59%
10	Total Income	$ 339,000	100.00%
11	Cost of Goods Sold		
12	Cost of goods sold	131,200	38.70%
13	Total Cost of Goods Sold	$ 131,200	38.70%
14	Gross Profit	$ 207,800	61.30%
15	Expenses		
16	Advertising & marketing	2,500	0.74%
17	Insurance	1,000	0.29%
18	Interest paid	2,500	0.74%
19	Payroll expenses	10,931	3.22%
20	Rent	6,000	1.77%
21	Utilities	1,800	0.53%
22	Total Expenses	$ 24,731	7.30%
23	Net Operating Income	$ 183,069	54.00%
24	Other Expenses		
25	Depreciation expense	1,250	0.37%
26	Vehicle expenses	1,100	0.32%
27	Total Other Expenses	$ 2,350	0.69%
28	Net Other Income	-$ 2,350	-0.69%
29	Net Income	$ 180,719	53.31%

Balance Sheet

In this section, you will create a balance sheet that reports on your company's assets, liabilities, and stockholders' equity as of a specific date (not period). However, when creating this report, QBO provides you the ability to define the period in which underlying account balances will reflect in their transactions reports. QBO default is this Year-to-date.

To create a balance sheet, do the following:

1 Continue from where you left off.

2 Click **Reports** from the navigation bar.

3 Type **Balance Sheet** in the Find report by name search box, and then select the **Balance Sheet** text. Type **1/1/2027** and **1/31/2027** in the from to report dates text boxes, then click **Run report**. Then click **Collapse** to view a modified balance sheet shown in Figure 10.8.

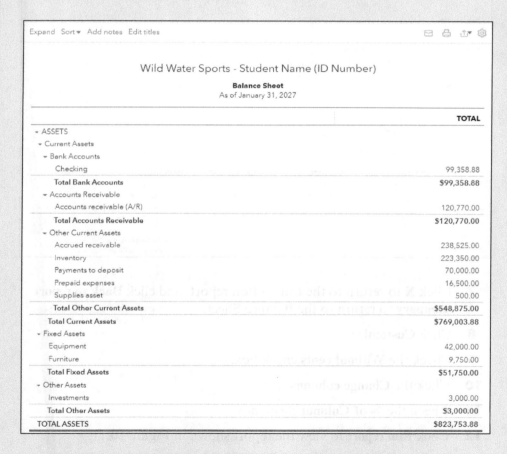

Figure 10.8

Balance Sheet (partial view)

4 Click the Accounts Receivable (A/R) balance **120,770.00** to view a transaction report for Accounts Receivable (A/R) for the month of January 2027 as shown in Figure 10.9.

Figure 10.9

Transaction Report for
Accounts Receivable (A/R)

5   Note the ending balance of 120,770.00 which matches the Balance Sheet
    report shown in Figure 10.8.

6   Click **–70,000.00** (a payment from Refugio) to view the Receive Payment
    window shown in Figure 10.10.

Figure 10.10

Payment received
(from Refugio)

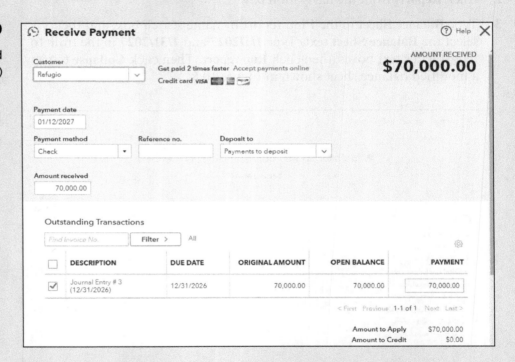

7   Click **X** to return to the transaction report, and click **Back to report
    summary** to return to the Balance Sheet.

8   Click **Customize**.

9   Check the **Without cents** check box.

10   Click the **Change columns** text.

11   Check the **% of Column** check box.

12   Click **Run report** to view the report shown in Figure 10.11.

Wild Water Sports - Student Name (ID Number)

Balance Sheet
As of January 31, 2027

	TOTAL	
	AS OF JAN 31, 2027	**% OF COLUMN**
▾ ASSETS		
▾ Current Assets		
▾ Bank Accounts		
Checking	99,359	12.00 %
Total Bank Accounts	**$99,359**	12.00 %
▾ Accounts Receivable		
Accounts receivable (A/R)	120,770	15.00 %
Total Accounts Receivable	**$120,770**	15.00 %
▾ Other Current Assets		
Accrued receivable	238,525	29.00 %
Inventory	223,350	27.00 %
Payments to deposit	70,000	8.00 %
Prepaid expenses	16,500	2.00 %
Supplies asset	500	0.00 %
Total Other Current Assets	**$548,875**	67.00 %
Total Current Assets	**$769,004**	93.00 %
▾ Fixed Assets		
Equipment	42,000	5.00 %
Furniture	9,750	1.00 %
Total Fixed Assets	**$51,750**	6.00 %
▾ Other Assets		
Investments	3,000	0.00 %
Total Other Assets	**$3,000**	0.00 %
TOTAL ASSETS	**$823,754**	100.00 %

Figure 10.11

Customized balance sheet report (partial view)

13 Click **Save customization**.

14 Type **Balance Sheet Custom** as the report name.

15 Click **Save**.

16 Click the **Export** button and then select **Export to Excel** as you've done before.

17 Click **Save** after you've specified where you'd like to save the Excel worksheet.

18 Open the Excel file you just saved and click **Enable Editing** to view the Excel file shown in Figure 10.12.

Figure 10.12

Exported Excel File

	A	B	C
1	**Wild Water Sports - Student Name (ID Number)**		
2	**Balance Sheet**		
3	As of January 31, 2027		
4			
5		Total	
6		As of Jan 31, 2027	% of Column
7	ASSETS		
8	Current Assets		
9	Bank Accounts		
10	Checking	99,359	12.06%
11	Total Bank Accounts	$ 99,359	12.06%
12	Accounts Receivable		
13	Accounts receivable (A/R)	120,770	14.66%
14	Total Accounts Receivable	$ 120,770	14.66%
15	Other Current Assets		
16	Accrued receivable	238,525	28.96%
17	Inventory	223,350	27.11%
18	Payments to deposit	70,000	8.50%
19	Prepaid expenses	16,500	2.00%
20	Supplies asset	500	0.06%
21	Total Other Current Assets	$ 548,875	66.63%
22	Total Current Assets	$ 769,004	93.35%
23	Fixed Assets		
24	Equipment	42,000	5.10%
25	Furniture	9,750	1.18%
26	Total Fixed Assets	$ 51,750	6.28%
27	Other Assets		
28	Investments	3,000	0.36%
29	Total Other Assets	$ 3,000	0.36%
30	TOTAL ASSETS	$ 823,754	100.00%

Statement of Cash Flows

In this section, you will create a statement of cash flows, which reports on a company's operating, investing, and financing activities.

To create a statement of cash flows, do the following:

1 Continue from where you left off.

2 Click **Reports** from the navigation bar.

3 Type **Statement of Cash Flows** in the Find a report by name search box, and then select the **Statement of Cash Flows** text.

4 Type **1/1/2027** and **1/31/2027** in the from and to report dates text boxes, then click **Run report** to view Statement of Cash Flows shown in Figure 10.13.

Figure 10.13

Statement of Cash Flows
(partial view)

Wild Water Sports - Student Name (ID Number)

Statement of Cash Flows

January 2027

	TOTAL
OPERATING ACTIVITIES	
Net Income	180,719.22
Adjustments to reconcile Net Income to Net Cash provided by operations:	
Accounts receivable (A/R)	-50,770.00
Accrued receivable	-238,525.00
Inventory	-50,550.00
Prepaid expenses	-1,500.00
Supplies asset	-500.00
Equipment:Accumulated depreciation	1,000.00
Furniture:Accumulated Depreciation	250.00
Accounts Payable (A/P)	134,250.00
Mastercard	1,600.00
Accrued liabilities	2,500.00
Florida Department of Revenue Payable	9,915.00
Payroll wages and tax to pay	2,944.66
Sales tax to pay	13,525.00
Unearned revenue	52,000.00
Total Adjustments to reconcile Net Income to Net Cash provided by operations:	-123,860.34
Net cash provided by operating activities	**$56,858.88**
INVESTING ACTIVITIES	
Equipment:Original Cost	-13,000.00
Furniture:Original cost	-10,000.00
Investments	-3,000.00
Net cash provided by investing activities	**$ -26,000.00**
FINANCING ACTIVITIES	
Long-term business loans	105,000.00
Common stock	10,000.00
Opening balance equity	0.00
Retained Earnings	-1,500.00
Net cash provided by financing activities	**$113,500.00**
NET CASH INCREASE FOR PERIOD	**$144,358.88**
Cash at beginning of period	25,000.00
CASH AT END OF PERIOD	**$169,358.88**

5 Scroll down the report and click the Common stock amount **(10,000.00)** to view a transaction report for Common stock as shown in Figure 10.14.

Figure 10.14

Transaction Report
(for Common stock)

Wild Water Sports - Student Name (ID Number)

Transaction Report

January 2027

DATE	TRANSACTION TYPE	NUM	NAME	MEMO/DESCRIPTION	ACCOUNT	SPLIT	AMOUNT	BALANCE
Common stock								
01/21/2027	Deposit		WB Investments		Common stock	Checking	10,000.00	10,000.00
Total for Common stock							$10,000.00	
TOTAL							$10,000.00	

6 Click **10,000.00** in the Common Stock Transaction Report to view Bank Deposit (the source of the entry shown in Figure 10.15).

Figure 10.15

Bank deposit to record $10,000 received from WB Investments for the purchase of common stock.

▼ Add funds to this deposit

#	RECEIVED FROM	ACCOUNT	DESCRIPTION	PAYMENT METHOD	REF NO.	AMOUNT
1	WB Investments	Common stock		Check	56000	10,000.00

7 Click **X** to return to the transaction report, and click **Back to report summary** to return to the Statement of Cash Flows.

8 Click **Customize**.

9 Check the **Without cents** check box.

10 Click **Run report**.

11 Click the **down arrow** next to the text Adjustments to reconcile.... to collapse the detail. Your screen should look like Figure 10.16.

Figure 10.16

Customized statement of cash flows

Wild Water Sports - Student Name (ID Number)	
Statement of Cash Flows	
January 2027	
	TOTAL
OPERATING ACTIVITIES	
Net Income	180,719
Adjustments to reconcile Net Income to Net Cash provided by operations:	-123,860
Net cash provided by operating activities	$56,859
INVESTING ACTIVITIES	
Equipment:Original Cost	-13,000
Furniture:Original cost	-10,000
Investments	-3,000
Net cash provided by investing activities	$ -26,000
FINANCING ACTIVITIES	
Long-term business loans	105,000
Common stock	10,000
Opening balance equity	0
Retained Earnings	-1,500
Net cash provided by financing activities	$113,500
NET CASH INCREASE FOR PERIOD	$144,359
Cash at beginning of period	25,000
CASH AT END OF PERIOD	$169,359

12 Click **Save customization**.

13 Type **Statement of Cash Flows Custom** as the report name.

14 Click **Save**.

Accounts Receivable Aging Summary

In this section, you will create an accounts receivable aging summary, which reflects unpaid invoices for the current period and for the last 30, 60, and 90+ days as of a specific date. Aging summaries help find customers who may be delinquent in their payments and help a company estimate the need for an allowance for uncollectible accounts. Aging information must take into consideration the company's normal terms for a customer. For example, it would not be an issue if many customers are in the 60+ category, but the normal terms for those customers are net 60. However, it would be an issue if the normal terms are net 30 and the same situation existed.

To create an accounts receivable aging summary report, do the following:

1   Continue from where you left off.

2   Click **Reports** from the navigation bar.

3   Type **Accounts receivable aging summary** in the Find a report by name search box, and then select the **Accounts receivable aging summary** text, which appears below the search text box to view the accounts receivable (A/R) aging report. Type **1/31/2027** in the as of report date text box, then click **Run report** to view the A/R Aging Summary report shown in Figure 10.17. Save this customized report as A/R Aging Summary 1/31/27.

Wild Water Sports - Student Name (ID Number)

A/R Aging Summary
As of January 31, 2027

	CURRENT	1 - 30	31 - 60	61 - 90	91 AND OVEF	TOTAL
Florida Ski School	2,000.00					$2,000.00
Performance Rentals	118,770.00					$118,770.00
TOTAL	$120,770.00	$0.00	$0.00	$0.00	$0.00	$120,770.00

Figure 10.17

A/R Aging Summary

4   Click on the **118,770.00** owed by Performance Rentals shown in Figure 10.17 to view A/R Aging Detail report shown in Figure 10.18.

Wild Water Sports - Student Name (ID Number)

A/R Aging Detail
As of January 31, 2027

DATE	TRANSACTION TYPE	NUM	CUSTOMER	DUE DATE	AMOUNT	OPEN BALANCE
Current						
01/06/2027	Invoice	1002	Performance Rentals	02/05/2027	118,770.00	118,770.00
Total for Current					$118,770.00	$118,770.00
TOTAL					$118,770.00	$118,770.00

Figure 10.18

Accounts Receivable (A/R) Aging Detail report (partial view)

5   Click **118,770.00** to view invoice #1002 shown in Figure 10.19.

Figure 10.19

Invoice #1002 to Performance Rentals

6   Click **X** to return to the detail report, and click **Back to report summary** to return to the A/R Aging Summary report.

Accounts Payable Aging Summary

In this section, you will create an accounts payable aging summary, which reflects unpaid bills for the current period and for the last 30, 60, and 90+ days as of a specific date. Aging summaries help prioritize the payment of bills. Aging information must take into consideration the company's normal terms from a vendor. For example, it would not be an issue if a large amount of vendors bills are in the 60+ category, but the normal terms for those vendors are net 60. However, it would be an issue if the normal terms are net 30, and the same situation existed.

To create an accounts payable aging summary report, do the following:

1   Continue from where you left off.

2   Click **Reports** from the navigation bar.

3   Type **Accounts payable aging summary** in the Find a report by name search box, and then select the **Accounts payable aging summary** text, which appears below the search text box to view the accounts payable aging report. Type **1/31/2027** in the as of report date text box, then click **Run report** to view the A/P Aging Summary report shown in Figure 10.20. Save this customized report as A/P Aging Summary 1/31/27.

Wild Water Sports - Student Name (ID Number)

A/P Aging Summary
As of January 31, 2027

	CURRENT	1 - 30	31 - 60	61 - 90	91 AND OVER	TOTAL
Allstate Insurance	2,500.00					$2,500.00
Best Buy Geek Squad	6,000.00					$6,000.00
Malibu Boats	1,750.00					$1,750.00
Tige	180,000.00					$180,000.00
TOTAL	$190,250.00	$0.00	$0.00	$0.00	$0.00	$190,250.00

Figure 10.20

Accounts Payable (A/P) Aging Summary

4   Click on the **6,000.00** owed to Best Buy Geek Squad shown in Figure 10.20 to view A/P Aging Detail report shown in Figure 10.21.

Wild Water Sports - Student Name (ID Number)

A/P Aging Detail
As of January 31, 2027

DATE	TRANSACTION TYPE	NUM	VENDOR	DUE DATE	PAST DUE	AMOUNT	OPEN BALANCE
Current							
01/19/2027	Bill		Best Buy Geek Squad	02/18/2027	-1489	6,000.00	6,000.00
Total for Current						$6,000.00	$6,000.00
TOTAL						$6,000.00	$6,000.00

Figure 10.21

Accounts Payable (A/P) Aging Detail report

5   Click **6,000.00** to view the bill shown in Figure 10.22.

BALANCE DUE

Vendor

Best Buy Geek Squad

$6,000.00

Schedule online payment   Mark as paid

Mailing address	Terms	Bill date	Due date	Bill no.
Best Buy Geek Squad	Net 30	01/19/2027	02/18/2027	

Permit no.

Tags   Manage tags

Start typing to add a tag

▼ Category details

#	CATEGORY	DESCRIPTION	AMOUNT
1	Rent: Equipment rental		6,000.00

Figure 10.22

Bill (from Best Buy Geek Squad)

6   Click **X** to return to the detail report, and click **Back to report summary** to return to the A/P Aging Summary report.

Inventory Valuation Summary

In this section, you will create an inventory valuation summary that reflects each inventory item's quantity on hand, its average cost, and the resulting valuation as of a specific date.

To create an inventory valuation summary report, do the following:

1   Continue from where you left off.

2   Click **Reports** from the navigation bar.

3   Type **Inventory** in the Find a report by name search box, and then select the **Inventory Valuation Summary**. Change the as of date to **1/31/2027**. Then click **Run report** to view the report shown in Figure 10.23.

Figure 10.23

Inventory Valuation Summary

Wild Water Sports - Student Name (ID Number)

Inventory Valuation Summary
As of January 31, 2027

	SKU	QTY	ASSET VALUE	CALC. AVG
▼ Boats				
2023 Vi22		0.00	0.00	
Malibu Sportster LX		1.00	41,600.00	41,600.00
Malibu Sunset LX		0.00	0.00	
Tige 25 zx		1.00	180,000.00	180,000.00
Total Boats			**221,600.00**	
▼ Parts				
Tige Thruster Control Package		0.00	0.00	
Wake Accessory Package		5.00	1,750.00	350.00
Total Parts			**1,750.00**	
TOTAL			$223,350.00	

4   Click on the **5.00** representing the number of wake accessory packages on hand shown in Figure 10.23 to view an Inventory Valuation Detail report shown in Figure 10.24.

Figure 10.24

Inventory Valuation Detail

Wild Water Sports - Student Name (ID Number)

Inventory Valuation Detail
As of January 31, 2027

DATE	TRANSACTION TYPE	NUM	NAME	QTY	RATE	FIFO COST	QTY ON HAND	ASSET VALUE
▼ Parts								
▼ Wake Accessory Package								
01/18/2027	Inventory Starting Value	START		0.00	350.00	0.00	0.00	0.00
01/18/2027	Bill		Malibu Boats	5.00	350.00	1,750.00	5.00	1,750.00
Total for Wake Accessory Package				**5.00**		**$1,750.00**	**5.00**	**$1,750.00**
Total for Parts				**5.00**		**$1,750.00**	**5.00**	**$1,750.00**

5 Click **Bill** reflecting the purchase of five wake accessory packages shown in Figure 10.24 to view the bill shown in Figure 10.25.

Figure 10.25

Bill (from Malibu Boats)

6 Click **Cancel** to return to the detail report, and click **Back to report summary** to return to the Inventory Valuation Summary report. Save this report customization as Inventory Summary 1/1/27.

End Note

In this chapter, you did not add business events, but you did create the basic financial statement reports: profit and loss, balance sheet, and statement of cash flows. In addition, you drilled down beyond those reports to transaction detail reports and to source documents like payments, invoices, bills, and so on. You created some analytical reports to learn more about accounts receivable, accounts payable, and inventory.

Chapter 10 Questions

View the Wild Water Sports company QBO file to answer these questions by creating reports:

1   Invoice 1002 was created for which customer?

2   What was the first item sold on invoice 1002?

3   What document created an Advertising & Marketing expense?

4   Who did you send a check to for phone service?

5   How many Malibu Sunset LX boats are currently on hand?

6   What is the average cost per unit of a Wake Accessory Package?

7   How much cash was used for purchase equipment?

8   When is the bill from Allstate Insurance due?

9   When is the invoice to Florida Ski School due?

10   What amount of cash was provided by financing activities?

Chapter 10 Matching

a. Income statement

b. Balance sheet

c. Statement of cash flows

d. AR aging report

e. AP aging report

f. Inventory valuation report

g. Profit and Loss report

h. To view a transaction report

i. To view a source document

j. % of income check box

_____   Click on an event in any transaction report

_____   Click an account on any report

_____   Click to add a new column in a report

_____   Reflects unpaid bills for the current period

_____   Reports revenues and expenses

_____   Includes operating, investing, and financing activities

_____   Reports inventory quantities on hand

_____   Reports assets, liabilities, and equities

_____   Another name for the income statement

_____   Reflects unpaid invoices for the current period

Chapter 10 Cases

The following cases require you to open the company you updated in Chapter 9. Each of the following cases continues throughout the text in a sequential manner. Each of the following cases is similar in concepts assessed but differs in amounts and transactions.

To reopen your company, do the following:

1   Open your Internet browser.

2   Type **https://qbo.intuit.com** into your browser's address text box.

3   Type your user ID and password into the text boxes as you have done earlier.

Case 1

Now it is time to create, customize, and print some new reports. Based on what you learned in the text using the Wild Water Sports company, you are to make the following changes to the Case 1 company you modified in Chapter 9:

1   Create, print, and export to Excel a Profit and Loss report for January 2024. Customize this report by adding a percent of income column and saving and by sharing your customization as Profit and Loss Jan 2024.

2   Using the Profit and Loss report created above, drill down to a Transactions Report for the Sales account. Print and export this report to Excel. Save and share this report as a Sales Transaction Report.

3   Create, print, and export to Excel a Balance Sheet report as of 1/31/24. Customize this report by adding a percent of column and saving and sharing your customization as Balance Sheet Jan 2024.

4   Using the Balance Sheet report created above, drill down to a Transactions Report for the Checking account. Print and export this report to Excel. Save and share this report as Checking Report.

5   Create, print, and export to Excel a Statement of Cash Flows report as of 1/31/24. Save and share your customization as Statement of Cash Flows Jan 2024.

6   Using the Statement of Cash Flows report created above, drill down to a Transactions Report for the Accounts Receivable account. Print and export this report to Excel. Save and share this report as an A/R SCF Report.

7   Create, print, and export to Excel an A/R Aging Summary report for the month of January 2024. Save and share your customization as A/R Aging Summary Jan 2024.

8   Create, print, and export to Excel an A/P Aging Summary report for the month of January 2024. Save and share your customization as A/P Aging Summary Jan 2024.

9   Create, print, and export to Excel an Inventory Valuation Summary report for the month of January 2024. Save and share your customization as an Inventory Valuation Summary Jan 2024.

Case 2

Now it is time to create, customize, and print some new reports. Based on what you learned in the text using the Wild Water Sports company, you are to make the following changes to the Case 2 company you modified in Chapter 9:

1   Create, print, and export to Excel a Profit and Loss report for January 2025. Customize this report by adding a percent of income column. Save and share your customization as Profit and Loss Jan 2025.

2   Using the Profit and Loss report created above, drill down to a Transactions Report for the Insurance account. Print and export this report to Excel. Save and share this report as an Insurance Transaction Report.

3   Create, print, and export to Excel a Balance Sheet report as of 1/31/25. Customize this report by adding a percent of column. Save and share your customization as Balance Sheet Jan 2025.

4   Using the Balance Sheet report created above, drill down to a Transactions Report for the Inventory Asset account. Print and export this report to Excel. Save and share this report as Inventory Report.

5   Create, print, and export to Excel a Statement of Cash Flows report as of 1/31/25. Save and share your customization as Statement of Cash Flows Jan 2025.

6   Using the Statement of Cash Flows report created above, drill down to a Transactions Report for the Prepaid Expenses account. Print and export this report to Excel. Save and share this report as PPE SCF Report.

7   Create, print, and export to Excel an A/R Aging Summary report for the month of January 2025. Save and share your customization as an A/R Aging Summary Jan 2025.

8   Create, print, and export to Excel an A/P Aging Summary report for the month of January 2025. Save and share your customization as an A/P Aging Summary Jan 2025.

9   Create, print, and export to Excel an Inventory Valuation Summary report for January 2025. Save and share your customization as Inventory Valuation Summary Jan 2025.

Case 3

Now it is time to create, customize, and print some new reports. Based on what you learned in the text using the Wild Water Sports company, you are to make the following changes to the Case 3 company you modified in Chapter 9:

1   Create, print, and export to Excel a Profit and Loss report for the month of January 2026. Customize this report by adding a percent of income column and saving and sharing your customization as Profit and Loss Jan 2026.

2   Using the Profit and Loss report created earlier, drill down to a Transactions Report for the Advertising & Marketing account. Print and export this report to Excel. Save this report as Advertising & Marketing Transaction Report.

3   Create, print, and export to Excel a Balance Sheet report as of 1/31/26. Customize this report by adding a percent of column and saving your customization as Balance Sheet Jan 2026.

4   Using the Balance Sheet report created earlier, drill down to a Transactions Report for the Accounts Receivable (A/R) account. Print and export this report to Excel. Save this report as AR Report.

5   Create, print, and export to Excel a Statement of Cash Flows report for the month of January 2026. Save your customization as Statement of Cash Flows Jan 2026.

6   Using the Statement of Cash Flows report created earlier, drill down to a Transactions Report for the Payroll Tax Payable to pay account. Print and export this report to Excel. Save this report as Payroll Tax SCF Report.

7   Create, print, and export to Excel an A/R Aging Summary report for the month of January 2026. Save your customization as A/R Aging Summary Jan 2026.

8   Create, print, and export to Excel an A/P Aging Summary report for the month of January 2026. Save your customization as A/P Aging Summary Jan 2026.

9   Create, print, and export to Excel an Inventory Valuation Summary report for the month of January 2026. Save your customization as Inventory Valuation Summary Jan 2026.

Case 4

Now it is time to create, customize, and print some new reports. Based on what you learned in the text using the Wild Water Sports company, you are to make the following changes to the Case 4 company you modified in Chapter 9:

1   Create and print a Profit and Loss report for the month of January 2027. Customize this report by adding a percent of income column and saving your customization as Profit and Loss Jan 2027.

2   Using the Profit and Loss report you just created, drill down to a Transactions Report for the Advertising & Marketing account. Print and save this report as Advertising Transaction Report.

3   Create and print a Balance Sheet report as of 1/31/27. Customize this report by adding a percent of column. Collapse, print, and save this report as Balance Sheet Jan 2027.

4   Using the Balance Sheet report you just created, drill down to a Transactions Report for the Accounts Receivable (A/R) account. Print and save this report as AR Report.

5   Create and print a Statement of Cash Flows report as of 1/31/27. Save your customization as Statement of Cash Flows Jan 2027.

6   Using the Statement of Cash Flows report you just created, drill down to a Transactions Report for the Payroll wages and tax to pay account. Print and save this report as Payroll Tax SCF Report.

7   Create and print an Accounts Receivable Aging Summary report for the month of January 2027. Save your customization as A/R Aging Summary Jan 2027.

8   Create and print an Accounts Payable Aging Summary report for the month of January 2027. Save your customization as A/P Aging Summary Jan 2027.

9   Create and print an Inventory Valuation Summary report for the month of January 2027. Save your customization as Inventory Valuation Summary Jan 2027.

Case 5

Now it is time to create, customize, and print some new reports. Based on what you learned in the text using the Wild Water Sports company, you are to make the following changes to the Case 5 company you modified in Chapter 9:

1   Create and print a Profit and Loss report for the month of January 2022. Customize this report by adding a percent of income column and saving your customization as Profit and Loss Jan 2022.

2   Using the Profit and Loss report you just created, drill down to a Transactions Report for the Advertising & Marketing account. Print and save this report as Advertising Transaction Report.

3   Create and print a Balance Sheet report for the month of January 2022. Customize this report by adding a percent of row column. Collapse, print, and save this report as Balance Sheet Jan 2022.

4   Using the Balance Sheet report you just created, drill down to a Transactions Report for the Accounts Receivable (A/R) account. Collapse, print, and save this report as AR Transaction Report.

5   Create and print a Statement of Cash Flows report as of 01/31/22. Save your customization as Statement of Cash Flows Jan 2022.

6   Using the Statement of Cash Flows report you just created, drill down to a Transactions Report for the Payroll Tax Payable account. Print and save this report as Payroll Tax SCF Report.

7   Create and print an Accounts Receivable Aging Summary report for the month of January 2022. Save your customization as AR Aging Summary Jan 2022.

8   Create and print an Accounts Payable Aging Summary report for the month of January 2022. Save your customization as AP Aging Summary Jan 2022.

9   Create and print an Inventory Valuation Summary report for the month of January 2022. Save your customization as Inventory Valuation Summary Jan 2022.

Case 6

Now it is time to create, customize, and print some new reports. Based on what you learned in the text using the Wild Water Sports company, you are to make the following changes to the Case 6 company you modified in Chapter 9:

1 Create and print a Profit and Loss report for the month of January 2023. Customize this report by adding a % of income column and saving your customization as Profit and Loss Jan 2023.

2 Using the Profit and Loss report you just created, drill down to a Transactions Report for the Payroll account. Print and save this report as Payroll Transaction Report.

3 Create and print a Balance Sheet report as of 1/31/23. Customize this report by adding a % of row column. (This is done in a similar manner to adding a % of income column done for the Profit and Loss report.) Collapse, print, and save this report as Balance Sheet Jan 2023.

4 Using the Balance Sheet report you just created drill down to a Transactions Report for the Prepaid Expenses account. Collapse, print, and save this report as Prepaid Expenses Transaction Report.

5 Create and print a Statement of Cash Flows report as of 1/31/23. Save your customization as Statement of Cash Flows Jan 2023.

6 Create and print an Accounts Receivable Aging Summary report for the month of January 2023. Save your customization as A/R Aging Summary Jan 2023.

7 Create and print an Accounts Payable Aging Summary report for the month of January 2023. Save your customization as A/P Aging Summary Jan 2023.

8 Create and print an Inventory Valuation Summary report for the month of January 2023. Save your customization as Inventory Valuation Summary Jan 2023.

Sales Tax

Some companies are required to collect sales tax from customers depending on the state(s) in which they do business. Collecting sales tax in QBO has gotten easier! Through the new Automated Sales Tax experience, you just need to answer a few simple questions and QBO will know what taxes apply to your business, set them up, and automatically track your sales taxes.

This means you no longer need to select a tax rate when you create an invoice or other transaction. As long as your Sales Tax Center and all applicable tax agencies are set up, the system will automatically do it for you!

Be advised that end-of-chapter Cases 1 and 2 do not require the collection of sales tax. Cases 3 to 6 do require the collection of sales tax using the new Automated Sales Tax system. Keep in mind that sales tax rates change year to year, state to state. The solutions provided by the author for each case were based on tax rates in effect for that particular year. If a rate changes your answers for sales tax payable and related accounts may be different.

At the time of publication, Intuit had two different procedures for setting up sales tax. The first works for regular companies students and instructors. This is the process used in prior editions of QBO and this text. The second works for the Sample Company and is the new process used going forward. At some point this new process will be implemented and work for both types of companies.

The following are steps to set up the new Automated Sales Tax system. The following example assumes the company is in California. That is not true in all cases. Your case may be in a different state, and thus, your steps to create a company's sales tax will be different.

Navigate your browser to the Video Tutorials provided by Intuit (See web site address specified in the Preface to this text) and then search on How to Set Up and use Automatic Sales Tax.

To set up a company's sales tax (QBO regular companies):

1   Click **Taxes** from the navigation bar.

2   Click the **Use Automatic Sales Tax** button (assuming you've already entered your company's address during the setup process), and then click **Next** to confirm your company's business address. Click **No** when asked if you need to collect sales tax out of the state and then click **Next**. Now view the window shown in Figure A.1.

Figure A.1

Sales Tax Center

Automatic sales tax is all set up

Give it a spin by creating your first invoice.

Create invoice

3 Do not click **Create invoice**. Instead click the **X** to close this window.

4 Select **Quarterly** from the Filing frequency drop-down text box, and then click **Save**.

5 From the Sales Tax Center, click **Sales Tax Settings**.

6 Click **Edit** from the Agency Action column.

7 Type **01/01/20xx** replacing XX with the start date of your company. For example, see Figure A.2.

Navigate your browser to the Video Tutorials provided by Intuit (see website address specified in the Preface to this text) and then search on How to Set Up and use Automatic Sales Tax.

Figure A.2

Example of changing the start
date for the sales tax center

8   Click **Save** to accept changes.

9   Click **Back to sales tax center**.

10   Click **Dashboard** to return to the Dashboard.

Comprehensive Case Problems

Your instructor may assign you these comprehensive case problems after you complete all 10 chapters of the text. These are an *extension* of the cases assigned at the end of Chapters 3 to 10 of the *QuickBooks Online for Accounting*, fifth edition, text. Because QBO only allows you access to one company, Case 1 can be used by students only if they have *successfully completed* Case 1 through Chapter 10, Case 2 can be used by students only if they have *successfully completed* Case 2 through Chapter 10, Case 3 can be used by students only if they have *successfully completed* Case 3 through Chapter 10, and Case 4 can be used by students only if they have *successfully completed* Case 4 through Chapter 10. There is no Case 5 comprehensive problem. Case 6 can be used by students only if they have *successfully completed* Case 6 through Chapter 10.

Case 1 Comprehensive Problem

Case 1, which begins in Chapter 3, is a company that distributes surfboards and is in La Jolla, California. Business events in Case 1 occurred from 12/31/23 to 1/31/24 when presented in Chapters 3 to 10. The following is a description of business events that occurred in the month of February 2024.

Date	Description of Event	Chapter	Event
2/1/24	Add a new product	4	Add a new product with quantity tracked – Biscuit Bonzer, initial quantity on hand: 0, as of date: 2/1/24, price: $1,000, cost: $675, income account: Sales, expense account: Cost of Goods Sold. Vendor: Channel Islands.
2/1/24	Edit the chart of accounts	3	Change the name of the account Notes Payable to Notes Payable – Bank of CA.
2/1/24	Add a new service	4	Add a new service – Repairs, rate: $85, income account: Services.
2/1/24	Modify budget	8	Modify the following monthly budgeted amounts (Budget 1) for February 2024 through December 2024 as follows: sales: $35,000, services: $2,000, cost of goods sold: $21,500, interest expense: $800, payroll: $13,000, rent or lease: $2,500, travel: $500, utilities: $300.
2/1/24	Add a new employee	7	Add a new employee – Jane Price, 65 Ocean View Lane, La Jolla, CA 92037, Employee ID No.: 555-15-3537.
2/1/24	Add a new customer	4	Add a new customer – Awesome Surf, 501 Boardwalk Place, Santa Cruz, CA 95060.
2/5/24	Add a sales receipt	4	Add a new sales receipt #1005 for $2,810 – Customer: Awesome Surf, payment method: Check, reference no.: 984, deposit to: Undeposited Funds, product: The Water Hog, quantity: 1, and product: Rook 15, quantity: 3.
2/6/24	Add a new invoice	4	Add a new invoice #1006 for $820 – Customer: Surf Rider Foundation, terms: Net 30, service: Repairs, quantity: 2, and product: Rook 15, quantity: 1.
2/7/24	Add a cash receipt	4	Add a new cash receipt – Customer: Blondie's Boards, payment method: Check, reference no.: 1003, deposit to: Undeposited Funds, amount received: $8,000, applied to invoice #1003.
2/8/24	Make a bank deposit	4	Add a bank deposit to the checking account in the amount of $15,810, which represents payments from Blondie's Boards for $5,000 and $8,000 and Awesome Surf for $2,810.
2/9/24	Add a new vendor	5	Add a new vendor – BoardsWest, 36 Anacapa St., Santa Barbara, CA 93101, terms: Net 30.

Date	Action		Description
2/9/24	Add a new product	5	Add a new product with quantity tracked – Wiley One, initial quantity on hand: 0, as of date: 2/9/24, price: $4,000, cost: $2,400, income account: Sales, expense account: Cost of Goods Sold. Vendor: BoardsWest.
2/9/24	Add a new account	3	Add a new account – Account type: Other Current Assets, detail type: Other Current Assets, name: Employee Loans.
2/9/24	Add a new purchase order	5	Add a new purchase order #1003 for $9,600 to purchase 4 Wiley One boards from vendor BoardsWest.
2/10/24	Use credit card	5	Add a credit card charge – Vendor: Village Travel, using credit card: VISA, category Travel, amount: $775.
2/11/24	Record a check	5	Add check no. 1013 – Vendor: Office Depot, amount: $575, category: Supplies Asset.
2/11/24	Add a new purchase order	5	Add a new purchase order #1004 for $12,400 – Vendor: Channel Islands, ordered 10 Fred Rubbles, 6 Rook 15, and 8 The Water Hog boards.
2/12/24	Add a new bill	5	Add a new bill based on a purchase order #1002 for $4,700 – Vendor: Stewart Surfboards, terms: Net 30. All items ordered were received.
2/13/24	Add a new bill	5	Add a new bill without a purchase order – San Diego Gas & Electric, terms: Net 15, category: Utilities, amount: $150.
2/14/24	Add a new bill	5	Add a new bill without a purchase order – Prime Properties, terms: Net 15, category: Rent or Lease, amount: $2,500.
2/14/24	Pay a bill with a check	5	Pay bill $7,500 due to Prime Properties using check no. 1012.
2/15/24	Add new fixed asset accounts	6	Create four new fixed asset accounts – Account type: Fixed Assets, detail type: Buildings and Accumulated Depreciation (where appropriate), account names: Original Cost (a sub account of Building) and Accumulated Depreciation (a sub account of Building), and Land with Account type: Fixed Asset, detail type: Land.
2/15/24	Purchase land and building	6	Add the purchase of land and a warehouse building from Prime Properties, check no. 1014, amount: $2,000, as a down payment on land $5,000 and a building $15,000. The balance was paid by signing a long-term note for $18,000 (create a new account called Notes Payable – Chase, Account type: Long-Term Liabilities, detail type: Notes Payable).
2/19/24	Sell common stock	6	Add the sale of common stock to shareholders as a deposit of a $15,000 check.
2/19/24	Pay dividends	6	Add the payment of dividends to shareholders on 2/19/24, check no. 1015, in the amount of $500.
2/20/24	Make a loan payment	6	Add the payment of $339.68 to Chase Bank (a new vendor) as an installment on the land and building purchase made on 2/15/24, which included interest expense of $75 and principal amount of $264.68 using check no. 1016.
2/20/24	Make a loan payment	6	Record the payment of $1,132.27 to Bank of CA on 2/20/24 (as an installment on a loan received last month), which included interest expense of $250 and principal amount of $882.27 using check no. 1017.
2/20/24	Pay first payroll	7	Add payroll (as you did in the chapter) based on the information shown in Figure 1. (This payroll covers work through 2/15/24 but wasn't paid until 2/20/24.)
2/27/24	Add a new bill	6	Add a new bill based on purchase order #1003 on 2/9/24 – Vendor: BoardsWest, terms: Net 30. All items ordered were received.
2/27/24	Add a new invoice	4	Add invoice #1007 for $12,000 to Blazing Boards, terms: Net 30, for 3 Wiley One boards.
2/28/24	Pay second payroll	7	Add payroll (as you did in the chapter) based on the information shown in Figure 2 as follows.
2/28/24	Add a new bill	5	Add a new bill based on purchase order #1004 for $12,400 – Vendor: Channel Islands, terms: Net 15. All items ordered were received. (*Hint:* First clear all lines in the Item details section of the bill that are left over from a previous bill from Channel Islands.)
2/28/24	Add a new invoice	4	Add an invoice #1008 for $12,990 to Blondie's Boards, terms: Net 30, for 8 Fred Rubble, 3 Rook 15, and 4 The Water Hog boards.

2/28/24	Add a sales receipt	4	Add a sales receipt #1009 for Sarah Hay at Hey Hays Surf for $12,210 to record their check no. 988, which was deposited to the checking account, for 1 California Nose Rider, 3 Fred Rubble, 1 Wiley One, 1 Water Hog, and 2 Rook 15 boards.
2/28/24	Reconcile bank account	4	Reconcile your company's checking account. No service charges or interest were incurred or earned. The ending bank statement balance on 2/28/24 was $39,896.91. All checks cleared the bank except checks no. 1021 to 1023. All deposits cleared the bank except a check from Sarah Hay for $12,210.
2/28/24	Adjust supplies	9	$250 of supplies were used in February. Use journal entry 10.
2/28/24	Adjust prepaid rent	9	$800 of prepaid expenses expired (representing prepaid rent) in the month of February. Use journal entry 11.
2/28/24	Accrue expenses	9	A bill for $450 was received and recorded in the next month for travel consumed in the current month. Use journal entry 12. In January, you accrued $150 in maintenance costs, which remains unpaid. No adjustment is necessary, but payment needs to be made next month.
2/28/24	Defer revenue	9	Consulting services recorded on invoice #1004 for $2,500 to Surf Rider Foundation were unearned as of 1/31/24 but were performed in February 2024. Thus, the revenue was earned. This requires the reversal of journal entry 7 recorded on 1/31/24. (*Hint:* Look at journal entry 7, and use journal entry 13 to reverse it on 2/28/24.)
2/28/24	Accrue revenue	9	Consulting services of $8,500 (340 hours) were performed as of 1/31/24 for Blazing Boards but not invoiced to the customer or recorded into the accounting records. Revenue was accrued using journal entry 8. Add invoice #1010 to bill Blazing Boards for this service. This also requires reversal of journal entry 8 recorded on 1/31/24. (*Hint:* Look at journal entry 8, and use journal entry 14 to reverse it on 2/28/24.)
2/28/24	Accrue depreciation	9	Depreciation Expense of $675 ($100, $75, and $500 for Building, Equipment, and Furniture & Fixtures, respectively) needs to be recorded for the month. Use journal entry 15 to record this depreciation.
2/28/24	Accrue revenue	9	Consulting services of $10,200 were performed on 2/28/24 for a new customer, Kyle Hain, but not invoiced or recorded into the accounting records. Use journal entry 16 to accrue this revenue.

Pay/Tax/Withholding	Ben	Betsy	Jane	Total
Hours if applicable	n/a	62	60	
Annual salary or hourly rate	95,000.00	21.50	20.00	
Gross pay	3,958.33	1,333.00	1,200.00	5,291.33
Federal withholding	542.29	182.62	164.40	724.91
Social security employee (6.2%)	245.42	82.65	74.40	328.07
Medicare employee (1.45%)	57.40	19.33	17.40	76.73
Employee withholding	845.11	284.60	256.20	1,129.71
Social security employer (6.2%)	245.42	82.65	74.40	328.07
Medicare employer (1.45%)	57.40	19.33	17.40	76.73
Employer payroll tax expense	302.82	101.98	91.80	404.80
Net Check amount	3,113.22	1,048.40	943.80	5,105.42
Check number	**1018**	**1019**	**1020**	

Figure 1

First semimonthly payroll

Figure 2

Second semimonthly payroll

Pay/Tax/Withholding	Ben	Betsy	Jane	Total
Hours if applicable	n/a	52	45	
Annual salary or hourly rate	95,000.00	21.50	20.00	
Gross pay	3,958.33	1,118.00	900.00	5,076.33
Federal withholding	542.29	153.17	123.30	695.46
Social security employee (6.2%)	245.42	69.32	55.80	314.74
Medicare employee (1.45%)	57.40	16.21	13.05	73.61
Employee withholding	845.11	238.70	192.15	1,083.81
Social security employer (6.2%)	245.42	69.32	55.80	314.74
Medicare employer (1.45%)	57.40	16.21	13.05	73.61
Employer payroll tax expense	302.82	85.53	68.85	388.35
Net Check amount	3,113.22	879.30	707.85	3,992.52
Check number	1021	1022	1023	

Requirements:

1   Create, save, and print a Profit and Loss report for February 2024.
2   Create, save, and print a Sales Transaction report for February 2024.
3   Create, save, and print a Balance Sheet report for February 28, 2024, with a % of column.
4   Create, save, and print a Checking report for February 2024.
5   Create, save, and print a Statement of Cash Flows report for February 2024.
6   Create, save, and print an A/R Aging Summary report for February 2024.
7   Create, save, and print an A/P Aging Summary report for February 2024.
8   Create, save, and print an Inventory Valuation Summary report for February 2024.
9   Create, save, and print a Transactions List by Date report for February 2024.
10 Create, save, and print a Budget vs. Actuals report for February 2024.

Case 2 Comprehensive Problem

Case 2, which begins in Chapter 3, is a company that distributes remote controlled toys and is in La Jolla, California. Business events in Case 2 occurred from 12/31/24 to 1/31/25 when presented in Chapters 3 to 10. The following is a description of business events that occurred in the month of February 2025.

Date	Description of Event	Chapter	Event
2/1/25	Add a new product	4	Add a new product – Speedy Whit, initial quantity on hand: 0, as of date: 2/1/25, price: $1,500, cost: $925, income account: Sales, expense account: Cost of Goods Sold.

2/1/25	Add a new vendor	5	Add a new vendor – 3D Robotics, 36 Anacapa St., Santa Barbara, CA 93101, terms: Net 30.
2/1/25	Edit the chart of accounts	3	Change the name of the account Notes Payable to Notes Payable – Bank of San Diego.
2/1/25	Add a new service	4	Add a new service – Consulting, rate: $105, income account: Services.
2/1/25	Modify budget	8	Modify the following monthly budgeted amounts (Budget 1) for February 2025 through December 2025 as follows: sales: $22,000, services: $4,800, cost of goods sold: $11,000, interest expense: $400, payroll: $10,000, rent or lease: $2,500, travel: $500, utilities: $300. All other accounts remain the same.
2/1/25	Add a new employee	7	Add a new employee – Juan Perez, 65 Ocean View Lane, La Jolla, CA 92037, Employee ID No.: 555-15-3537.
2/1/25	Add a new customer	4	Add a new customer – Briggs Construction, 501 Boardwalk Place, Santa Cruz, CA 95060.
2/5/25	Add a sales receipt	4	Add a new sales receipt #1005 for $3,300 – Customer: Briggs Construction, payment method: Check, reference no.: 984, deposit to: Undeposited Funds, product: Broon F830 Ride, quantity: 1, and product: Sport Cub S, quantity: 3.
2/6/25	Add a new invoice	4	Add a new invoice #1006 for $2,250 – Customer: Hagen's Toys, terms: Net 30, service: Consulting, quantity: 10, and product: Sport Cub S, quantity: 2.
2/7/25	Add a cash receipt	4	Add a new cash receipt – Customer: Hagen's Toys, payment method: Check, reference no.: 5841, deposit to: Undeposited Funds, amount received: $1,425 (related to invoice #1002).
2/8/25	Make a bank deposit	4	Add a bank deposit to the checking account in the amount of $5,650 (Benson's RC $925, Brigg's Construction $3,300, and Hagen's Toys $1,425).
2/9/25	Add a new product	4	Add a new product – Pro View, initial quantity on hand: 0, as of date: 2/9/25, price: $2,500, cost: $1,200, income account: Sales, expense account: Cost of Goods Sold.
2/9/25	Add a new account	3	Add a new account – Account type: Other Current Assets, detail type: Other Current Assets, name: Security Deposits.
2/9/25	Add a new purchase order	5	Add a new purchase order #1003 for $11,550 to purchase 6 Speedy Whit and 5 Pro View drones from vendor 3D Robotics.
2/9/25	Use credit card	5	Add a credit card charge, new vendor: Village Travel, using credit card: AMEX, category: Travel, amount: $1,800.
2/11/25	Record a check	5	Add check no. 1011, vendor: Staples, Inc., amount: $750, account: Supplies Asset.
2/11/25	Add a new purchase order	5	Add a new purchase order #1004 for $3,695 – Vendor: E-flite for 5 Sport Cub S and 4 Mystique RES drones.
2/12/25	Add a new bill	5	Add a new bill based on a purchase order #1002 for $8,820 – Vendor: Kyosho, terms: Net 30. All items ordered were received.
2/13/25	Add a new bill	5	Add a new bill without a purchase order – San Diego Gas & Electric (a new vendor), terms: Net 15, category: Utilities, amount: $150.
2/13/25	Add a new bill	5	Add a new bill without a purchase order – Deluxe Properties (a new vendor), terms: Net 15, category: Rent & Lease, amount: $3,500.
2/13/25	Add new fixed asset accounts	6	Create four new fixed asset accounts – Account type: Fixed Assets, detail type: Buildings and Accumulated Depreciation (where appropriate), account names: Original Cost (a sub account of Building) and Accumulated Depreciation (a sub account of Building), and Land with Account type: Fixed Asset, detail type: Land.
2/13/25	Purchase land and building	6	Add the purchase of land and a warehouse building from Deluxe Properties, check no. 1012, amount: $10,000, as a down payment on land $15,000 and a building $35,000. The balance was paid by signing a long-term note for $40,000 to the Bank of San Diego (a new vendor).

2/15/25	Pay first payroll	7	Add payroll (as you did in the chapter) based on the information shown in Figure 1.
2/19/25	Sell common stock	6	Add the sale of common stock to shareholders as a deposit of a $10,000, check no. 3009.
2/19/25	Pay dividends	6	Add the payment of dividends to shareholders on 2/19/25, check no. 1016, in the amount of $500.
2/20/25	Make a loan payment	6	Add the payment of $1,216.88 to the Bank of San Diego as an installment on the land and building purchase made on 2/15/25, which included interest expense of $200 and principal amount of $1,016.88, using check no. 1017.
2/22/25	Add a new bill	5	Add a new bill based on a purchase order #1003 – Vendor: 3D Robotics, terms: Net 30, amount: $11,550. All items ordered were received.
2/25/25	Add a new invoice	4	Add invoice #1007 for $10,500 to Kelly's Awesome Copters, terms: Net 30, for 4 Speedy Whit and 3 Broon F830 Ride drones.
2/25/25	Pay a bill with a check	5	Pay bill $3,500 due to Deluxe Properties using check no. 1018.
2/26/25	Receive payment	4	Receive payment on account from Hagen's Toys of $4,500 for invoice #1003 using check no. 938 and deposited to the Undeposited Funds account.
2/27/25	Add a new invoice	4	Add an invoice #1008 for $4,755 to A+ Engineering (a new customer), terms: Net 30, for 15 hours of consulting, 2 Speedy Whit drones, and 4 hours of custom painting.
2/27/25	Add a new bill	5	Add a new bill based on purchase order #1004 for $3,695 – Vendor: E-flite, terms: Net 15. All items ordered were received. (*Hint:* First clear all lines in the Item details section of the bill that are left over from a previous bill from E-flite.)
2/27/25	Add a sales receipt	4	Add a sales receipt #1009 for Fly by Night (a new customer) for $2,700 to record cash received, which was deposited to the checking account for 3 Sport Cub S and 2 Mystique RES drones.
2/27/25	Make a deposit	4	Deposited Hagen's Toys check for $4,500 into the checking account.
2/28/25	Add a new invoice	4	Add invoice #1010 to record repair services performed for Kelly's Awesome Copters. This transaction had been accrued on 1/31/25 via journal entry 8. (A variety of rates were used on this repair; thus, just enter $6,298 as the Rate for this invoice and 1 as the QTY.)
2/28/25	Add a bill	5	Add a bill for legal services rendered by Galas & Associates (new vendor) for $750. This had been accrued on 1/31/25 using journal entry 6.
2/28/25	Pay second payroll	7	Add payroll (as you did in the chapter) based on the information shown in Figure 2 as follows.
2/28/25	Reconcile bank account	8	Reconcile your company's checking account. No service charges or interest were incurred or earned. The ending bank statement balance on 2/28/25 was $29,835.47. All checks cleared the bank except checks no. 1019 to 1021. All deposits cleared the bank except a deposit from Hagen's Toys for $4,500.
2/28/25	Adjust supplies	9	$250 of supplies were used in February. Use journal entry 10.
2/28/25	Adjust prepaids	9	$1,800 of prepaid expenses expired (representing prepaid insurance) in the month of February. Use journal entry 11.
2/28/25	Accrue expenses	9	A bill for $850 was received and recorded in the next month for travel consumed in the current month. Use journal entry 12.
2/28/25	Reverse accrual	9	Legal fees accrued on 1/31/25 for $750 via journal entry 6 were properly recorded in February. Use journal entry 13 to reverse it.
2/28/25	Defer revenue	9	Consulting services recorded on invoice #1008 for $1,575 to A+ Engineering were not yet performed and thus were unearned as of 2/28/25. Use journal entry 14 to defer this revenue.
2/28/25	Accrue depreciation	9	Depreciation Expense of $1,125 ($125, $375, and $625 for Building, Furniture, and Machinery & Equipment, respectively) needs to be recorded for the month. Use journal entry 15 to record this depreciation.

| 2/28/25 | Reverse accrual | 9 | $6,298 of revenue had been accrued on 1/31/25 via journal entry 8 for services rendered but not yet invoiced. These were then invoiced using invoice #1010 to Kelly's Awesome Copters. (*Hint:* Reverse journal entry 8 via a new journal entry 16.) |
| 2/28/25 | Accrue revenue | 9 | Consulting services of $15,000 were performed on 2/28/25 for a new customer, Wesley Ray, but not invoiced or recorded into the accounting records. Use journal entry 17 to accrue this revenue. |

Pay/Tax/Withholding	Frank	Sara	Juan	Total
Hours if applicable	n/a	80	65	
Annual salary or hourly rate	72,000.00	18.75	17.00	
Gross pay	**3,000.00**	**1,500.00**	**1,105.00**	**4,500.00**
Federal withholding	411.00	205.50	151.39	616.50
Social security employee (6.2%)	186.00	93.00	68.51	279.00
Medicare employee (1.45%)	43.50	21.75	16.02	65.25
Employee withholding	**640.50**	**320.25**	**235.92**	**960.75**
Social security employer (6.2%)	186.00	93.00	68.51	279.00
Medicare employer (1.45%)	43.50	21.75	16.02	65.25
Employer payroll tax expense	**229.50**	**114.75**	**84.53**	**344.25**
Net Check amount	2,359.50	1,179.75	869.08	3,539.25
Check number	**1013**	**1014**	**1015**	

Figure 1

First semimonthly payroll

Pay/Tax/Withholding	Frank	Sara	Juan	Total
Hours if applicable	n/a	75	70	
Annual salary or hourly rate	72,000.00	18.75	17.00	
Gross pay	**3,000.00**	**1,406.25**	**1,190.00**	**4,406.25**
Federal withholding	411.00	192.66	163.03	603.66
Social security employee (6.2%)	186.00	87.19	73.78	273.19
Medicare employee (1.45%)	43.50	20.39	17.26	63.89
Employee withholding	**640.50**	**300.24**	**254.07**	**940.74**
Social security employer (6.2%)	186.00	87.19	73.78	273.19
Medicare employer (1.45%)	43.50	20.39	17.26	63.89
Employer payroll tax expense	**229.50**	**107.58**	**91.04**	**337.08**
Net Check amount	2,359.50	1,106.01	935.93	3,465.51
Check number	**1019**	**1020**	**1021**	

Figure 2

Second semimonthly payroll

Requirements:

1 Create, save, and print a Profit and Loss report for February 2025.

2 Create, save, and print a Total Income Transaction report for February 2025. (*Hint:* Click the **Total Income amount** in the Profit and Loss report for February 2025.)

3 Create, save, and print a Balance Sheet report for February 28, 2025.

4 Create, save, and print a Checking report for February 2025.

5 Create, save, and print a Statement of Cash Flows report for February 2025.

6 Create, save, and print an A/R Aging Summary report for February 2025.

7 Create, save, and print an A/P Aging Summary report for February 2025.

8 Create, save, and print an Inventory Valuation Summary report for February 2025.

9 Create, save, and print a Transactions List by Date report for February 2025.

10 Create, save, and print a Budget vs. Actuals report for February 2025.

Case 3 Comprehensive Problem

Case 3, which begins in Chapter 3, is a company that sells and services cell phones to consumers (retail business) and is in La Jolla, California. Business events in Case 3 occurred from 12/31/25 to 1/31/26 when presented in Chapters 3 to 10. The following is a description of business events that occurred in the month of February 2026.

Date	Description of Event	Chapter	Event
2/2/26	Add new products	4	Add two new taxable products – iPhone 8, initial quantity on hand: 0, as of date: 2/1/26, inventory asset account: Inventory Asset, price: $850, cost: $650, income account: Sales of Product Income, expense account: Cost of Goods Sold (taxable) and iPhone 8 Plus, initial quantity on hand: 0, as of date: 2/1/26, inventory asset account: Inventory Asset, price: $1,050, cost: $850, income account: Sales of Product Income, expense account: Cost of Goods Sold (taxable).
2/2/26	Change the name of a product	4	Change the name of the Apple iPhone 7 to iPhone 7.
2/2/26	Add a new vendor	5	Add a new vendor – LG Baker Distributing Company, 36 Sequoia St., Redlands, CA 92374, terms: Net 30.
2/2/26	Add a new product	4	Add a new taxable product – LG V30, initial quantity on hand: 0, as of date: 2/2/26, inventory asset account: Inventory Asset, price: $830, cost: $600, income account: Sales of Product Income, expense account: Cost of Goods Sold (taxable).
2/3/26	Add a new service	4	Add a new service – LG Repairs, rate: $95, income account: Services (not taxable).
2/3/26	Modify budget	8	Modify the following monthly budgeted amounts (Budget 1) for February 2026 through December 2026 as follows: sales of product income: $25,000, services: $9,000, cost of goods sold: $18,000, advertising and marketing: $2,000, insurance: $750, interest paid: $200, meals: $0, payroll: $11,000, utilities: $300.
2/3/26	Add a new employee	7	Add a new employee – Obi-Wan Kenobi, 65 Ocean View Lane, La Jolla, CA 92037, Employee ID No.: 555-22-9741.

2/3/26	Add a bill	5	Add a bill from FixIt, Inc., terms: Net 15, for repairs made last month for $350. This bill was accrued as of 1/31/26. You will reverse this accrual at the end of this month.
2/4/26	Add a new customer	4	Add a new customer – United Air, 598 Terrace View, Santa Cruz, CA 95060.
2/5/26	Add a sales receipt	4	Add a new sales receipt #1004 for $1,293 – Customer: GHO Marketing, payment method: Check, reference no.: 1641, deposit to: Payments to deposit, product: iPhone 7, quantity: 1, and product: Samsung Galaxy 8, quantity: 1. (Click **See the math** to update amounts.)
2/6/26	Add a new purchase order	5	Add a new purchase order #1003 for $16,700 to purchase 10 iPhone 8 and 12 iPhone 8 Plus phones from vendor Apple Computer, Inc.
2/7/26	Add a new purchase order	5	Add a new purchase order #1004 for $9,000 to purchase 15 LG V30 phones from vendor LG Baker Distributing Company.
2/10/26	Add a new invoice	4	Add a new invoice #1005 for $9,751.38 – Customer: United Air, terms: Net 30, product: Pixel, quantity: 10, and product: Samsung Note, quantity: 3. (Click **See the math** to update amounts.)
2/10/26	Add a new invoice	4	Add a new invoice #1006 for $1,800 – Customer: Graham Engineering, Inc., terms: Net 30, service: Phone Consulting. Use 1 as the QTY and $1,800 as the Rate. (Not taxable.)
2/11/26	Add a cash receipt	4	Add a new cash receipt – Customer: Diamond Girl, Inc., payment method: Check, reference no.: 7419, deposit to: Payments to deposit, amount received: $6,728.88 (related to invoice #1003).
2/11/26	Pay bills	5	Pay $8,900 in bills from Hathaway Insurance, Google, Inc., and the News-Press, using checks no. 330 to 332.
2/11/26	Make a bank deposit	4	Add a bank deposit to the checking account in the amount of $8,021.88 to deposit previously received payments from GHO Marketing ($1,293) and Diamond Girl, Inc. ($6,728.88).
2/12/26	Record a credit card purchase	5	Purchase supplies from Staples, Inc. using the AMEX credit card $800. (Be sure to use the Supplies Asset account.)
2/12/26	Record a check	5	Add check no. 333 to E-Trade for $15,000 in additional investments.
2/12/26	Record a check	5	Add check no. 334 to Property, Inc. (a new vendor) for $12,000 to prepay one-year rent on a storage facility.
2/12/26	Add a new purchase order	5	Add a new purchase order #1005 for $16,500 – Vendor: Samsung, Inc. for 10 Samsung Galaxy 8 and 20 Samsung Note phones.
2/13/26	Add a new bill	5	Add a new bill based on a purchase order #1004 for $9,000 – Vendor: LG Baker Distributing Company, terms: Net 30. All items ordered were received.
2/14/26	Add a new bill	5	Add a new bill based on a purchase order #1003 for $16,700 – Vendor: Apple Computer, Inc., terms: Net 30. All items ordered were received.
2/14/26	Add a new bill	5	Add a new bill without a purchase order – San Diego Gas & Electric (a new vendor), terms: Net 15, category: Utilities, amount: $300.
2/15/26	Modify fixed asset accounts	6	Modify the Furniture & Fixtures account to track depreciation of this asset by adding two subaccounts: Original Cost and Accumulated Depreciation.
2/15/26	Record a credit card purchase and bank loan using a journal entry.	6	Add the purchase of $25,000 in furniture from Staples, Inc. On this purchase, $5,000 was charged to the AMEX credit card, and the $20,000 balance was paid by signing a note payable using journal entry 10. (Be sure to indicate Rabobank in the Name section of the notes payable entry and to record the purchase in the original cost sub account of Furniture & Fixtures.)
2/15/26	Pay first payroll	7	Add payroll (as you did in the chapter) based on the information shown in Figure 1. (Use checks no. 335 to 337.)

2/17/26	Additional owner's investment	6	Received additional owner's investment and recorded it as a deposit of $10,000 (check no. 283) from owners.
2/17/26	Withdrawals	6	Record a withdrawal by owners using check no. 338, in the amount of $200.
2/18/26	Make a loan payment	6	Add the payment of $590.38 made to Rabobank as an installment on the furniture purchased on 2/15/26, which included interest paid of $66.67 and principal amount of $523.71, using check no. 339.
2/19/26	Make a loan payment	6	Add the payment of $944.77 to Chase Bank as an installment on the note payable on 1/16/26, which includes interest paid of $106.67 and principal amount of $838.10, using check no. 340.
2/20/26	Add a new bill	5	Add a new bill of $16,500 based on a purchase order #1005 – Vendor: Samsung, Inc., terms: Net 30. All items ordered were received. (*Hint:* First clear all lines in the Item details section of the bill that are left over from a previous bill from Samsung, Inc.)
2/25/26	Pay bills	5	Pay bills from Samsung, Inc. ($6,950) and Apple Computer, Inc. ($16,700) using checks no. 341 and 342.
2/25/26	Add a new invoice	4	Add invoice #1007 for $16,809 to Surfer Sales, terms: Net 30, for 10 iPhone 8 Plus and 6 iPhone 8 phones plus tax. (Click **See the math** to update amounts.)
2/25/26	Receive payment	4	Receive payment on account from Graham Engineering, Inc. of $1,800 from invoice #1006 using check no. 1641 into the Payments to deposit account.
2/27/26	Add a new invoice	4	Add an invoice #1008 for $13,738.13 to Diamond Girl, Inc., terms: Net 30, product: Samsung Note, quantity: 15. (Click **See the math** to update amounts.)
2/27/26	Add a new invoice		Add an invoice #1009 for $875 to Rooney Enterprises (a new customer), for 25 hours of Phone Consulting @ $35/hour, terms: Net 30.
2/27/26	Make a deposit	4	Deposited Graham Engineering, Inc.'s check for $1,800 into the checking account.
2/28/26	Pay second payroll	7	Add payroll (as you did in the chapter) based on the information shown in Figure 2 as follows. (Use checks no. 343 to 345.)
2/28/26	Reconcile bank account	8	Reconcile your company's checking account. No service charges or interest were incurred or earned. The ending bank statement balance on 2/28/26 was $6,043.24. All checks cleared the bank except checks no. 343 to 345. All deposits cleared the bank except a deposit from Graham Engineering, Inc. for $1,800.
2/28/26	Adjust supplies	9	Supplies worth $700 were used in February. Use journal entry 11.
2/28/26	Adjust prepaids	9	Prepaid expenses of $2,800 expired in the month of February ($1,800 related to insurance expense and $1,000 related to rent). Use journal entry 12.
2/28/26	Accrue expenses	9	A bill for $2,550 was received and recorded in the next month for legal fees consumed in the current month. Use journal entry 13.
2/28/26	Reverse accrual	9	Repair fees accrued on 1/31/26 for $350 via journal entry 6 were properly recorded in February. Use journal entry 14 to reverse this accrual.
2/28/26	Defer revenue	9	Phone Consulting services recorded on invoice #1009 for $875 for Rooney Enterprises were deemed unearned as of 2/28/26. Use journal entry 15 to defer this revenue.
2/28/26	Reverse deferral	9	Phone Consulting services deferred in the prior month of $210 were earned in February. Use journal entry 16 to reverse journal entry 7 recorded on 1/31/26.
2/28/26	Accrue depreciation	9	Depreciation Expense of $1,700 ($850, $500, and $350 for Computers, Furniture & Fixtures, and Machinery & Equipment, respectively). Use journal entry 17 to record this depreciation.
2/28/26	Accrue revenue	9	Phone Consulting services of $3,500 were performed on 2/28/26 for a new customer, Rigel Works, but not invoiced or recorded into the accounting records. Use journal entry 18 to accrue this revenue.

Pay/Tax/Withholding	Kira	Jedi	Obi-Wan	Total
Hours if applicable	n/a	72	80	
Annual salary or hourly rate	48,000.00	17.00	22.00	
Gross pay	**2,000.00**	**1,224.00**	**1,760.00**	**4,984.00**
Federal withholding	274.00	167.69	241.12	682.81
Social security employee (6.2%)	124.00	75.89	109.12	309.01
Medicare employee (1.45%)	29.00	17.75	25.52	72.27
Employee withholding	**427.00**	**261.33**	**375.76**	**1,064.09**
Social security employer (6.2%)	124.00	75.89	109.12	309.01
Medicare company employer (1.45%)	29.00	17.75	25.52	72.27
Employer payroll tax expense	**153.00**	**93.64**	**134.64**	**381.28**
Net Check amount	1,573.00	962.67	1,384.24	3,919.91

Figure 1

First semimonthly payroll

Pay/Tax/Withholding	Kira	Jedi	Obi-Wan	Total
Hours if applicable	n/a	65	85	
Annual salary or hourly rate	48,000.00	17.00	22.00	
Gross pay	**2,000.00**	**1,105.00**	**1,870.00**	**4,975.00**
Federal withholding	274.00	151.39	256.19	681.58
Social security employee (6.2%)	124.00	68.51	115.94	308.45
Medicare employee (1.45%)	29.00	16.02	27.12	72.14
Employee withholding	**427.00**	**235.92**	**399.25**	**1,062.17**
Social security employer (6.2%)	124.00	68.51	115.94	308.45
Medicare company employer (1.45%)	29.00	16.02	27.12	72.14
Employer payroll tax expense	**153.00**	**84.53**	**143.06**	**380.59**
Net Check amount	1,573.00	869.08	1,470.75	3,912.83

Figure 2

Second semimonthly payroll

Requirements:

1 Create, save, and print a Profit and Loss report for February 2026 that includes a % of income column.

2 Create, save, and print a Total Income Transaction report for February 2026. (*Hint:* Click the **Total Income amount** in the Profit and Loss report for February 2026.)

3 Create, save, and print a Balance Sheet report for February 28, 2026.

4 Create, save, and print a Checking report for February 2026.

5 Create, save, and print a Statement of Cash Flows report for February 2026.

6 Create, save, and print an A/R Aging Summary report for February 2026.

7 Create, save, and print an A/P Aging Summary report for February 2026.

8 Create, save, and print an Inventory Valuation Summary report for February 2026.

9 Create, save, and print a Transactions List by Date report for February 2026.

10 Create, save, and print a Budget vs. Actuals report for February 2026.

Case 4 Comprehensive Problem

Case 4, which begins in Chapter 3, is a sports gym that sells month-to-month memberships and related merchandise. Business events in Case 4 occurred from 12/31/26 to 1/31/27 when presented in Chapters 3 to 10. The following is a description of business events that occurred in the month of February 2027.

Date	Description of Event	Chapter	Event
2/2/27	Add new product	4	Add a new taxable product – Bowflex Xtreme Home Gym, initial quantity on hand: 0, as of date: 2/1/27, inventory asset account: Inventory Asset, price: $1,199, cost: $700, income account: Sales of Product Income, expense account: Cost of Goods Sold (taxable).
2/2/27	Change the name of a product	4	Change the name of the Yoga pants to Xtreme Yoga pants.
2/2/27	Add a new vendor	5	Add a new vendor – Sole Fitness LLC, 1844 Raven Rd., Diana, TX 75640, terms: Net 30.
2/2/27	Add a new product	4	Add a new taxable product – Sole E98 Elliptical, initial quantity on hand: 0, as of date: 2/1/27, inventory asset account: Inventory Asset, price: $2,300, cost: $1,500, income account: Sales of Product Income, expense account: Cost of Goods Sold (taxable).
2/3/27	Add a new service	4	Add a new service – Annual Fee – Individual, rate: $1,620, income account: Sales (not taxable).
2/3/27	Modify budget	8	Modify the following monthly budgeted amounts (Budget 1) for February 2027 through December 2027 as follows: sales of product income: $6,000, sales: $60,000, cost of goods sold: $3,000, advertising & marketing: $3,000, insurance: $2,100, interest expense: $325, payroll: $16,000, repairs & maintenance: $700.
2/3/27	Add a new employee	7	Add a new employee – Sammy Watkins, 300 Westwood Blvd., Westwood, CA 90037, Employee ID: 555-22-9741.
2/3/27	Add a bill	5	Add a bill from Supreme Marketing, terms: Net 15, for advertising performed last month for $675. This bill was accrued as of 1/31/27. You will reverse this accrual at the end of this month.
2/4/27	Add a new customer	4	Add a new customer – Fox Broadcasting Company, 10201 West Pico Blvd., Los Angeles, CA 90064, terms: Net 30.

2/5/27	Add a sales receipt	4	Add a new sales receipt #1005 for $6,480 – New customer: Harrison Ford, payment method: Check, reference no.: 1987, deposit to: Payments to deposit, service: Annual Fee – Individual, quantity: 4.
2/5/27	Add a new purchase order	5	Add a new purchase order #1003 for $2,100 to purchase 3 Bowflex Xtreme Home Gyms from vendor Bowflex, Inc.
2/5/27	Add a new purchase order	5	Add a new purchase order #1004 for $7,500 to purchase 5 Sole E98 Elliptical machines from vendor Sole Fitness LLC.
2/8/27	Add a new invoice	4	Add a new invoice #1006 for $29,453.10 – Customer: Fox Broadcasting Company, terms: Net 30, service: Monthly Fee – Corporate Membership 50 Employees, quantity: 4, and product: Bowflex Dumbbells, quantity: 20.
2/9/27	Add a new invoice	4	Add a new invoice #1007 for $12,000 – Customer: ABC Studios, terms: Net 30, service: Monthly Fee – Corporate Membership 50 Employees, quantity: 2.
2/10/27	Add a new invoice	4	Add a new invoice #1010 for $750 – Customer: Jules, Inc., terms net 30, service: Training – Individual, quantity: 10.
2/11/27	Receive payment	4	Receive payment – Customer: ABC Studios, payment method: Check, reference no.: 98745, deposit to: Payments to deposit, amount received: $7,368.75 (related to invoice #1002).
2/11/27	Pay bills	5	Pay $6,800 in bills from Bowflex, Inc. and Supreme Marketing, using checks no. 25511 and 25512.
2/11/27	Make a bank deposit	4	Add a bank deposit to the checking account in the amount of $13,848.75 to deposit previously received payments from ABC Studios ($7,368.75) and Harrison Ford ($6,480).
2/12/27	Record a credit card purchase	5	Purchase supplies from Wal-Mart (a new vendor) using the VISA credit card $1,800. (Be sure to use the Supplies asset account.)
2/12/27	Record a check	5	Add check no. 25513 to Barber Investments, Inc. for $10,000 in long-term investments.
2/12/27	Record a check	5	Add check no. 25514 to Leaseco, Inc. (a new vendor) for $6,000 to prepay one-year rent on a storage facility (Prepaid Rent).
2/12/27	Add a new purchase order	5	Add a new purchase order #1005 for $25,000 – Vendor: NordicTrack, Inc. for 5 new treadmills for use in the facility and not for resale (You will need to create 3 new Fixed Asset accounts; Equipment, Original Cost, and Accumulated Depreciation like you did in Chapter 3. Be sure to record this purchase to the Original Cost account).
2/15/27	Add a new bill	5	Add a new bill based on a purchase order #1003 for $2,100 – Vendor: Bowflex Inc., terms: Net 15. All items ordered were received. Be sure to delete any other items from this bill other than the 3 Bowflex Xtreme Home Gym.
2/15/27	Add a new bill	5	Add a new bill without a purchase order – LADWP (a new vendor), terms: Net 15, category: Utilities, amount: $900.
2/15/27	Add new fixed asset accounts	6	Create 3 new Fixed Asset accounts; Computers, Original Cost, and Accumulated Depreciation like you did in Chapter 3.
2/15/27	Record a credit card purchase and bank loan using a journal entry	6	Add the purchase of $45,000 in computers from Best Buy (a new vendor) for which $10,000 was charged to the VISA credit card and the $35,000 balance was paid by signing a long-term business loan using journal entry 11. (Be sure to indicate Coast Bank in the Name section of the notes payable entry and to record the purchase in the original cost sub account of Computers.)
2/15/27	Pay first payroll	7	Using recurring transactions (as you did in the chapter), pay Graham, Beckett, and Allegra based on the information shown in Figure 1. Using the Check function, pay Sammy based on the information shown in Figure 1. Be sure to indicate that Sammy's check is a recurring transaction. (Use checks no. 25515 to 25518.)
2/17/27	Sell common stock	6	Add the sale of common stock as a deposit of $25,000, check no. 1974, from shareholders.
2/17/27	Pay dividends	6	Add the payment of dividends to shareholders, check no. 25519, in the amount of $1,000.
2/18/27	Make a loan payment	6	Add the payment of $2,000 made to Coast Bank as an installment on long-term business loans, which included interest expense of $300 and principal amount of $1,700, using check no. 25520.

Date	Action		Description
2/19/27	Add a new bill	5	Add a new bill of $2,985 based on a purchase order #1002 – Vendor: Precor, terms: Net 30. All items ordered were received.
2/25/27	Pay bills	5	Pay bills from LADWP ($900) and Supreme Marketing ($675) using checks no. 25521 and 25522.
2/26/27	Add a bill	5	Add a new bill of $7,500 based on purchase order #1004 – Vendor: Sole Fitness LLC, terms: Net 30.
2/27/27	Add a new invoice	4	Add invoice #1008 for $7,555.50 to Jules, Inc., terms: Net 30, for 3 Sole E98 Elliptical machines plus tax.
2/27/27	Receive payment	4	Receive payment on account from ABC Studios of $12,000 from invoice #1007 using check no. 19981 into the Payments to deposit account.
2/27/27	Add a new bill	5	Add a new bill of $25,000 based on purchase order #1005 – Vendor: NordicTrack Inc., terms: Net 30.
2/27/27	Add a sales receipt	4	Add a new sales receipt #1009 for $3,280.62 to Taylor Swift (a new customer), product: Bowflex Xtreme Home Gym, quantity: 2, and product: Power Block Elite Dumbbells, quantity: 2, deposit check 948 to: Payments to deposit. (Click **See the math** to update amounts.)
2/27/27	Make a deposit	4	Deposited ABC Studios check for $12,000 into the checking account.
2/28/27	Pay second payroll	7	Add payroll (as you did in the chapter) based on the information shown in Figure 2 as follows. (Use checks no. 25523 to 25526.)
2/28/27	Reconcile bank account	8	Reconcile your company's checking account. No service charges or interest were incurred or earned. The ending bank statement balance on 2/28/27 was $19,173.16. All checks cleared the bank except checks no. 25524 and 25526 for $1,671.31 and $1,286.41, respectively. All deposits cleared the bank except a deposit from ABC Studios for $12,000.
2/28/27	Adjust supplies	9	Supplies worth $1,700 were used in February. Use journal entry 12.
2/28/27	Adjust prepaids	9	Prepaid rent of $3,000 expired in the month of February (rent & lease). Use journal entry 13.
2/28/27	Reverse accrual	9	Reverse journal entry 7 made on 1/31/27 to accrue advertising & marketing expenses of $675 to Supreme Marketing using journal entry 14.
2/28/27	Accrue expenses	9	A bill for $1,300 was received and recorded in the next month for legal & professional services consumed in the current month from a new vendor Legal Beagles. Use journal entry 15.
2/28/27	Reverse accrual	9	Sales accrued on 1/31/27 for $750 via journal entry 9 were properly recorded in February. Use journal entry 16 to reverse this accrual.
2/28/27	Defer revenue	9	Sales of product income recorded on sales receipt #1009 for $2,996 to Taylor Swift were deemed unearned as of 2/28/27. Use journal entry 17 to defer this revenue.
2/28/27	Reverse deferral	9	Training services recorded on invoice #1003 for $3,750 to Flyer Corporation were only partially performed even though invoiced. Sales of $2000 had not been earned and thus were deferred in the prior month. Use journal entry 18 to reverse journal entry 8 recorded on 1/31/27.
2/28/27	Accrue depreciation	9	Record Depreciation Expense of $1,600 ($500, $600, $400, and $100 for Vehicles, Furniture, Equipment, and Computer, respectively). Use journal entry 19 to record this depreciation.
2/28/27	Accrue revenue	9	Training (Sales) of $2,500 was performed for ABC Studios on 2/28/27 but not invoiced or recorded into the accounting records. Use journal entry 20 to accrue this revenue.

Pay/Tax/Withholding	Graham	Allegra	Beckett	Sammy	Total
Hours if applicable	n/a	70	80	90	
Annual salary or hourly rate	75,000.00	25.00	22.00	20.00	
Gross pay	**3,125.00**	**1,750.00**	**1,760.00**	**1,800.00**	**8.435.00**
Federal withholding	428.13	239.75	241.12	246.60	**1,155.60**
Social security employee (6.2%)	193.75	108.50	109.12	111.60	**522.97**
Medicare employee (1.45%)	45.31	25.38	25.52	26.10	**122.31**
Employee withholding	**667.19**	**373.63**	**375.76**	**384.30**	**1,800.87**
Social security employer (6.2%)	193.75	108.50	109.12	111.60	**522.97**
Medicare company employer (1.45%)	45.34	25.38	25.52	26.10	**122.34**
Employer payroll tax expense	**239.09**	**133.88**	**134.64**	**137.70**	**645.31**
Net Check amount	2,457.81	1,376.37	1,384.24	1,415.70	**5,218.42**

Figure 1

First semi-monthly payroll

Pay/Tax/Withholding	Graham	Allegra	Beckett	Sammy	Total
Hours if applicable	n/a	85	72	83	
Annual salary or hourly rate	75,000.00	25.00	22.00	20.00	
Gross pay	**3,125.00**	**2,125.00**	**1,584.00**	**1,660.00**	**8,494.00**
Federal withholding	428.13	291.13	217.01	246.60	**1,182.86**
Social security employee (6.2%)	193.75	131.75	98.21	102.92	**526.63**
Medicare employee (1.45%)	45.31	30.81	22.97	24.07	**123.16**
Employee withholding	**667.19**	**453.69**	**338.18**	**373.59**	**1,832.65**
Social security employer (6.2%)	193.75	131.75	98.12	102.92	**526.63**
Medicare company employer (1.45%)	45.34	30.81	22.97	24.07	**123.19**
Employer payroll tax expense	**239.09**	**162.56**	**121.18**	**126.99**	**649.82**
Net Check amount	2,457.81	1,671.31	1,245.82	1,286.41	**6,661.35**

Figure 2

Second semimonthly payroll

Requirements:

1   Create, save, and print a Trial Balance report for February 2027.

2   Create, save, and print a Profit and Loss report for February 2027.

3   Create, save, and print a Budget vs. Actuals report for February 2027 without cents and reflecting accounts vs. total.

4   Create, save, and print a Balance Sheet report for February 28, 2027.

5   Create, save, and print a Checking report for February 2027.

6   Create, save, and print a Statement of Cash Flows report for February 2027.

7   Create, save, and print an A/R Aging Summary report for February 2027.

8   Create, save, and print an A/P Aging Summary report for February 2027.

9   Create, save, and print an Inventory Valuation Summary report for February 2027.

10   Create, save, and print a Transactions List by Date report for February 2027.

Case 5 Comprehensive Problem

Note: Be aware that there is no Case 5 comprehensive problem provided in this text.

Case 6 Comprehensive Problem

Case 6, which begins in Chapter 3, is a Recreational Vehicle (RV) dealership in the state of Washington. They sell new RVs and related accessories to individuals and businesses. In addition, they repair and service RVs. Business events in Case 6 occurred from 12/31/22 to 1/31/23 when presented in Chapters 3 to 10. The following is a description of business events that occurred in the month of February 2023.

Date	Description of Event	Chapter	Event
2/1/23	Add a new vendor	5	Add a new vendor – R-Pod, 888 SE Sheridan Road, Sheridan, OR 97378, terms: Net 30.
2/2/23	Add new product	4	Add a new product – Name/Description/Purchasing information: RP-171, initial quantity on hand: 0, as of date: 2/2/23, inventory asset account: Inventory, Sales price: $26,900, cost: $21,520, income account: Sales of Product Income, expense account: Cost of Goods Sold, Sales tax category: Taxable – standard rate, Preferred vendor: R-Pod.
2/2/23	Change the name of a product	4	Change the name/description of the service Basic 6,000-mile service to Basic 8,000-mile service.
2/2/23	Add a new product	4	Add a new product – Name/Description/Purchasing information: RP-179, initial quantity on hand: 0, as of date: 2/2/23, inventory asset account: Inventory, Sales price: $22,800, cost: $18,240, income account: Sales of Product Income, expense account: Cost of Goods Sold, Sales tax category: Taxable – standard rate, Preferred vendor: R-Pod.
2/3/23	Add a new service	4	Add a new service – Detailing, rate: $50, income account: Sales, Sales tax category: Nontaxable.
2/3/23	Modify budget	8	Modify the following monthly budgeted amounts (Budget 1) for February 2023 as follows: sales of product income: $400,000, sales: $15,000, cost of goods sold: $320,000, advertising & marketing: $18,000, contractors: $3,000, insurance: $4,000, interest expense: $600, payroll: $22,000, repairs: $700, utilities: $5,000, and depreciation: $1,200. Leave budgets for March through December as is.
2/3/23	Add a new employee	7	Add a new employee – Anastasia Quinn, 507 N 169th St., Shoreline, WA 98133, Social Security No.: 555-54-1111.
2/3/23	Add a bill	5	Add a bill from Pacific Marketing, terms: Net 15, for advertising performed last month, for $1,800. This bill was accrued as of 1/31/23. You will reverse this accrual at the end of this month.
2/4/23	Add a new customer	4	Add a new customer – Apple Travel, terms: Net 30.
2/6/23	Add a sales receipt	4	Add a new sales receipt #1003 – New customer: Rose Ski, 241 St., Andrews Way, Santa Maria, CA 93454, payment method: Check, reference no.: 355, deposit to: Undeposited Funds, product: 2022 Winnebago Revel 44E, price: $150,000 quantity: 1, amount received: $163,950.
2/7/23	Add a new purchase order	5	Add a new purchase order #1003 to purchase two RP-171 and three RP-179 trailers from vendor R-Pod for a total cost of $97,760.
2/8/23	Add a new purchase order	5	Add a new purchase order #1004 to purchase two 2023 Thor Motor Coach Palazzo 33.2 motorhomes from vendor Thor Motor Coach for a total cost of $288,000.
2/8/23	Add a new invoice	4	Add a new invoice #1004 for $108,207 – Customer: Apple Travel, terms: Net 30, product: one 2023 Airstream Flying Cloud 27FB TWIN. (Click **See the math** to update amounts.)
2/10/23	Add a new invoice	4	Add a new invoice #1005 for $700 – Customer: Rose Ski, terms: Net 30, service: one Basic 8,000-mile service and five hours of Detailing.
2/13/23	Receive payment	4	Receive payment – Customer: Deja Smith, payment method: Check, deposit to: Undeposited Funds, amount received: $153,020 (related to invoice: #1002).
2/14/23	Pay bills	5	Pay $322,000 in bills from Winnebago, Inc., and Pacific Marketing, using checks no. 601 and 602.

2/15/23	Make a bank deposit	4	Add a bank deposit to the checking account in the amount of $316,970 to deposit previously received payments from Deja Smith and Rose Ski.
2/15/23	Record a credit card purchase	5	Purchase supplies from Best Buy using the AMEX credit card $3,000. (Be sure to use the Supplies Asset account.)
2/15/23	Record a check	5	Add check no. 603 to McConnel Investments, Inc. for $20,000 in additional investments.
2/15/23	Record a check	5	Add check no. 604 to Global Leasing (a new vendor) for $24,000 to prepay one-year rent on a warehouse (Prepaid Expenses).
2/15/23	Add a new bill	6	Add a new bill without a purchase order – Seattle City Light (a new vendor), terms: Net 15, category: Utilities, amount: $3,000.
2/15/23	Add new fixed asset accounts	6	Create new fixed asset accounts – Account type: Fixed Assets, detail type: Vehicles, name: Vehicles. Track depreciation of this asset. Be sure to change the name of the Vehicles accumulated depreciation account from Depreciation to Accumulated Depreciation.
2/15/23	Record a vehicle purchase and bank loan using a journal entry	6	Add the purchase of a truck for $95,000 from Seattle Ford (a new vendor) and the signing a note payable to Seattle Bank for the full purchase price using journal entry 10.
2/15/23	Pay first payroll	7	Using recurring transactions (as you did in the chapter), pay Rhett, Oliver, and Emelia based on the information shown in Figure 1. Using the check function, pay Anastasia. Be sure to indicate that Anastasia's check is a recurring unscheduled transaction. (Use checks no. 605 to 608.)
2/17/23	Sell common stock	6	Add the sale of common stock as a deposit of $20,000 from shareholders (Common stock $200, Paid-In Capital $19,800).
2/20/23	Pay dividends	6	Add the payment of dividends to shareholders, check no. 609, in the amount of $500.
2/21/23	Make a loan payment	6	Add the payment of $3,542.88 made to Seattle Bank as an installment on notes payable, which included interest expense of $390 and principal amount of $3,152.88, using check no. 610.
2/22/23	Add a new bill	5	Add a new bill of $97,760 based on a purchase order #1003 – Vendor: R-Pod, terms: Net 30. All items ordered were received.
2/25/23	Pay bills	5	Pay bills from State Farm Insurance ($18,000), National Covers ($4,000), and Airstream, Inc. ($180,000) using checks no. 611 to 613.
2/27/23	Add a new invoice	4	Add invoice #1006 for $29,401.70 to Donald Biden, terms: Net 30, for one RP-171 plus tax. (Click **See the math** to update amounts.)
2/27/23	Receive payment	4	Receive payment on account from Apple Travel of $108,207 from invoice #1004 recorded into the Undeposited Funds account.
2/27/23	Add a sales receipt	4	Add a new sales receipt #1007 for $153,020 to Ebony Williams for one 2022 Winnebago View 24G deposited to Undeposited Funds. (Click **See the math** to update amounts.)
2/27/23	Add a new invoice	4	Add invoice #1008 for $950 to Deja Smith, terms: Net 30, for a transmission service ($350) and sewer system inspection and repair ($600).
2/28/23	Make a deposit	4	Deposited Apple Travel and Ebony William's checks for a total of $261,227 into the checking account.
2/28/23	Add a new bill	5	Add a new bill without a purchase order, vendor: Pacific Marketing, terms: Net 15, category: Advertising & Marketing, amount: $1,800.
2/28/23	Pay second payroll	7	Add payroll using recurring transactions for Rhett, Oliver, Emelia, and Anastasia based on the information shown in Figure 2. (Use checks no. 614 to 617.)
2/28/23	Reconcile bank account	8	Reconcile your company's checking account. No service charges or interest were incurred or earned. The ending bank statement balance on 2/28/23 was $182.49. All checks cleared the bank except checks no. 613 through 617. All deposits cleared the bank except a deposit made on 2/28/23 for $261,227.
2/28/23	Adjust supplies	9	Supplies worth $1,200 were used in February. Use journal entry 11.
2/28/23	Adjust prepaids	9	Prepaid expenses of $4,400 expired in the month of February ($2,400 related to insurance and $2,000 related to rent & lease). Use journal entry 12.

2/28/23	Reverse accrual	9	Reverse journal entry 7 made on 1/31/23 to accrue advertising & marketing expenses of $1,800 to Pacific Marketing using journal entry 13.
2/28/23	Accrue expenses	9	A bill for $2,500 was received from Elite Events and recorded in March 2023 for contractors expense consumed in the current month. Use journal entry 14 to accrue this liability.
2/28/23	Reverse accrual	9	Sales accrued on 1/31/23 for $950 via journal entry 8 were properly recorded in February. Use journal entry 15 to reverse this accrual.
2/28/23	Defer revenue	9	The sale of a motorhome to Donald Biden on 2/27/23 for $29,401.70 was deemed unearned as of 2/28/23 since it wasn't delivered until March. Use journal entry 16 to defer this revenue to a new Unearned Revenue account and reduce sales tax payable. You'll need to review invoice #1006 to determine amounts by account.
2/28/23	Accrue depreciation	9	Record Depreciation Expense of $3,000 ($1,000, $300, $800, and $900 for Buildings, Computers, Machinery & Equipment, and Vehicles, respectively). Use journal entry 17 to record this depreciation.
2/28/23	Accrue revenue	9	Services of $16,000 were performed for Sam Ski on 2/28/23 but not invoiced or recorded into the accounting records until the next month. Use journal entry 18 to accrue Sales and Accrued Receivables.

Pay/Tax/Withholding	Oliver	Rhett	Emelia	Anastasia	Total
Hours if applicable	n/a	n/a	83	65	
Annual salary or hourly rate	85,000.00	60,000.00	35.00	40.00	
Gross pay	**3,541.67**	**2,500.00**	**2,905.00**	**2,600.00**	**8,946.67**
Federal withholding	485.22	342.50	397.99	356.20	1,225.70
Social security employee (6.2%)	219.58	155.00	180.11	161.20	554.69
Medicare employee (1.45%)	51.35	36.25	42.12	37.70	129.73
Employee withholding	**756.15**	**533.75**	**620.22**	**555.10**	**1,910.11**
Social security employer (6.2%)	219.59	155.00	180.11	161.20	554.70
Medicare company employer (1.45%)	51.38	36.28	42.12	37.70	129.79
Employer payroll tax expense	**270.97**	**191.28**	**222.23**	**198.90**	**684.48**
Net Check amount	2,785.52	1,966.25	2,284.78	2,044.90	7,036.55

Figure 1

First semimonthly payroll

Pay/Tax/Withholding	Oliver	Rhett	Emelia	Anastasia	Total
Hours if applicable	n/a	n/a	73	72	
Annual salary or hourly rate	85,000.00	60,000.00	35.00	40.00	
Gross pay	**3,541.67**	**2,500.00**	**2,555.00**	**2,880.00**	**8,596.67**
Federal withholding	485.22	342.50	350.04	394.56	1,177.75
Social security employee (6.2%)	219.58	155.00	158.41	178.56	532.99
Medicare employee (1.45%)	51.35	36.25	37.05	41.76	124.65
Employee withholding	**756.15**	**533.75**	**545.49**	**614.88**	**1,835.39**
Social security employer (6.2%)	219.59	155.00	158.41	178.56	533.00
Medicare company employer (1.45%)	51.38	36.28	37.05	41.76	124.71
Employer payroll tax expense	**270.97**	**191.28**	**195.46**	**220.32**	**657.71**
Net Check amount	2,785.52	1,966.25	2,009.51	2,265.12	6,761.27

Figure 2

Second semimonthly payroll

Requirements:

1 Create, save, and print a Bank Reconciliation report as of 2/28/23 (click **Hide additional information** when generating this report).

2 Create, save, and print a Trial Balance report as of 2/28/23.

3 Create, save, and print a Profit and Loss report for the month of February 2023 with a % of income column.

4 Create, save, and print a Balance Sheet report as of 2/28/23 with a % of row column.

5 Create, save, and print a Statement of Cash Flows report for February 2023.

6 Create, save, and print an A/R Aging Summary report as of 2/28/23.

7 Create, save, and print an A/P Aging Summary report as of 2/28/23.

8 Create, save, and print an Inventory Valuation Summary report as of 2/28/23.

9 Create, save, and print a Transactions Detail by Account report for all dates.

10 Create, save, and print a Budget vs. Actuals report for the two months ended 2/28/23.

Overview—Do I Need to Become QuickBooks Online Certified?

There are two schools of thought here. The first is that becoming certified provides employers/clients independent confirmation of an individual's skill and proficiency in using QBO. Thus, certification is a good résumé builder. The second is that any employer/client that relies solely on certification to assure competency in using QBO will eventually find themselves looking for a new QBO professional.

Does it hurt? No. Does it help? Maybe. Is it necessary? No. What is important is the knowledge, skill, and proficiency in using QuickBooks as a tool to help businesses better understand the financial implications of their decisions.

In the author's opinion, certification takes a back seat to accounting education and experience. Thus, it is in the student's best interest to gain accounting knowledge (the more, the better) through courses at accredited institutions in the topics of bookkeeping, financial accounting, managerial accounting, cost accounting, and tax accounting, as well as the application of QuickBooks to different business situations. The next step is to gain experience through internships or part-time jobs working under a QuickBooks/Accounting professional. Add that to certification and you're ready for gainful employment.

The following is a summary overview of the topics covered by the QuickBooks certified user online exam.

What Topics Are Covered in the QBCU Certification Exam?

1 QuickBooks setup and maintenance
    a. List management
    b. Sales and money-in
    c. Purchases and money-out
    d. Basic accounting
    e. Reports
    f. Customization and saving time
    g. The Intuit QBCU Desktop exam covers the following topics:

2 QuickBooks set-up
    a. QuickBooks utilities and general product knowledge
    b. List management
    c. Items
    d. Sales
    e. Purchases

    f.   Payroll

    g.   Reports

    h.   Basic accounting

    i.   Customization and shortcuts

Links to QuickBooks Certification Information

https://certiport.pearsonvue.com/Certifications/QuickBooks/Certified-User/Overview

https://quickbooks.intuit.com/accountants/training-certification/

Index